THE LOST TOMB
OF VIRACOCHA

THE LOST TOMB
OF VIRACOCHA

Unlocking the Secrets of the Peruvian Pyramids

Maurice Cotterell

Bear & Company
Rochester, Vermont

Bear & Company
One Park Street
Rochester, Vermont 05767
www.InnerTraditions.com

Bear & Company is a division of Inner Traditions International

Library of Congress Cataloging-in-Publication Data
Cotterell, Maurice.
  The lost tomb of Viracocha : unlocking the secrets of the Peruvian
pyramids / Maurice Cotterell.
      p. cm.
Originally published: London : Headline, 2001.
Includes bibliographical references and index.
  ISBN 1-59143-005-4
  1. Incas. 2. Pyramids—Peru. 3. Viracocha, Inca of Peru. 4.
Viracocha (Inca deity) 5. Peru—Antiquities. I. Title.

F3429.C883 2003
985'.019—dc21
                              2003000621

Printed and bound in the United States at Lake Book Manufacturing, Inc.

10 9 8 7 6 5 4 3 2 1

Contents

Illustrations

All illustrations, drawings and artwork by M. Cotterell; photographs, A. J. Perry and M. Cotterell and graphics by K. Burns, except those specified below.

Figure 11, after H. Carter; 23, Corel 131042; 24a, 24b, 24c, after Augustus Villagra; 26a,The Griffith Institute (Howard Carter Archive); 46a, after Arthur Posnansky; 47, Corel 90045; 61c, Corel 142097; 66b, Corel 139020; 68c, Corel 163063; 69c, after geometrician Patricia Villiers-Stuart; 71b, Corel 139039; 72c (vase) and 79c, American Museum of Natural History #313605; 77e, Corel 247047; 80, Bettany, G. T., *The World's Religions* (Ward Lock and Co., London, 1890); 87, after a line drawing from Documentary Media Resources, Cambridge, Mass., USA.

Plate 18a, after Arthur Posnansky; 19b, Corel 53048; 19e, Corel 90036; 22e, Corel 33024; 22f Corel 33023; 29 (boxed jade mask), after Vautier de Nanxe; 32b, Corel 8026.

Transparency packs and specialised museum publications containing the transparencies may be obtained directly from the author, Maurice Cotterell, at:

'Garryndruid'
c/o Timoleague Post Office
Timoleague
West Cork
Republic of Ireland

Acknowledgments

With sincere thanks, as always, to G; to my wife Ann for her continuing support; to Kevin Burns for help with the graphics and artwork; to editor Hugh Morgan; to Amanda Ridout and her production team; to my literary agent Robert Kirby and all at Peters Fraser & Dunlop; to Dr Walter Alva, Director of the Museo Arqueologico Nacional Bruning De Lambayeque, for permission to photograph the exhibition of Sipan at the Museum of Archaeology and Anthropology, Lima.

Introduction

When the body is gone the soul moves on. It is imperishable, indestructible, immortal and everlasting. It was never born and it will never cease to be. The ancients learned this from their fathers, and before that from their fathers' fathers, and before that, their legends say, from a white man with a beard who taught that heaven awaits the pure and that rebirth on earth awaits the rest.

In *The Supergods* I explained how Lord Pacal of Mexico was a Supergod, a teacher who taught his people the higher orders of science and spirituality. In *The Tutankhamun Prophecies* I went further, explaining how Tutankhamun and Lord Pacal were one and the same, different incarnations of the same being at different moments in time.

This book shows that two more Supergods, the Lords of Sipan, walked among the Peruvians and the Tiahuanacos of Bolivia. They, too, taught the higher orders of science and spirituality, the mysteries of the heavens, the laws of astronomy and mathematics. They taught their people the super-science of the sun, how it controls behaviour (astrology) and fertility (the rise and fall of civilisations) and how it brings periodic catastrophic destruction to earth, erasing each civilisation in turn from the annals of history.

They built the mighty pyramids of Peru and their great cities of stone as a message to future generations; to tell us that we have been here, and have experienced life on earth, before.

They encoded their secrets into their treasures, locked them into their monuments, hid them in the mountains and scratched them in the deserts to give us another chance of redemption, of becoming a star, 'the next time around'.

The message is clear. We are spiritual beings by nature, entombed for a time in a body, imprisoned in a hell from which no one escapes – except for those who know the secrets of the sun-kings.

CHAPTER ONE

The Mochica

The Lost Tribes of Central America, Peru and Bolivia

'You mark my words, Juan Alvarez Aguillar, one day your luck will run out, one day you will pay – and then you will not be so clever.'

So many times his mother had said these words during his 25 years and each time he dismissed her without so much as a 'who cares?'. But today was different . . .

'One more time I ask you, Alvarez, where did you get the gold?'

The inspector wiped his brow with the back of his hand and turned away, dragging his hulk across the open doorway. The makeshift room of reeds, grass, a few poles and bits of old string went some way to shield the desert sun and abrasive sands that scoured the ground in whirlwinds. After two days without food, Juan Alvarez Aguillar began to believe that today was to be that fateful day.

'. . . Water,' he groaned, '. . . water.'

The inspector turned, snapping his fingers at the armed guard by the doorway who scurried away, returning a few seconds later with half a can of brackish fluid. If there was one thing that all Peruvians agreed on, it was that every human being, no matter how bad, or how poor, had a God-given right to water – even grave robbers like Alvarez would not be denied this.

The inspector sat down, two inches from his quarry, arms across the chair-back, gums smacking at the toothpick that teased his teeth. His hot, stale breath stirred the nostrils of Alvarez, who ruefully eyed the rope that bound his wrists. His ankles, too, were caked in blood, blackened and congealed since he was first anchored down 36 hours ago.

'. . . If you cooperate you'll be a free man in five years . . .' He paused.
'. . . We have the gold – the guards found it buried inside your place. We have a statement from the g-r-e-e-n-g-o who bought the necklace for ten-thousand dollars . . . We know it was you, Alvarez.'

The inspector stood up astride the chair which he lifted slowly into the air with one finger, allowing it to rest gently on one of Alvarez's bare feet. He was a big man, all of 127 kilogrammes (20 stone). Alvarez winced. Sapped in strength, and broken in spirit, he knew it was over.

'OK . . . OK,' he sighed. '. . . Sipan . . . Sipan . . . The flat-topped huaca three kilometres (two miles) east of the village.'

The inspector pulled a mobile phone from his breast pocket, punched in a few numbers and gave the orders:

'. . . Huaca three kilometres east of Sipan. Clear the area . . . as many guards as you like. I'll be there at sunrise.'

This was no one-off case. Pillaging tombs in the deserts of northern Peru provided locals with much-needed cash to compensate for the loss of income between sugar harvests. The flat-topped *huacas*, mud-brick pyramid shrines, attracted gangs of looters from miles around. These three, near Sipan, had not been thought of as especially noteworthy until the gold began appearing on the black market, eagerly purchased by fair-skinned Westerners – those with green eyes, so untypical of the indigenous Indians, descendants of the sun-worshipping Mochica (sometimes referred to as the Moche).

From around AD 100–700 as many as 50,000 Mochica lived and farmed the narrow fertile valleys fed by the rivers that flowed from the Andes through the desert to the sea. Using ingenious irrigation methods, along 355 kilometres (220 miles) of coastline, they raised a wide variety of fruit and vegetables, including corn, squash, peanuts and beans. Meats, too, were plentiful in the form of llama and guinea

Figure 1. The Lost Tribes of Central America, Peru and Bolivia

pig, as was fish from the rivers and the sea. This little-known civilisation thrived simultaneously with that of the Maya of Mexico, declining at around the same time, AD 700, the time of a known sunspot minimum that brought infertility to the region (see figure 41).

On 3 February 1987 archaeologist Dr Walter Alva, Director of the Bruning Archaeological Museum, received a call from the chief inspector of the antiquities police. Together they inspected the mud-brick pyramid mounds at Sipan, honeycombed with tunnels dug by hordes of looters. This discovery would, in time, turn out to be the most important ever made in Peruvian archaeology.

The first phase of excavation lasted until June 1987. This revealed the tomb of a Mochica sun-king whom they named the Lord of Sipan. His richly attired body was found together with a treasure-trove of gold, panned from the beds of the Amazon; silver, from mines in the south; lapis lazuli, from Chile; turquoise, again from the south, and seashells from Ecuador, which lay on the equator to the north. Together, hundreds of priceless artefacts – including 13 pectorals, each made from thousands of fine seashell pieces, a solid gold bat-mask, golden facial features including eyes, nose and mouth, golden necklaces, a golden rod-like sceptre, shields, bells, bracelets, blankets of gold foil, and others of copper – exposed a breathtaking legacy of one of the world's greatest civilisations. From now on archaeologists would view the Mochica alongside the Mayas and the Egyptians.

From the top of the Huaca Rajada 28 more huacas can be seen in the valley, suggesting that the area has much more to reveal. But the Mochica were not the only sun-worshipping culture to flourish in Peru; the Chavín thrived before them, the Tiahuanacos of Tiahuanaco,* near Lake Titicaca, Bolivia, thrived alongside them and, later, the Incas came after them. Despite the years between them they had much in common; each worshipped the sun as the source of fertility; each worshipped the bat-god as the god of death; each worshipped a feathered snake; and each worshipped a white man with a beard.

---

* Also spelled Tiwanaku and Tihuanacu.

Figure 2. Time Chart of the Principal Lost Tribes of Central America, Peru and Bolivia

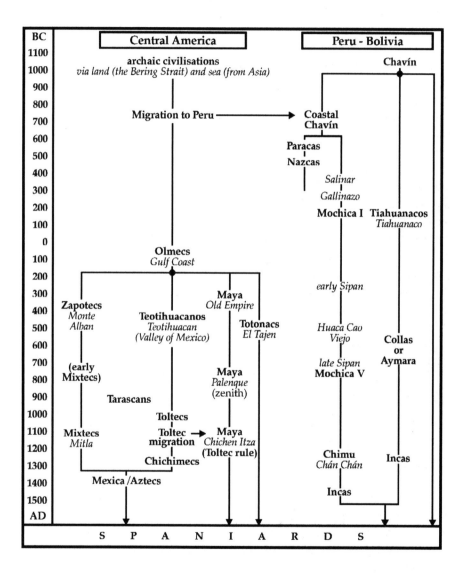

The Battle Against Nature

The nineteenth-century explorer Alexander von Humboldt was the first to identify the ice-cold currents that run from the Antarctic to the equator along the coast of Chile and Peru. These waters, home to penguins, fur seals and other cold-water species, eventually collide with hot tropical surface currents just south of the equator, causing a blanket of haze to settle along the Peruvian coast. This leads to a mini-greenhouse effect, trapping in the equatorial heat. The cold waters also cause premature condensation of Pacific air flows and with it precipitation offshore at sea, instead of inland along the warmer coastline. The effect is most noticeable around the Santa Valley region of central coastal Peru, where the coastal current sweeps back into the Pacific. There's an old saying that 'the sun never shines in Lima', or indeed anywhere along this inhospitable stretch of coastline where next to nothing grows in the barren deserts.

The coastal deserts further exacerbate the problem of drought by warming what little moisture-laden air reaches the land, defeating the normal process of condensation and rainfall common to other coastal areas around the world. Instead, heavy grey clouds rise high into the westernmost chain of the Andes, the black mountains. At high altitude and cold temperatures the clouds burst, sending torrents of water down mountain rivers into the valleys and the ocean below.

Swollen rivers cut their way through the coastal deserts, forming rich fertile regions in the valleys themselves, radiating like green fingers from the foothills of the mountains to the sea. It was in these valleys (*figure 3*), along the northern coast of Peru, that the Mochica decided to settle. Here they established their farms and communities. The one east of Sipan, Pampa Grande, in the Lambayeque Valley, sustained a population of some 10,000 people, while as many as 40,000 established themselves in other valleys.

Off the coast, the cold upwelling waters of the Humboldt current carry nutrients from the depths of the Pacific to the surface, supporting billions of light-sensitive plankton. These stimulate a rich food chain of marine herbivores, fish, shellfish and crustaceans, that in turn attract a wide range of sea fowl, including pelicans and cormorants that nest on the many barren offshore islands. This was another major factor that both attracted and persuaded the Mochica to settle on the coast.

Figure 3. Early Settlements in the River Valleys of Peru

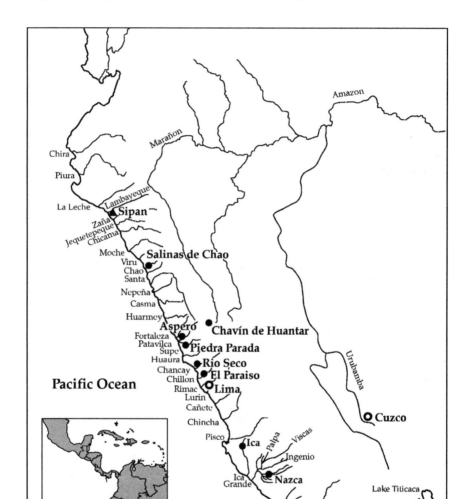

Figure 4. Elevations and Rivers of the Andes

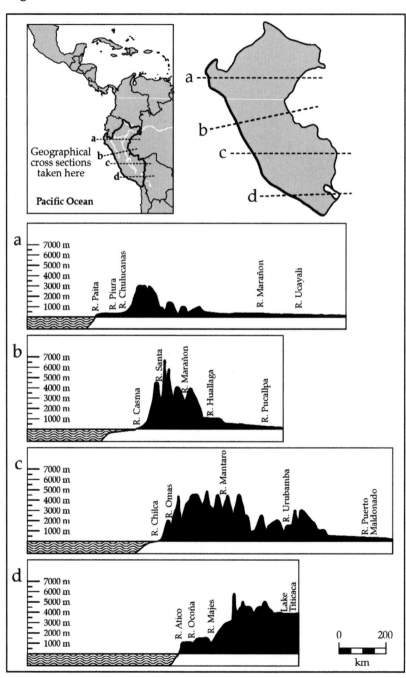

As little as 1.25 centimetres (0.5 inches) of rain falls on the coastal deserts each year, apart from rains brought by *El Niño*. 'The Baby', so called because its worst effects are felt around Christmas (coinciding with the time of the birth of Jesus), arrives annually. The decreased intensity of trade winds at that time of year allows the warmer Ecuadorian counter-current to extend further southwards than usual along the northern Peruvian coastline, bringing with it not only dolphins and flying fish from the north but also heavy rains along the coast. The counter-current varies in intensity each year, reaching a maximum cyclically every 17 years or so on average. Today, global warming seems to be varying the cyclical periodicity of the effect.

The rains fall with great intensity, dropping inches of water in torrential downpours along the coast, causing devastating erosion to the mud-brick pyramids of Sipan and elsewhere in Peru.

Damaged road bridges, washed to the sea by heavily swollen rivers, bring chaos to the region. Visitors travelling the coastal route of modern-day Peru are forced repeatedly to leave the road and embark on a hazardous and uncomfortable detour over some makeshift bridge, through fields of vegetables, while sandwiched between an armada of intercontinental trucks that bounce along, lurching first from one side and then to the next. With a sigh of relief, through clouds of desert dust, they return to the Pacific coast highway before thundering on their way. All of this while the washed-away sections of highway are repaired and reinstated. These disasters, along with earthquakes and disease that might overwhelm lesser mortals in the West, are borne by the indigenous Indians with sublime dignity, as though the battle against nature and the elements were all part of their own unavoidable predestiny.

The First Stone-Builders

Little is known about the first settlers who built monumental quarried stone structures in both the valleys and highland areas. One of the first to appear was at Huaca de los Idolos at Aspero, in the Supe Valley just north of Lima, at around 2,750 BC. Other contemporaneous sites flourished at El Paraiso, in the Chillon Valley; Rio Seco, in the Chancay Valley; Bandurria, in the Huara Valley; Piedra Parada, in the Supe Valley, and Salinas de Chao, in the Chao Valley. Radiocarbon evidence, from Aspero, suggests dates even further into antiquity to

3,000 BC, superseding the appearance of the first monumental structures in Egypt. Such constructions imply the organisation of a complex
society abundant in labour at that time.

The ancient stone city of Chavín de Huantar, c. 900 BC, is 3,150 metres
(10,335 feet) high, in between peaks of the 'white' mountains, the second
Andean range inland from the Pacific. This highland 'valley' is blessed
with fertile land and abundant rainfall and served by the River
Huachesca, which flows into the Marañon, the Amazon and eventually
to the Atlantic in the east. Both the black and the higher white (snow-
capped) mountain ranges run inland, parallel to the coast, dividing
Peru down the middle, presenting a formidable obstacle to east–west
communications. The ceremonial centre is also located at the junction
of two, of only ten, mountain passes, strategically placed to take
advantage of Andean trade. The two ranges come together inland at a
latitude just south-east of Lima before dividing again into three parallel
sections down through Peru: the western range, the central range and
the eastern range. These three again merge, just south of Cuzco in the
highlands, before splitting again, this time into two; the western range
goes to the south, while the royal range continues to the south-east,
providing a highland route to Tiahuanaco in today's Bolivia.

The coastal Chavín appeared slightly later than their highland
ancestors, at around 800 BC. They developed trade facilitated by boat,
taking advantage of vast deposits of white bird-droppings, locally
known as guano, that have accumulated over thousands of years on
many of the small offshore islands. Guano was used to fertilise
Peruvian farmland and for export to neighbouring Ecuador in
exchange for a variety of goods, including warm-water shells of the
oyster, conch and cone varieties, salted meats and other foodstuffs.

There is little doubt that trade links operated between coastal and
highland regions. Ocean salt was frequently carried inland together
with fish and molluscs, a source of valuable iodine, effective in the
prevention and cure of cretinism and goitre common in mountain
regions. The trade worked both ways, with highlanders providing
much-needed goods to compensate for El Niño catastrophes along
the coast.

The Long-Lost Pyramids of Peru

On 14 September 1988 Dr Walter Alva announced the discovery of the

Figure 5. The Lost Tombs of the Mochica

On 14 September 1988 the world's press announced the discovery of the lost tombs of Sipan, the final resting place of the Mochica sun-kings. The spectacular treasure-trove of gold, silver, bronze and semi-precious stones was compared to that of Tutankhamun's in Egypt.

undisturbed tomb of a hitherto unknown Mochica king buried 1,700 years ago in a pyramid at Sipan. For some time he and other archaeologists suspected that a secret cache of Mochica treasure may lie buried around the Lambayeque region following the appearance of looted antiquities on the open market around the end of 1986.

The Huaca Rajada mud-brick pyramid complex lies at the foot of the black mountains in the Lambayeque Valley on Peru's northern coast. It consists of three large adobe (mud-brick) pyramid platforms *(plate 1)* built by the Mochica in several stages from around AD 100 to 700. The pyramids, lashed by the torrential rains of El Niño for almost 2,000 years, are today barely recognisable as man-made structures *(plate 1a)*.

An archaeological reconstruction of the complex *(plate 1b)* suggests that the taller central platform was built in around AD 100 and the more distant one in around AD 700. In the foreground, to the left of the taller pyramid, the Mochica constructed another platform 70 metres long, 50 metres wide and 10 metres high (230 feet by 165 feet by 33 feet), with a smaller pyramid-shaped temple on top at one end. This dated from around AD 100 to 300 and contained the long-lost tombs of the Mochica.

A nearby lake is all that remains of a clay pit excavated during the construction phase. In those days brick-makers from the nearby administration centre of Pampa Grande would have laboured without the wheel, or motive power, scooping mud from the valley floor into wooden moulds before laying them in the sun to bake rock-hard. Others, working from scaffolding, rendered the outside walls of the platform with a coat of mud and sand to give a smooth finish. The dusty bed of a wide high-banked irrigation canal that stretched from Pampa Grande to Sipan gives some clue as to the engineering abilities and achievements of the Mochica.

Excavations at the top of the burial platform revealed its relatively recent use as a cemetery for locals. Loose dirt from shallow graves near the surface contrasted sharply with compacted earth nearby. As Walter Alva and his team dug deeper, they could never have anticipated what lay ahead. Two more undisturbed Mochica tombs were discovered within three years *(plate 1)*; the tomb of the Lord of Sipan was the first to emerge, in 1987, on the uppermost level. Radiocarbon dating placed the age of roof timbers at around AD 290. Next, a year later, came the tomb of the Priest on the same level and then, in 1990, the tomb of the Old Lord of Sipan (c. AD 100) at the base of the platform. Another tomb was found looted and virtually emptied of its contents on the third level down. Whether this was ever occupied is not known.

When I examined the tombs and treasures of the Mochica it was clear that they, like the Mayas and Egyptians, possessed a cosmological understanding of a very high order. They understood the super-science of the sun, which they worshipped as the god of fertility, astrology and destruction. This knowledge is only just dawning on modern man in our own age of space exploration (see figures A1 and A3–7 in the appendices and figures 32, 41, 44 and 45) and, like the Mayas and Egyptians, the Mochica were aware of the higher orders of spirituality, and they went to great lengths, just like them, to encode their super-knowledge into their treasures at Sipan.

The Tomb of the Lord of Sipan

The tomb of the Lord of Sipan differed markedly from the others in two important respects: roof construction and coffin construction (compare plate 4 with plates 2 and 3). Firstly, the roof of the Lord of Sipan's tomb comprised 17 wooden transverse horizontal beams, but only 16 of these actually supported the roofing materials. The remaining beam (shown in the foreground of plate 4) was embedded into the adobe wall construction and was, as far as structural support of the roof was concerned, curiously redundant. The 16 supporting beams were themselves supported by 5 short Y-shaped vertical prop-beams. These figures (quantities of beams) at first appear to be unexceptional; however, examining the roof beams in the sequence in which archaeologists uncovered them (figure 6), we note that another Y-shaped prop-beam was found on top of the roof (shown in the top centre of figure 6). Why would builders of the tomb place a roof support beam on top of a roof instead of in situ in its proper place underneath as a support? Could the Mochica be attempting to convey a message? If we recall (figure 7), the entrance leading to Tutankhamun's tomb consisted of 16 quarried limestone steps, 6 of which had been chiselled away and removed to permit access of larger pieces of furniture into the tomb. The missing 6 steps were later reinstated in soft plaster by the burial party just before the entrance-way to the tomb was sealed. This raised the question of 'why would a burial party seal a tomb and then repair a broken stairway prior to filling the stairway with rubble to prevent entry in the future?' It didn't make sense; it would simply

Figure 6. The Sunspot Cycle Message of the Lord of Sipan

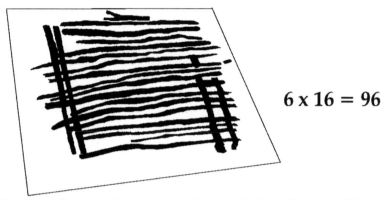

$$6 \times 16 = 96$$

Sixteen wooden beams *(above)* supported the roof of Lord Sipan's tomb *(plate 4)*. Five Y-shaped wooden beams supported these. 5 x 16 is not astronomically significant; however, we note that one Y-shaped beam was found on top of the roof *(top centre, above)*. Why would tomb-builders place one of six supports on top of the roof? The message here is that 6 is important; 6 x 16 = 96, the number of magnetic cycles in one sunspot cycle *(figure 8)*. One more transverse beam was embedded in the bricks (making a total of 97) but this did not support the roof *(plate 4)*.

Figure 7. The Sunspot Cycle Message of Tutankhamun

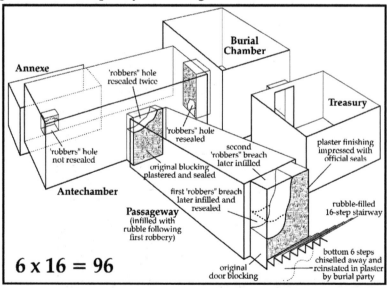

The bottom 6 steps of the 16-step stairway, which led to the tomb of Tutankhamun, were chiselled away by the burial party, according to archaeologists, to permit access of larger pieces of furniture into the tomb.The steps, originally stone, were reinstated in plaster by the same burial party. But why would a burial party seal a tomb and then repair a broken stairway before filling the stairway with rubble behind themselves? This would simply invite others to use the steps in the future, to gain access to a solid wall. The 6 and the 16 are astronomically significant; 6 x 16 = 96, the number of magnetic cycles in one sunspot cycle *(figure 8)*.

Figure 8. The Sunspot Cycle Message of Lord Pacal

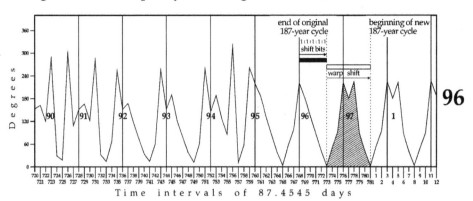

96

The computer-calculated version of the sunspot cycle shows that 96 microcycles of magnetic activity take place on the sun every 187 years (the 97th cycle leads to an even longer cycle of 18,139 years). The 96-cycle sequence was known by ancient sun-worshipping civilisations who encoded the secret super-science of the sun into their treasures. (Note: *to save space the first 89 microcycles are not shown*).

Figure 9. The Palace at Palenque

96

(*a*) Overview of the Palace at Palenque. (*b*) Tablet of 96 glyphs from the steps of the Palace at Palenque. (*c*) The Temple of Inscriptions, Palenque, burial place of Lord Pacal and his tombstone, the Lid of Palenque.

invite others to gain unauthorised access to the tomb at a later date. Those familiar with the super-science of the sun will already have realised the astronomical significance of these two numbers: 16 x 6 = 96, the number of cycles of magnetic activity which take place on the sun during one 187-year sunspot cycle *(figure 8)*. In drawing our attention to the numbers 16 and 6, Tutankhamun was telling us that he taught his people the super-science of the sun almost 3,500 years ago on the banks of the Nile.

In the same way, a stone tablet at Palenque *(see figure 9b)*, the burial place of Lord Pacal, carried 96 glyphs (carved characters); Lord Pacal also taught his people the super-science of the sun.

The 16 roof timbers in the tomb of the Lord of Sipan therefore, taken together with the (total of) 6 Y-shaped beams, tell us that the Lord of Sipan, like Tutankhamun and Lord Pacal, taught his people the super-science of the sun; 16 x 6 = 96. The extra curiously redundant beam, the seventeenth, goes one step further by adding 1 to the total of 96; 1 + 96=97, the number of magnetic cycles in one sunspot cycle *(see figure 8, magnetic cycle number 97)* that need to be recognised when the longer solar magnetic reversal period of 3,740 years is under consideration.

The Temple of Inscriptions at Palenque *(figure 9c)* contained other astronomical numerical indicators. In 1952 Mexican archaeologist Alberto Ruz climbed the stairway that led to the temple at the top of the Pyramid of Inscriptions. He noticed 4 pairs of circular holes in one of the flooring slabs at the top of the pyramid. Removing the mortar filling that blocked the holes, he was able to insert hooks and lift the paving stone clear of the floor. In so doing he exposed a secret rubble-filled stairway running down through the pyramid.

At the bottom of the excavated stairway he was confronted by a stone wall which carried a box containing 11 jade beads, 3 red-painted shells, 3 clay plates and a pearl in a seashell filled with red cinnabar. Demolishing the wall, the excavators found themselves in a small square chamber where their flickering torches picked out the skeletons of 5 men and 1 woman. To the left, a 3-sided door blocked access to the tomb. Opening the door, for the first time in 1,250 years, Ruz was confronted by an enormous ornately carved limestone slab *(figure 24)* which had two of its corners missing. The chamber, supported by 5 roof beams, was filled with treasures; two plaster heads rested on the floor of the tomb, one with a high hairstyle *(plate 7e)* and another, with a low hairstyle, personified the man in the tomb. The stone

Figure 10. The 9 9 9 9 9 Message of Lord Pacal

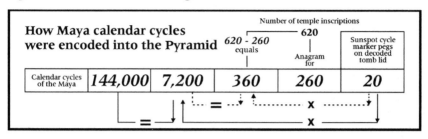

	144,000	7,200	360	260	20
1	Pearl in seashell	Female skeleton in antechamber	Single long bead on necklace	Single long bead on necklace	Single long bead on necklace
2	Holes in paving slab	Holes in paving slab	Holes in paving slab	Holes in paving slab	Plaster heads on tomb floor
3	Clay plates in stone chest	Red shells in stone chest	-sided tomb door	Jade beads (1 in each hand, 1 in mouth)	-tiered jade necklace
4	Steps down into tomb	Jade rings on left hand	Jade rings on right hand	Sets of holes in paving slab	Cylindrical plugs in sarcophagus
5	Pyramid stairway landings	Temple doorways	Male skeletons	Ceiling beams	Sarcophagus sides
6	Temple pillars	Sides to tomb lid	missing **6**	missing **6**	missing **6**
7	missing **7**	Necklace beads	**7** = 13 Necklace beads	**7** = 13 Necklace beads	**7** = 13 Necklace beads
8	**8** = 15 Necklace beads	Dash-dot beads •••	Dash-dot beads •••	Dash-dot beads •••	Dash-dot beads •••
9	Bottom steps of pyramid	Pyramid levels	Top steps of pyramid	Lords painted on tomb walls	9 / 9* Codes on left / right sides of lid

Decoding the clues of the Pyramid and Temple of Inscriptions

Decoding in relation to calendar cycles used by the Maya:

$$9 \times 144{,}000 + 9 \times 7{,}200 + 9 \times 360 + 9 \times 260 + 9 \times 20$$

$$= 1{,}366{,}560 \text{ days}$$

Lord Pacal encoded the number of the sun-king Supergods 9, 9, 9, 9, 9 into his treasures in the Temple of Inscriptions, Palenque *(figure 9c)*. The number cleverly conceals astronomical information; 9 multiplied by the Maya calendar cycles of time, in days, amounts to 1,366,560 days, the duration of 20 sunspot cycles, one solar magnetic reversal.

Figure 11. The 9 9 9 9 9 Message of Tutankhamun

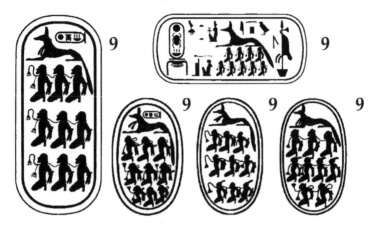

Door seals and object seals from the tomb of Tutankhamun *(figure 7)* showing the 'prisoners', groups of 9 individuals (9, 9, 9, 9, 9) bound by rope around the neck and arms. Each rope terminates with a lotus flower, the epitome of sun-worship, suggesting that the 'prisoners' were in 'divine captivity' on earth.

Figure 12. The 9 Layers of Tutankhamun's Coffin

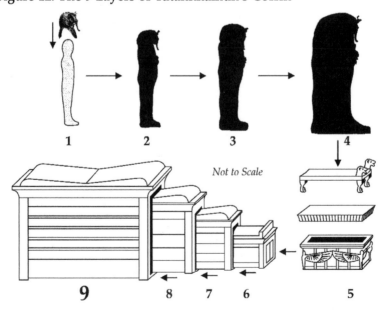

Tutankhamun was entombed in 9 layers of coffin *(see The Tutankhamun Prophecies, Chapter 3)*. 9 is symbolic in that it is the highest number that can be reached before becoming (one) 1 (as in 10) with God. Tutankhamun, like the other sun-king Supergods, was second only to God.

sarcophagus had one corner missing, and the lid was tied down by 4 stone plugs. The skull of the dead man was covered by a mosaic jade face mask *(plate 29, boxed, top right)*. He carried a jade bead in each palm and another in his mouth. He wore a 3-tiered jade necklace around his neck, 4 jade rings on his left hand and again 4 on his right. What was it all about?

Analysis of the information reveals a remarkable legacy left by the Maya. They were playing a game of numbers. Setting the numbers down, it becomes clear what they were trying to say *(figure 10)*; they had left modern man a secret message encoded into their jewellery and architecture which, when broken, reveals the duration of magnetic reversals on the sun. These affect the earth, sometimes causing infertility cycles *(figures 32 and 41)* and sometimes catastrophic destruction *(figures 44 and 45)*. The numbers matrix finishes at 9, 9, 9, 9, 9, the highest number before becoming 1 (100000) with God. The number 9, 9, 9, 9, 9 hence represents the number of a spiritual teacher, a Supergod *(figure 30)*.

Door seals and object seals found in the tomb of Tutankhamun *(figure 12)* pointed to the same numbers, 9, 9, 9, 9, and he was buried in 9 levels of coffin, confirming that Tutankhamun was a Supergod.

It was on 20 June 1987, four months after digging began, that archaeologists reached the untouched tomb of the Lord of Sipan. To the untrained eye his simple wooden coffin betrayed the status of a once-great leader. There was a message concealed in the lid (*figure 13)*, which nobody knew or has since, until now, realised; the lid was fixed to the sides by 9 copper straps (9, 9, 9, 9). The corners, too, carried the same number of ties (9, 9, 9, 9), and his bones, untouched for more than 1,700 years, were accompanied by 8 others, 9 in all. This was no accident and no coincidence; the Lord of Sipan, like Tutankhamun and Lord Pacal, was both a sun-king and a Supergod.

Just above the mausoleum, 30 metres (98 feet) below the summit of the pyramid, the bones of a 'guard' *(plate 4g)* with severed feet were the first to emerge. The message was clear: this man would never walk upon the earth again, would never reincarnate. But this had little to do with the messenger; it was meant for the man below him, the man he pointed to with his head, the king *(a)*, wrapped in red.

Beneath the bones of the guard lay the 16 wooden beams of the burial chamber. A recess in the wall concealed a meditating priest *(l)* who prayed for the soul of the king. The skeletons of two men *(d and*

Figure 13. The 9 9 9 9 9 Message of the Lord of Sipan

The lid of the coffin of the Lord of Sipan *(plates 4 and 5)* was tied to the sides by three sets of copper straps (3, 3, 3), 9 in all, along each side (9, 9, 9, 9). The corners were likewise tied together, and to the floor of the coffin, with the same number of straps, 9 at each corner (9, 9, 9, 9). The tomb was the final resting place of the Lord of Sipan and 8 companions, 9 in all.

j), aged about 40 at the time of death, lay on either side of the king, and between each of these and the king lay a llama *(e and i)*, each with its head and neck severed from the body. These 'sacrificial lambs' (identical to sheep without the head and neck) suggest the king, who lay in between, was the lamb of God, a spiritual teacher.

At the king's feet a 'concubine' *(k)*, aged around 20, faced west, while at the head end another *(b)* of the same age faced east. A third female *(c)*, the 'fortune-teller', lay beneath the one that faced east; she would foretell good fortune for the king in the afterlife. In the corner a young boy *(f)*, aged around 10, sits with outstretched legs facing the king. The Mochica believed that for seven days following physical death the soul revisits familiar places, bidding farewell to old friends, during which time relatives collect possessions of the deceased to furnish the tomb. The young boy probably died of natural causes during this seven-day period and was placed in the tomb to symbolise eternal youthfulness in the afterlife. On the eighth day the soul departed accompanied by a dog *(h)* which would guide his master

Figure 14. The Gods of Heliopolis

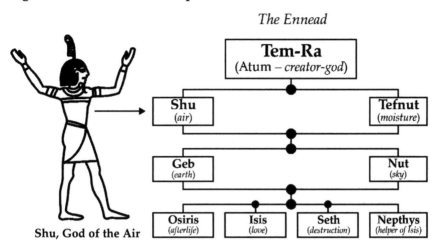

Shu, God of the Air

across the first level of the underworld, a swift-flowing river.

The 'platform'-style tomb, with its horizontal beams and Y-shaped prop-supports, was commonly found throughout North and South America. Historian Donald A. Mackenzie, in *Myths of Pre-Columbian America*, comments:

> In America the dead who are disposed of in platform tombs are protected in wooden boxes, canoes or wrapped between flat boards. They are then supported by Y-shaped stakes. The 'Y' symbol, in ancient Egypt, is associated with one of the creator gods, Shu, who supports the firmament *(figure 14)*. Four 'Y' symbols represent the sky-pillars of the four cardinal points of the heavens. Platforms supported on Y-formed stakes appear to be symbols of heaven.

This, again, seems to suggest that the Lord of Sipan was associated with heaven, confirming his status as a Supergod.

The Treasures of the Tomb

The burial party was surrounded by 1,137 ceramic pots. Many, according to archaeologists, depicted naked prisoners bound with rope around their necks, a common Mochica preoccupation curiously paralleled by those on the tomb seals of Tutankhamun. Others were fashioned as warriors carrying weapons, and others as men at play.

Virtually all the contents of the coffin *(plate 5a)* were wrapped within a thin sheet of copper approximately 3 metres (10 feet) square. An embroidered woollen blanket insulated this from a red outer fine woollen blanket, symbolic of sacrifice, that secured the bundle. The copper sheet carried a copper strap that extended across the copper-clad feet of the dead man.

The cache of treasure (briefly mentioned earlier) included 13 pectoral collars, many of which were made of thousands of seashell beads each drilled with holes measuring only 0.4 millimetre (1/1,000 inch) in radius. These sun-ray-style collars were worn around the neck, over the shoulders *(plate 5b)*, and were similar in style to the one worn by Tutankhamun *(figure 26a)*, confirming the status of the Lord of Sipan as a sun-king. Another large necklace, made up of 10 large gold 'peanuts' (draped across the left-hand shoulder to the breastbone) and 10 silver peanuts (across the right), hung from his neck. Gold represented, on the one hand, the flesh of the gods, while silver represented the bones. At the same time gold was synonymous with the sun and silver with the moon. Peanut shells contain two spheres; it is therefore likely that the necklace of gold and silver peanut shells epitomises the sun and the moon. The man who wore the necklace is hence associated with the sun and the moon, day and night, life and death.

Solid gold plates covered the eyes, nose and mouth. Another crescent-shaped bat-mask *(plate 7f)*, similar to the one worn by Lord Pacal *(plate 7d)*, covered the mouth and cheeks. In his right hand he carried an ornate golden rod-like sceptre *(seen in more detail in plate 8b)* and in his left a silver knife. Seventy-two individual hollow gold spheres, arranged in a semicircle, were positioned to follow the outer edge of the pectorals. Another necklace, made of 16 circular golden discs, was draped across his chest. Those familiar with the super-science of the sun will have realised that these quantities are all astronomically significant; there are 20 (peanuts) magnetic cycles in one solar magnetic reversal; there are 16 (golden discs) sunspot cycles in one 187-year sunspot cycle (16 x 6 magnetic cycles = the 96 magnetic cycles of one 187-year cycle mentioned earlier) and there are 72 'calendar rounds' (used by the Maya) in one 3,740-year solar magnetic reversal.

His body rested on two objects that archaeologists describe as golden crescent-shaped *(figure 15)* 'knives', that more likely represent the 'radiating soul' *(figure 16)*. The reconstruction *(plate 5b)* suggests that these two ornaments hung from his waist-belt at the back. Two more golden ornaments hung from his waist-belt at the front *(plates 5b and 8b)*. These were made from eight golden spheres, attached to each other in a semicircle. The centre of each carried a tiny model of Ai Apaec, the supreme jaguar-god of the Mochica, depicted in anthropomorphic form with huge fangs and a cat-like wrinkled face. In his right hand he carries a rope from which hangs a decapitated human head, and in his left he carries what archaeologists describe as a 'sacrificial knife'. Because of this he is often referred to as the 'decapitator'.

It seems that archaeologists have confused Ai Apaec's crescent-shaped 'sacrificial knife' with similarly shaped crescent-shaped 'knives' used by the Mochica. A more likely explanation is that Ai Apaec, with his arms outstretched, weighs, like scales, the bound (prisoner's) head (the physical body) against the crescent shape of the soul *(figures 15 and 16)*, concentrating the mind on the afterlife possibilities of either divine bondage, on earth, like the depictions found on the tomb seals of Tutankhamun and those found on the 1,137 ceramic pots, as against the corollary of spiritual purification of the soul and a promise of everlasting life in the spirit world.

The cat-like face of Ai Apaec depicts the jaguar, with its golden coat and brown spots, that was also revered by the Maya as an embodiment of the golden sun covered in brown spots (sunspots) on earth.

Another so-called golden 'knife' *(figure 5b, headdress)* was found beneath the skull of the Lord of Sipan. However, close examination shows that the crescent shape again corresponds to that of the radiating soul *(figures 15 and 16)*; the underside edge comprises two tight crescents that clearly refer to the halo or spirit as depicted by the Maya in their carvings *(figure 16)*, while the upper outer edge is clearly elliptical, showing the path of the earth around the sun (light) in one year. The outer edge and underside crescents hence together show that the halo that radiates from those who are purified is one and the same energy as the energy that radiates from the sun; meaning that the light within us is the same light as that of the sun, which is God, creator of the universe. The golden crescent carried above the head of the Lord of Sipan hence tells us that he was both pure in spirit and that he *was* the sun. His feathered headdress also shows that he ruled the four corners of the sky, the heavens. The two crescent

Figure 15. The Halo of the Sun-King

The underside of the head-gear worn by the Mochica depicts a halo, as shown in figure 16 *(below)*. The outer edge describes an ellipse, which in turn describes the motion of the earth around the sun. The head-gear thus suggests that the spirit (light) in man is one and the same as the spirit (light) of the sun. Normally the light (the soul) resides inside the body. But purified souls are often depicted with light radiating from the head.

Figure 16. The Halo of the Priest

Drawing of a Mayan priest, from a Yucatán rock carving, shown in a meditative position. When the physical, emotional and intellectual bodies achieve coordinated equilibrium, electromagnetic energy flows up the spinal column and radiates from the crown chakra centre at the top of the head *(figure 88)*. The Maya represented this as a fountain of light, representing high levels of soul energy leaving (radiating from) the body.

'knives' that hang from the waist go one step further in telling us, once again, that he was both the sun and the moon; gold and silver, night and day, life and death.

He wore large gold and turquoise earrings *(figure 17)* that were remarkable for their detail. The outer edge of each carried 42 golden spheres. Inside this a mosaic circle of turquoise circumscribed a central disc of gold, cut out to accommodate three inlaid characters: two mosaic turquoise warriors flanking a central golden figure. The central, three-dimensional figure resembled a miniature Lord of Sipan in all his refinery carrying a golden sceptre in his right hand, a gold shield in his left, a gold bat-mask across his face, a golden crescent halo radiating from his head, and four Ai Apaec semicircles hanging from the waist.

The attire of the central miniature differed from that worn by the Lord of Sipan *(as shown in plate 5)*; the miniature wears a necklace of owl heads identical to a necklace worn by the *Old* Lord of Sipan (discussed later) who was buried at the bottom level of the pyramid, suggesting that the Lord of Sipan was a descendant of the Old Lord. Another curiosity is that the silhouette, cut into the disc to accommodate the three inlaid miniature figures, does not in any way match the periphery of the inlaid figures, as though to labour the point that 'the characters depicted here do not fit (belong) *here'*, but belong in another tomb – that of the Old Lord, who wears a necklace of owl heads. It is almost as if the complex construction of the ear-pieces suggests that the Lord of Sipan is in the wrong tomb, so to speak.

Archaeologists' reconstruction of the Lord of Sipan *(figure 5b)* shows him wearing his golden tunic, fringed in conical bells, that he wore on top of his white shroud-vest *(detailed in plate 5a)* and copper sandals.

Two banner-like golden shields covered the contents of the coffin. One showed, in the centre, a mysterious small man wearing a hat who appeared again in each of the corners of the other shield *(figure 18)* and again on the chest of the Lord of Sipan *(plate 8a, b, and c)*. The style of the hat resembles that of the Spanish priests who came to Peru with the conquistadores in the sixteenth century, which might not be considered unusual, except that the Lord of Sipan was buried 1,250 years earlier. Examination of other pieces of jewellery from the Sipan complex *(see plate 11h)* suggests the hat may in fact represent the sun. The small man with the hat may therefore be considered as representing the sun, the Lord of Sipan, who ruled the four corners.

This notion of dominion over the four corners of the sky was

Figure 17. Golden Earring Inlaid with Mosaic Turquoise
from the Tomb of the Lord of Sipan

another feature shared by sun-king Supergods. A picture on the backrest of the gold-foil throne found in the tomb of Tutankhamun *(figure 19)* shows Tutankhamun together with his loving wife Ankhesenamun. In the picture both wear the 'scarf tails' that represent the four corners. Ankhesenamun touches Tutankhamun saying 'he is the four corners'. That the scarf tails represent this is in little doubt; the same symbolism was used by the Mexicans to depict the first four sky-gods who ruled the heavens, the four Tezcatlipocas *(figure 20)*. The feathered headdress of the Lord of Sipan similarly shows the four corners, and Lord Pacal carries the same four-corners mark on his forehead in a picture from the decoded Amazing Lid of Palenque *(figure 21)*.

(a)

(b)

Figure 18. The Lord of Sipan, King of the Four Corners

(a) The Sipan sun-king carries both the mark of the sun (halo) and the feathers of the four corners on his head. In his hand he carries the golden rod-like sceptre, shaped with the four corners. (b) The attendant carries a golden shield, the corners of which (see main text) are occupied by a mysterious small man wearing a hat. It seems that the hat epitomises the sun (plate 11h). The Lord of Sipan, like Lord Pacal of Mexico and Tutankhamun of Egypt, ruled the four corners of the sky, the heavens.

Figure 19. Tutankhamen, King of the Four Corners

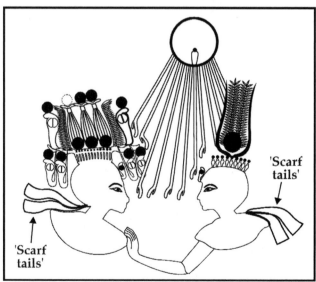

Treasures from the tomb of Tutankhamun show the young king and his wife, Ankhesenamun, wearing the symbols of the four corners. Ankhesenamun is saying that Tutankhamun, like the Lord of Sipan, ruled the four corners of the heavens (north, south, east and west).

Figure 20. The Mexican Gods of the Four Corners

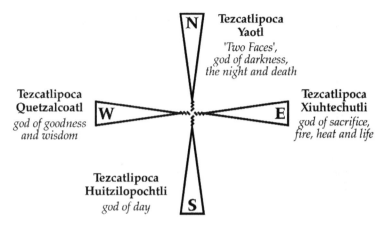

N

**Tezcatlipoca
Yaotl**
*'Two Faces',
god of darkness,
the night and death*

**Tezcatlipoca
Quetzalcoatl**
*god of goodness
and wisdom*

W

E

**Tezcatlipoca
Xiuhtechutli**
*god of sacrifice,
fire, heat and life*

**Tezcatlipoca
Huitzilopochtli**
god of day

S

In Mexican mythology four gods ruled the four quarters of the sky. These were known as the four Tezcatlipocas, the first four brothers of creation.

Figure 21. Lord Pacal of the Four Corners

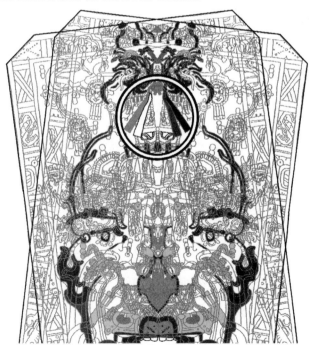

The decoded composite picture of Lord Pacal from *The Amazing Lid of Palenque (plate 7d)* reveals that he was also king of the four corners (which hang from his head, *circled*) like the Lord of Sipan *(plate 7f)*, who carries the four corners as a headdress.

31

The Amazing Lid of Palenque and the Lord of Sipan

Both the Mayas and the Egyptians believed that the human constitution may be broken down into four distinct areas *(figure 22)*: the astral (spiritual), the physical, the intellectual and the emotional. They believed that these four bodies were created simultaneously and that on death the physical body returned to dust, taking with it the emotional body (an adjunct of the heart) and the intellectual body (an adjunct of the brain). Destination of the soul depended on the purity of the soul at the time of physical death; pure souls would journey to the heavens and become stars, everlasting gods. Impure souls would journey through the underworld and purgatory before reincarnating on earth for another try at soul purification through physical, emotional and intellectual suffering. It was for this reason that the Egyptians preserved only some of their internal organs (liver, lungs, stomach and intestines) in canopic jars on physical death. The practice was allegorical; there was no need to preserve the heart and brain – if they did reincarnate they would receive a new heart and a new brain, thereby remembering nothing of their previous emotional and intellectual lifetimes.

The mechanics of the reincarnation process imply that the super-knowledge, which had taken many lifetimes to accumulate, could have been acquired more quickly had they been able to build on the knowledge with each successive incarnation. But a new brain and heart each incarnation precluded such gains. So the purification process takes many more lifetimes than it otherwise might. To overcome this, the ancients encoded their super-knowledge into their treasures. Rediscovery of the same knowledge, in the next incarnation, would enable a higher starting level of purification, giving the soul a better chance of transmigration and transmutation into a star the next time around.

But how could the knowledge be 'written down' so as to guarantee its transmission over vast epochs of time?

Throughout history nations and languages have been wiped out by conquering armies and political regimes eager to impose their own beliefs on defeated nations. Ideas and cultures are lost through ideological succession. Natural disasters, floods, fire and earthquake likewise erase all evidence of earlier civilisations. Solar-inspired catastrophe cycles that periodically cause the earth to tilt on its axis *(figures 44 and 45)* likewise defeat the transmission of knowledge.

Figure 22. How Ancient Civilisations Perceived Human Life
the true nature of man

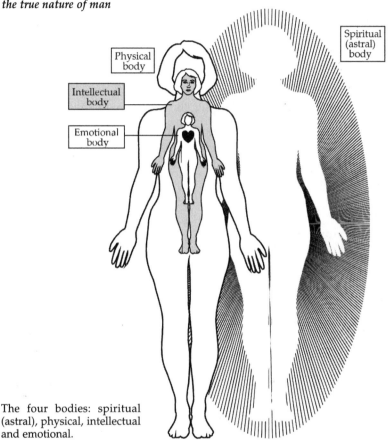

The four bodies: spiritual (astral), physical, intellectual and emotional.

There are two ways to 'write down' knowledge for posterity without the use of words. One way is by using numbers, the cultural common denominator; the number 10 is common to all mankind, because all of mankind has 10 fingers. This is why Lord Pacal chose to use numbers in his encoding of solar magnetic cycles into the pyramid clues at Palenque *(figure 10)* and why Tutankhamun used numbers to encode his knowledge into his sun-ray necklace *(figure 26)*. A second way of encoding information is through the use of pictures; one picture tells a thousand words, and all pictures are common to all people.

Some pictures convey information more efficiently and effectively than others; if we ask ourselves the question 'what's so special about the jigsaw picture *(figure 23, top)* of an English country garden?', we quickly realise that the human brain finds it difficult to reconcile such a loosely defined interrogation criterion. However, if we ask the same question about the lower picture *(figure 23, bottom)* the answer becomes immediately apparent: several pieces of the puzzle are missing. This demonstrates that the human brain finds difficulty in attaching meaning to what it sees; rather, it is much easier for it to attach meaning to what it does not see – the exception rather than the rule. This is why we are quick to see the faults in others around us but often fail to see merit where merit is due. It also explains why we are slow to see defects in our own character, because we have no perfect picture of ourselves against which we can be compared. It was for these reasons that the ancients chose to *omit* information from their treasures. *Omission* served as the fundamental mechanism that facilitated the encoding of information. Decoding hence involved a search for, assimilation of and (once located) reorganisation of the missing pieces. The fact that information had been *encoded* itself conveyed a special meaning that differentiated it from other less important information that had not.

In 1989, while working at Cranfield University, I successfully calculated the duration of the long-term sunspot cycle. The university computer, one of the most powerful in the world, had predicted that the sun would reverse its magnetic field every 3,740 years (1,366,040 days). I was later astonished to learn that the Maya of Mexico worshipped a number virtually identical to this (1,366,560), more than a thousand years ago in the jungles of Mexico. It soon became clear that this ancient sun-worshipping civilisation knew more about the magnetic cycles of the sun than we did in 1989.

So I travelled to their ceremonial centre of Palenque, deep in the Mexican jungle, to take a closer look at the treasures they left behind. I was impressed by the lid that covered the sarcophagus of Lord Pacal. But I saw something, it seems, that nobody else had ever noticed: two corners of the lid were missing *(figure 24)*. I showed how, by finding the missing corners, the surrounding border code could be decoded to reveal secret instructions that enabled the central carving itself to be decoded. Plate 6 shows one example of a border code instruction which refers to one specific picture hidden in the central carving *(plate 7d)*. This decoded composite picture shows the head of Lord Pacal, occupant of the tomb, with his mouth covered by a bat-mask. The bat represented death for the Maya. On his head, in

Figure 23. How the Brain Perceives Information

The brain sees nothing unusual in the top picture but immediately spots the defects in the lower picture.

accordance with the border code instruction contained in plate 6, sits a baby bird that carries a chain, from which hangs a conch shell. The conch shell was the symbol of the wind and the mark of Quetzalcoatl*, highest of gods of the Maya (the feathered snake, the perfect being. The eagle represented the wind and the soul in the sky while the snake represented the body on earth that sheds its skin). The baby bird hence depicts a baby quetzal bird, a brightly coloured bird of the rainforest. The message concealed in this decoded picture hence reads *'Lord Pacal died and was reborn as Quetzalcoatl'.*

This discovery is particularly interesting because in around AD 1710 a Dominican monk, Father Francisco Ximenex, stumbled across an ancient manuscript concealed behind a group of loose stones in the thick whitewashed walls of his parish church at Santo Tomas Chichicastenango, about 322 kilometres (200 miles) up the River Ucamacinta from Palenque, in today's Guatemala. The crumbling pages of the manuscript had been written by an unknown Quiche Maya Indian in around AD 1550 in an attempt to set down the history and traditions of his people. The document was a later version of an earlier 'book of the people', the *Popol Vuh*, which had been 'lost'. It begins and ends with the same few words: '. . . the original book written long ago existed, but its sight is hidden from the *searcher* and the *thinker.'* The limestone lid that covered the sarcophagus of Lord Pacal was hidden from archaeologists *(searchers)* inside the Temple of Inscriptions. We now know it contains highly complex encoded

---

* The name Quetzalcoatl is the Nahuatl (Aztec) translation of the words 'feathered snake'. The Quiche (Maya) translation of the words 'feathered snake' is Ku-kul-kan.

The naming of the gods of Mexico is a complex subject. Many of essentially the same gods were given different names at different times throughout Mesoamerican history. For example, the god of rain during the Maya period was known as Chaac, during the Zapotec period Cocijo, and during the Aztec period Tlaloc. Additionally, many of the gods once thought to have been uniquely Aztec appear in the recently decoded Amazing Lid of Palenque meaning, therefore, that the same gods must have been known during the period of the Maya but that their names are unknown.

There are other difficulties. Many of the gods change roles at different times. Quetzalcoatl was the god of the wind (and the west, as well as goodness and wisdom) and perceived as presiding, like the wind, over all space, the four corners of the sky. When he journeyed into the southern sky he was associated with Huitzilopochtli, the god of day, who lived in the southern quarter of the sky, and hence was associated with daylight (sunlight) and the sun. When Quetzalcoatl journeyed into the underworld he was associated with darkness and hence the god of darkness (and death) Tezcatlipoca Yaotl, of the north. When Quetzalcoatl occupied the eastern sky he was associated with Xiuhtechutli, the god of fire. Some commentators insist that Quetzalcoatl was the brother of Huitzilopochtli, Yaotl and

information (hidden from the *thinker*). Is the Amazing Lid of Palenque the long-lost book of the Maya? I believe it is. Plate 7d is just one of around 200 secret pictures contained in the lid. *(Plates 23 and 25b, 26–31 and 32a show a few more which will be featured later in this book.)*

It was nine years after the first decoding of the Amazing Lid of Palenque that I travelled to Peru and first laid eyes on the Lord of Sipan *(plate 7f)*. He bore an uncanny and remarkable resemblance to Lord Pacal's decoded image from the Amazing Lid of Palenque *(plate 7d)*. Plate 7d was only one in a series which showed the death and rebirth of Lord Pacal. Another of the images from the series *(plate 28)* showed a picture of dying Pacal carried away by the 'god of death', a skeleton wearing a cloak and, curiously, a hat, which raises the same question raised earlier: how could a priest-like hat be featured in an artefact of such antiquity?

Returning home from Peru, I took another look at the Amazing Lid of Palenque, this time mindful of the small man with the hat, and soon discovered what I had suspected *(plate 9)*: the bat-mask that covered the face of Lord Pacal was supported by a picture of the mystery man with the hat. I had missed him during the first decoding of the lid *(plate 7d)*. What could be more conclusive? The Lord of Sipan and Lord Pacal must have been one and the same *(plate 10)*; only time, 500 years, separated these two great kings, reincarnations of the same being.

Remarkably, the small man with the hat, which covers the face of Lord Pacal, wears a tiny bat-mask across his own face. His heart can

Xiuhtechutli while others believe that they were different emanations of Quetzalcoatl as he occupied the different cardinal points. Because he was the highest of gods he was seen as the sun itself, or the sun-god. Huitzilopochtli, as the god of day, was also seen as the sun-god. Tonatiuh, another ostensible god of the Aztecs (who also appears on the Amazing Lid of Palenque), was also a sun-god.

To overcome these difficulties, firstly, Mesoamerican gods mentioned throughout this book have been given names known to have been used during the Aztec period, irrespective of the historical period they were thought to subsist. Secondly, to avoid confusion, generic names are used wherever possible, for example the 'sun-god' may be used in place of the name of a particular god. Thirdly, to help the reader, pronunciation of the names, where necessary, is given in brackets following their first appearance in the main text.

It is also worth mentioning that the words *Maya* and *Mayan* are interchangeable, as are the plurals *Maya, Mayans* and *Mayas* and that the word *Inca* can be used in two ways: to refer to the race, or to an individual belonging to the race, of South American people of that name, or to the leader of that race, the *Inca*, king (emperor). Similarly, the word *Incas* may refer to either the race, or to individuals belonging to the race, of South American people of that name, or to more than one king (emperor) of those people.

Figure 24. The Amazing Lid of Palenque

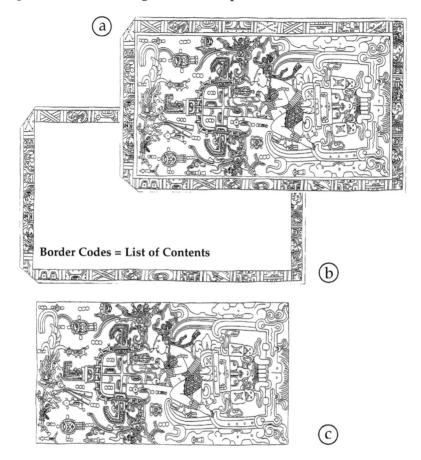

Border Codes = List of Contents

Central Carving = Sacred Book of the Maya
encoded in stone

(a) Line drawing of the Lid of Palenque, the five-tonne limestone lid that covered Lord Pacal's sarcophagus in the Temple of Inscriptions at Palenque, Mexico. We note that the corners of the lid are missing. If a transparent copy of the drawing is made, the patterns that should be carried by the missing corners, of the original drawing, can be repaired (by overlaying the transparency end to end on the original). Decoding of the lid can now begin, utilising both the original together with the transparent facsimile. Using this method, we discover that the border code pattern (b) contains secret pictures which provide a list of contents of more secret stories hidden in the central carving (c). Plate 6 shows one example. The central carving contains hundreds of secret pictures which tell many stories. The one shown in plate 7d corresponds with the border code (instruction) featured in plate 6. Plates 25b, 26 – 31 and 32a feature more stories using different orientations of the drawings. Other stories (not shown here) use moving pictures (animations) to explain the story-line.

Figure 25. The 144,000 Message
of Lord Pacal and the Lord of Sipan
(see plate 9)

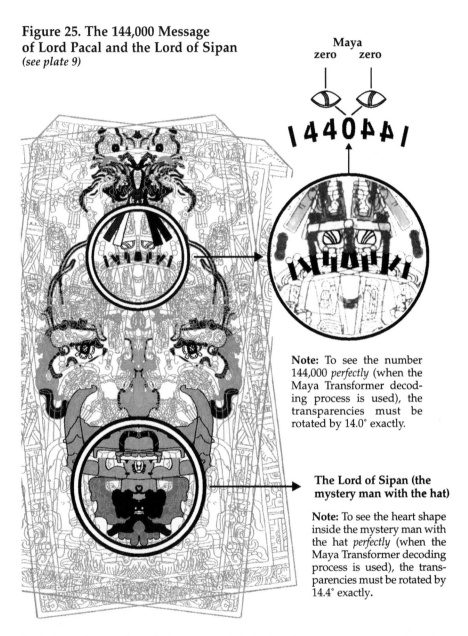

Note: To see the number 144,000 *perfectly* (when the Maya Transformer decoding process is used), the transparencies must be rotated by 14.0° exactly.

The Lord of Sipan (the mystery man with the hat)

Note: To see the heart shape inside the mystery man with the hat *perfectly* (when the Maya Transformer decoding process is used), the transparencies must be rotated by 14.4° exactly.

In the Bible those with 144,000 written on their foreheads represent the chosen few who will enter the Kingdom of Heaven. Lord Pacal carries the number 144,000 on his forehead *(above, top, circled)*. The perfect heart shape, contained within the composite picture of the mystery man with the hat *(bottom, circled)* can be completed only when the transparencies are inverted, overlaid and juxtaposed by 14.4°. These messages taken together tell us that only the pure of heart will become one of the 144,000, like Lord Pacal and the Lord of Sipan.

Figure 26. The 144,000 Message of Tutankhamun

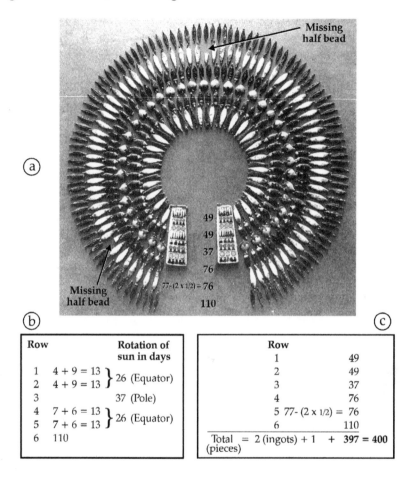

Row		Rotation of sun in days
1	4 + 9 = 13 ⎫	26 (Equator)
2	4 + 9 = 13 ⎭	
3		37 (Pole)
4	7 + 6 = 13 ⎫	26 (Equator)
5	7 + 6 = 13 ⎭	
6	110	

Row	
1	49
2	49
3	37
4	76
5	77- (2 x 1/2) = 76
6	110
Total (pieces)	= 2 (ingots) + 1 + 397 = 400

The Tutankhamun Prophecies explained how the sun-ray necklace *(a)* of Tutankhamun contained astronomical and spiritual information. *(b)* The count of beads on each row of the necklace refers to the rotational rates of the sun's equatorial and polar magnetic fields (26 and 37 days respectively). *(c)* The total number of beads adds up to 397, which is also astronomically significant (the solar pole rotates 360° in 37 days; 360 + 37 = 397). Multiplying 360 by 400 produces the 144,000 mentioned in the Book of Revelation in the Bible. That this is so is confirmed by table *(b)*; two rows do not add to 13, row 3 and row 6. The Book of Revelation (chapter xiii, verse 18) goes on to say: *'...here is wisdom, let him that hath understanding count the number of the beast; for it is the number of a man; and his number is six hundred three score and six...'* Row 6 multiplied by 110 = 660 on row 6 = 666. That this is so may be confirmed by multiplying row 3 (the only other row which does not add to 13) by 37, which equals 111. Hence the necklace carries both 144,000 and 666, as mentioned in Revelation. The same numbers can be found by decoding the clues in the Temple of Inscriptions at Palenque. Moreover, Tutankhamun carried 143 pieces of jewellery wrapped within the bandages of his mummy; he was object number 144.

be seen clearly in the middle of his naked chest, while another bat (the mark of death) covers his genitals. The stance of the small man, revealing his heart through his open chest, tells us that only the purified of heart will carry the number of 144,000 on their foreheads. At the same time the bat (symbol of death), covering his genital area, suggests that those who procreate find only death.

Another interesting fact emerged from the latest computer-aided decoding: the transparencies need to be juxtaposed at 14.0 degrees *exactly (figure 25)* before the number 144,000 appears *clearly* on the forehead of Lord Pacal. However, in this position the heart mark, of the man with the hat, does not form a *perfect* heart shape. The heart shape only completes when the transparencies are positioned exactly 14.4 degrees apart. This seems to imply that purity of heart (becoming one of the 144,000) can be achieved only by those who forgo sexual activity. Purification is therefore a two-step process – celibacy first and purification second – which explains why spiritual seekers subscribe to celibacy. These more precise angular measurements were made possible by the use of modern computer graphic techniques that were previously unavailable.

The sun-ray collar, from the tomb of Tutankhamun *(figure 26)*, shows that he, too, encoded the 144,000 message of the Supergods into his treasures, again showing concurrence between Supergod teaching.

The new decoding of the Amazing Lid of Palenque *(plate 9)* differs from the earlier one *(plate 7d)* in two other ways: the bat-mask worn by the Lord of Sipan can be seen more clearly by picking out and colouring in different areas of the lid and, secondly, Lord Pacal can be shown, again by selecting different areas of the design, wearing the grey beard of a white man.

The Tomb of the Priest

The tomb of the priest *(plate 2)* was the next to be discovered. This lay at the south end of the top platform. The remains of a 'guardian' with severed feet, similar to the one that watched over the tomb of the Lord of Sipan, were the first to appear in a cane coffin. Beneath these, the disintegrated remains of a timber roof formed a depression that sank into the tomb below. Around the tomb, hundreds of sculpted ceramic jugs, many of men with missing limbs, lay in disarray. The missing ceramic arms and legs were found in piles further away. Ceramic warrior jugs watched over the entourage from each of the four corners of the tomb.

Again, the tomb was stocked with all kinds of treasures, along the lines of those found in the tomb of the Lord of Sipan, although not quite so lavishly. He was given the name 'priest' by archaeologists who believed his elaborate headdress (plate 11a, right) featured an owl, a bird closely associated with wisdom, knowledge and the night sky (astronomy). However, close examination shows the 'owl' to have very large protruding ears, like those of a bat, suggesting that the 'owl' is in fact a bat, representing the bat-god, the god of death.

The priest wore gold and turquoise earrings, similar to those of the Lord of Sipan except that the centre carried a golden head, now known to characterise the face of the Old Lord of Sipan, whose remains were discovered at the bottom layer of the pyramid complex.

Plate 11a shows the priest wearing two necklaces, each of which comprised nine gilded copper heads, the faces of which resemble a golden mask that covered the face of the Old Lord (figure 28). The heads along the top necklace showed the Old Lord smiling, exposing two rows of white shell teeth. The nine faces on the lower string showed the Old Lord frowning, perhaps illustrating the dichotomy of life against death. The gilded (gold-plated) copper heads, like all the gilded artefacts of the Mochica, were contrived using electrochemical plating techniques unknown in Europe until the seventeenth century. The 'priest', who wore a golden halo-crescent (not shown in plate 11), again featuring the Old Lord, was accompanied at the south end of the tomb by a cane coffin containing the remains of a child, a dog, and a serpent.

To his right lay a young woman, face-down, with a decapitated llama at her feet.

To his left lay a young woman who wore a copper crown, and beyond her a man in a cane coffin faced the feet of the priest.

One of the companions (plate 11a, left) wore two earrings which, remarkably, showed the radiating solar wind (plate 11b). That these artefacts intentionally depicted the super-science of the sun can be little in doubt; other pieces from the Sipan tombs complex show the sun as a hollow disc (plate 11c), as a cross (plate 11d), representing the cross-sectional magnetic structure of the sun (figure A1, i), as a radiating disc (plate 11e), as a solar system (plate 11f), as a polarised (positive and negative) cross-sectional view of the sun's magnetic field *(figure A1, ii)* and as a golden solar disc that distinguishes the solar polar field from that of the equator *(plate 11h)*.

Across his chest, beneath the necklace that featured the Old Lord, he wore two solar-style pectoral collars. A golden solar nose-disc covered his mouth. The significance of the disc is not clear; the bat-mask represents death, so perhaps the disc refers to life, meaning that the priest was 'alive' during the reign of the Old Lord, whose nine (9) smiling faces and nine (9) frowning faces hang from the necklaces around his shoulders. He may have thus loyally served the Old Lord, through good times and bad times during his life.

Like the Lord of Sipan he carried a crescent-shaped, so-called knife, half of which was made of gold and the other half silver either side of a centre line down the middle. His body was covered with a cotton robe strung with gilded plates, and the entire coffin was wrapped in a red fine woollen blanket.

There is little doubt that the 'priest' was an important personage. He may well have been a priest, an astronomer, or a wise man, but the treasures in his tomb suggest that his rank was less than that of his neighbours found buried in the complex; the only 9s in his tomb refer to the Old Lord of Sipan and he did not rule the four corners; he could not, therefore, have been a Supergod.

The Tomb of the Old Lord of Sipan

The tomb of the Old Lord *(plate 3)* was found around 6 metres (19.68 feet) from the surface of the lowest of the six levels, at the base of the pyramid, and was therefore presumed to be the oldest, dating back to around AD 100.

The contents of the Old Lord's tomb matched, if not surpassed, in quantity and quality those of the Lord of Sipan. One of the most interesting pieces was a necklace of 10 gilded-copper saucer-shaped chambers *(figure 27)* scattered around across his chest. The top side of each was covered by a cage in the shape of a spider's web constructed of 20 spokes fixed to seven concentric rings by 140 spot-welds. A spider made of seven gold pieces was mounted astride the top of the cage. The face of the Old Lord, circumscribed by nine embossed oval egg-shaped spheres, appeared on the abdomen of each spider (9, 9, 9, 9, 9, 9, 9, 9, 9, 9), the egg-laying nucleus synonymous with fertility.

Figure 27. The Spider-Man Chambers
from the Tomb of the Old Lord

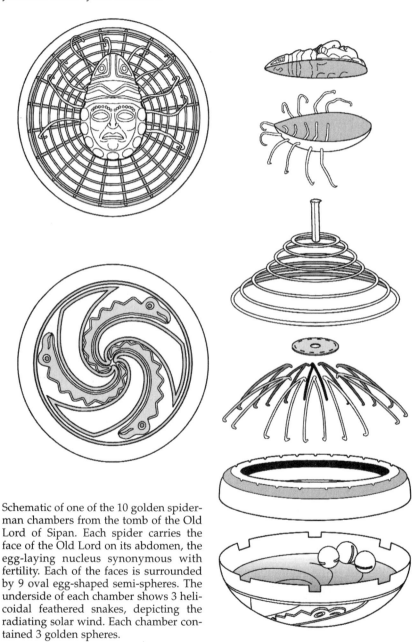

Schematic of one of the 10 golden spider-man chambers from the tomb of the Old Lord of Sipan. Each spider carries the face of the Old Lord on its abdomen, the egg-laying nucleus synonymous with fertility. Each of the faces is surrounded by 9 oval egg-shaped semi-spheres. The underside of each chamber shows 3 helicoidal feathered snakes, depicting the radiating solar wind. Each chamber contained 3 golden spheres.

Each of the spiders has 8 legs and 2 antenna-like appendages, which is perplexing. The 8s (legs) are straightforward; the duration of the 187-year sunspot cycle may be calculated easily without a computer using 6- and 8-sided shapes (hexagons and octagons), as explained in *The Tutankhamun Prophecies*. This is, no doubt, why the many 8-sphered semicircular pieces featuring Ai Apaec featured widely in the tomb of the Lord of Sipan and why so many other pieces featured 6s. The problem here is that spiders do not have antennae; only insects have antennae (although some have append-ages). Insects, on the other hand, do have antennae, but unlike spiders have only 6 legs. Moreover, insects consist of three separate body segments – head, thorax and abdomen – whereas spiders merge at the head and breast to form the cephalothorax, which is connected to the abdomen by a very narrow waist, unlike the spiders of the chambers which appear to be made of a single-piece body that does not narrow at the waist. Here again we have a dichotomy of 6s against 8s, again emphasising the astronomical importance of the numbers.

The spider featured on the chambers lies somewhere in between a true spider and an insect, and so emphasises the fact that 'the Old Lord is *different*', conveying the message that 'this man (pictured on the abdomen) is *different* from all other men'. The Old Lord was therefore not only associated with fertility; he was also '*different* from all other men'. At the foot of the stairs, in the Temple of Inscriptions at Palenque, the bones of 5 *male* skeletons were found alongside the bones of one *female* skeleton, making the point that 'the bones of *one skeleton* (the man in the tomb) was different from the bones of all other men'; meaning that Lord Pacal was a Supergod.

Spiders' eggs, wrapped in silk, mature, and the spider emerges, metamorphosing from egg to spider. (It is interesting to note that the practice of human mummification involves the wrapping of the body in bandages (analogous to silk) and therefore, in the same way, amounts to a statement of metamorphosis, rebirth or reincarnation.) The Old Lord therefore not only influenced fertility (birth) but also rebirth. This interpretation of the evidence is supported by the fact that each spider-chamber *(figure 27)* contains three golden spheres representing eggs. Each of the spheres is split, as though on the one hand delineating an 'equator', emulating the equatorial region of the sun (the prime mover in relation to fecundity), and on the other emphasising the emptiness of the egg, the fact that the host has successfully evacuated the shell.

So the Old Lord was different from other men. His number was 9, 9, 9, 9, 9, 9, 9, 9, 9. Not only was he a Supergod, but he was the only Supergod known to have reached 10 (ten nines).

The design on the underside of the spider-chambers *(figure 27)* shows three helicoidal 'feathered snakes' *(see also plate 11b, the solar wind)* – again confirming that the Old Lord *was* the sun (referred to as the 'feathered snake' by each of the sun-worshipping civilisations *(Appendix 3)*. Tutankhamun carried the feathers (vulture) and the snake (cobra) on his forehead *(figure A9)*. Decoded pictures from the Mosaic Mask of Palenque show Lord Pacal clearly *(figure 81)* as Quetzalcoatl, a feathered snake. The three eggs within each spider-chamber go one step further in saying that the Old Lord of Sipan was associated with the three aspects of the sun (light): the Father (God the creator), son (the physical manifestation of God the creator on earth) and the holy ghost (the spirit, the soul, within each man).

Modern science has shown electrical fields to be dependent on magnetic fields and magnetic fields to be dependent on electric fields but, so far, has failed to show an association between these two fields of nature and the third known field of gravity. Such an association would 'unify' the three important fields of nature. The helicoidal shape of the solar-serpents (feathered snakes) impressed into the underside of each chamber conveys further novelty; when shaken, the three balls race around the edge of the chamber like roulette balls. Eventually the decreasing velocity attracts the balls along the bodies of the serpents until they come to rest in the lowest point of the underside chamber, the locus of the three serpents. The chamber design therefore expresses a 'unified field' where the electric and magnetic (electromagnetic = light = the sun, epitomised by the feathered snakes) and gravitational fields equilibrate. The message of the spider-chambers is therefore both spiritual and super-scientific.

Components of another 10-piece gilded copper necklace were found scattered around one of the pectorals. The 10 pieces were similar in construction to the 10 spider-chambers, except that the top side featured feline (jaguar-style) faces *(plate 24b)* with sharp shell teeth. The underside of each chamber was embossed with only two, as against three, helicoidal feathered snakes. These clearly represented the sun as both jaguar and feathered snake.

Figure 28. The One-Eyed Man from Sipan

This life-size gilded copper mask covered the face of the Old Lord of Sipan. He wears a necklace of five owl faces and carries another owl face on his forehead. His left eye, which represents the moon and the right-hand side of the brain (femininity), is missing. His (closed) right eye represents the sun (at night), suggesting that the Old Lord was the sun. The owl (bird of the night and wisdom) motifs associate the wearer with wisdom.

Figure 29. The Crab-Man

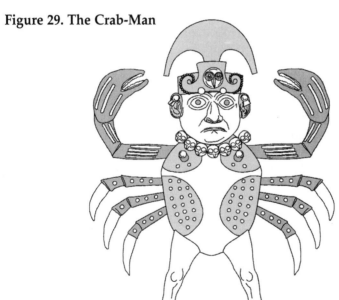

This 60-centimetre (2-foot) high gilded copper anthropomorphic figure, found in the tomb of the Old Lord of Sipan, depicts the Old Lord as a crab. His raised-arm posture copies that of the man with the hat found in the tombs of Sipan. A closer look at the man with the hat *(shown covering the mouth of Lord Pacal in plate 9)* reveals a pincer-like structure within the bat-mask. The crab, a creature that lives on the land and in the sea, represents the *foam of the sea*, the Spanish meaning of the name Viracocha, suggesting that the Old Lord of Sipan was an incarnation of Viracocha, the legendary white god of South America.

In his left hand the Old Lord carries a silver sceptre and in his right one of gold, the handle of which was cast with rays of the sun. Another particularly interesting piece was a gilded copper mask featuring the Old Lord *(figure 28)* wearing a halo-crescent, a necklace of five owl heads, an owl head on his forehead and earrings. The left eye (the moon) is missing from its socket, and the right eye (the sun) is infilled with shell, as though closed, representing the sun at night (darkness and death). The owl heads associate the Old Lord once again with wisdom (the number 5 is again significant; *The Tutankhamun Prophecies* showed how the solar magnetic reversal period can be calculated without a computer using 5-sided shapes (pentagons)).

The face of the Old Lord was again personified on an unusual crab-like anthropomorphic figure *(figure 29, and plate 3)*. This large 60-centimetre (2-foot) high gilded copper model astounded archaeologists when it was found. It carries a necklace of seven owl faces with one more featured on the forehead, eight in all. The crab adopts the posture of the small man with the hat found in the tomb of the Lord of Sipan and the Old Lord, with two front claws raised (like the Egyptian god Shu).

This crab-like association and depiction may seem odd but in fact is straightforward; the crab is a creature that lives both on land and in the sea, in the foam of the sea. The expression 'foam of the sea' is the popular Quechua translation of the name 'Viracocha', a creator-god who was worshipped by the later Incas. South American mythology describes him as a superior being, depicted as a bearded white man wearing the sun as a crown. This means that the Old Lord of Sipan (shown as a crab) and Lord of Sipan, whose tomb was also filled with representations of the small man with the hat with raised arms, must both be associated with the creator-god Viracocha.

The name Viracocha appears twice in South American mythology; once simply as Viracocha, and again as Viracocha Pachacamac, which translated means 'God of the World'. The eighth Inca ruler, Viracocha Inca, also carried the name but was a known living king as against the other two who were revered as *gods*.

Several legends tell stories of Viracocha. One says that he was a great spiritual leader, in olden times, who performed miracles throughout the land; that he established a temple close to today's modern city of Lima (at a place today called Pachacamac), before walking to the shore and disappearing into the foam of the sea; hence the name 'Foam of the Sea'. Other accounts say that he appeared much further back in antiquity, rising from the depths of Lake Titicaca in today's Bolivia to create the human race by breathing life into the colossal stone statues at Tiahuanaco. Which raises an interesting question: could the Lords of Sipan have actually been the lost gods of the Mochica, Viracocha, 'Foam of the Sea' and Viracocha Pachacamac, God of the World? Perhaps the stories of these two great gods were not a myth after all. Perhaps they really did walk the lands of Peru and Bolivia performing miracles. This possibility will be considered later, along with mythological stories of Peru.

The presence of the crab claws also sheds new light on the meaning of the small man with the hat that covers Lord Pacal's lower face *(featured in plate 9)*; his raised arms now become recognisably much more crab-like, associating Lord Pacal of the Maya with the crab, and with Viracocha. And Lord Pacal was also known to his people as 'the white man with the beard'.

This 'foam of the sea' interpretation also sheds more light on the significance of the golden spider-chambers found in the tomb of the Old Lord; the creature (spider or insect) is best described as somewhere in between, not insect or spider, not land or sea, analogous with the 'foam of the sea'.

The notion that the 'foam of the sea' refers to a spiritual teacher or spiritual sustenance is not unique to the Americas: the Indian holy book, the *Mahabharata (the Udyoga Parva, Roy's translation, pp. 309 et seq.)* comments:

A single jet only of her [the mother-goddess's] milk falling on the earth created what is known as the sacred and the excellent 'Milky Ocean'. The verge of that ocean all around is covered with white foam resembling a belt of flowers. Those best of ascetics that are known by the name of 'foam-drinkers' dwell around this ocean, subsisting on the foam only. They are called foam-drinkers because they live on nothing else save the foam.

Close examination of the crab-like effigy *(figure 29)* reveals two small circles, one above each eye socket. Note that each of the eyes of the owl face on the forehead is filled with star-bursts. The circles above each eye socket are thus associated with two star-bursts, suggesting that the two circles represent two stars, the 'twin star' of Venus.

Venus is actually a planet, second furthest from the sun after

Figure 30. The Supergods

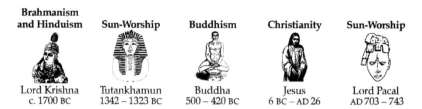

Brahmanism and Hinduism	Sun-Worship	Buddhism	Christianity	Sun-Worship
Lord Krishna c. 1700 BC	Tutankhamun 1342 – 1323 BC	Buddha 500 – 420 BC	Jesus 6 BC – AD 26	Lord Pacal AD 703 – 743

Several religious leaders, who taught the higher orders of spirituality, had much in common (see *The Supergods*). Each was the embodiment of the one living God who created the universe; each was born through an immaculate conception; each performed miracles; and each believed in reincarnation and everlasting life. When Krishna was born, a bright star appeared in the sky. Buddha, it was said, was a bright star in his mother's womb and when Jesus was born a bright star was seen in the sky. Revelation (xxii, 16) goes further, saying: 'I Jesus . . . am the root of David, and the bright and morning star.'

When Tutankhamun died he journeyed to the constellation of Orion to join Osiris, the god of resurrection, for everlasting life. Stories from the decoded Amazing Lid of Palenque *(plates 29, 30 and 31)* say that Lord Pacal became the twin star (planet) Venus on death. These two sun-kings shared even more in common; each encoded their knowledge of the super-science of the sun, together with the higher orders of spirituality, into their treasures.

Figure 31. The Twin Star (Planet) Venus

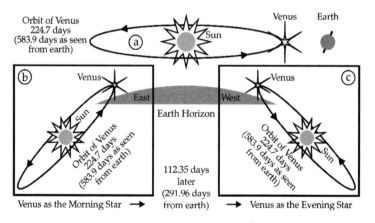

(a) The 224.7-day orbit of Venus falls between that of Mercury (not shown here) and earth. However, the interval between successive identical appearances of Venus, as seen from the moving earth, is 583.9 days. This means that Venus, in the position shown in *(b)*, appears brightly illuminated in the dark morning sky. In position *(c)* the sun sets before Venus which shines brightly in the darkening evening sky. Because of this, and because Venus, is the brightest heavenly body, she is referred to as the 'morning star' and the 'evening star', the twin star. Brightness (light) is synonymous with purity; hence, several spiritually pure teachers, including Jesus, Tutankhamun and Lord Pacal, were associated with Venus.

Mercury. It is the brightest of the night-time heavenly bodies. Spiritual leaders throughout history have been associated with Venus because brightness is associated with purity *(figures 30 and 31)*. The single 'star' (planet) can be seen clearly either in the morning (as the morning star) or in the evening (as the evening star), depending on its orbital position around the sun *(figure 31)*. Treasures in the tomb of Tutankhamun tell us that on physical death he journeyed to the constellation of Orion to live with Osiris, the god of resurrection. In Egyptian mythology Osiris was the consort of Isis, who lived in the star Sirius, the brightest (actual) star in the night sky. Sirius is also a twin star, which again associates Tutankhamun with a twin star. When Lord Pacal died (as we will see later), he journeyed to Venus to become the morning star. In the Bible (Revelation, xxii, 16) Jesus says: 'I Jesus . . . am the root of David, and the bright and morning star.' The other Supergods were also associated with bright stars *(figure 30)*.

The tomb of the Old Lord *(plate 3)* was filled with items very similar to those of the Lord of Sipan. Altogether there were 56 gold pieces; several banner-like shields showing the man with the hat; 9 golden nose ornaments; 2 gold ear ornaments; 10 semicircular pieces featuring Ai Apaec and several circular discs of gold; pectorals – one of which comprised three tiers with the third layer in the form of 8 octopus legs, and another made of snail and seashell pieces decorated with serpents; a bat headdress; a silver face-mask with the left eye missing, similar to the golden one discussed earlier but with the right eye open and eyeball exposed; several so-called sacrificial knives; more gold crescents and more semicircular pieces featuring Ai Apaec (similar to those on the front waistband of the Lord of Sipan *(plate 5b)*; arm bracelets; silver nose ornaments; and silver (not copper) sandals. The bundle was again wrapped, this time with 8 layers of cotton blankets, many of which were embroidered with serpent patterns. Twenty-six (26) ceramic jugs were stacked alongside the funerary bundle. Twelve (12) spears of gilded copper, together with scattered shells, were found beneath the bones of the dead king, who was aged around forty-five at the time of death. Curiously, the bundle of fabrics that cocooned the king, and his treasures, were far better preserved than those of the Lord of Sipan from the uppermost level of the pyramid, and there was no coffin.

Excavation at the head end of the tomb revealed the bones of a girl aged around 16 at the time of death, lying face-down next to a llama.

A fourth tomb, little mentioned by archaeologists, was found beneath that of the Old Lord. This contained the simple cane coffin and remains of a warrior adorned with copper and gold military ornaments.

Fertility Cult of the Andes

All of the pre-Columbian civilisations of Peru worshipped the sun as the god of fertility, as did the Mayas and Egyptians. We now know that the sun regulates fertility hormones in females *(figure 32)*; the sun, which spins on its axis once every 28 days, showers charged particles that collide with the Van Allen radiation belts that encircle the earth. The charged particles race up and down the Van Allen belts, from north to south, every second and then back again, causing the earth's magnetic field to vary in sympathy with particle bombardment. The varying magnetic field affects the pineal gland in the human brain. This converts the magnetic variations into chemical variations, which in turn affect the pituitary and hypothalamus glands. The hypothalamus varies the production of the follicle-stimulating hormone, regulating the fertility hormones oestrogen and progesterone in females throughout the 28-day solar cycle *(Appendix 2 explains why all females do not menstruate simultaneously)*. The ancient sun-worshipping civilisations were well aware of this process, which explains why they worshipped the sun as the god of fertility. On the shore of Lake Titicaca, a fifteenth-century Inca temple *(plates 12a and 12b)* was built in reverence to the erect penis, dozens of which monopolise the interior. These are accompanied by clover-shaped solar motifs *(similar to the one shown in plate 11g)*, proving that the same beliefs of sun-worship and fertility extended to the Inca around Lake Titicaca.

And they believed, in accordance with the scriptures of all the religions that subscribe to the notion of a creator-god, that God is light (electromagnetic energy). So they worshipped the sun as the creator of the universe. At the same time they believed that the body and soul were separate entities; that the soul was a tiny piece of godly energy (light) which attached to the biological body at the moment of conception. The biological body (born of biological parents) was simply a vehicle that gave the soul an opportunity to purify itself during its brief period on earth. Purification would in time lead to

Figure 32. How the Sun Controls Fertility in Females

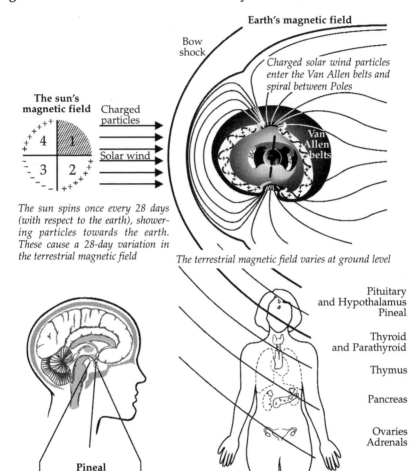

Earth's magnetic field

Bow shock

Charged solar wind particles enter the Van Allen belts and spiral between Poles

The sun's magnetic field

Charged particles

Solar wind

Van Allen belts

The sun spins once every 28 days (with respect to the earth), showering particles towards the earth. These cause a 28-day variation in the terrestrial magnetic field

The terrestrial magnetic field varies at ground level

Pituitary and Hypothalamus
Pineal

Thyroid and Parathyroid

Thymus

Pancreas

Ovaries
Adrenals

Pineal

Converts magnetic fields into the biorhythm hormone melatonin

Hypothalamus and Pituitary

These affect the manufacture and release of the fertility hormones oestrogen and progesterone

The endocrine system converts the modulating magnetic field into chemicals (hormones). This magnetic-to-chemical conversion process is termed 'electrochemical transduction' (Astrogenetics, 1988). The 28-day magnetic variations regulate menstruation in females. Research suggests that longer cycle variations (12-year cycles) trigger puberty and menopause (12 years and 48 (4 x 12) years after conception)

everlasting life as a star in the heavens, a sun, an everlasting living god. Failure to achieve purification in one lifetime would lead to reincarnation on earth in a new body, and another chance to progress spiritually.

Purification, they believed, could be achieved only through absolute devotion to God, placing the self and others second to God. It was as though they believed that human relationships somehow impede the pursuit and attainment of purification. It goes without saying that human sexual relationships therefore ultimately denied purification and transmigration of the soul. Sexual activity (pro-creation) therefore leads to bondage, an endless cycle of birth, death and reincarnation, on earth, for eternity. This must be why the man with the hat, that covers Lord Pacal's face *(plate 9)* carries a bat, the symbol of death, across his genital area.

The so-called 'prisoners', featured in the seals of Tutankhamun's tomb *(see figure 11)*, personify this very same paradigm; the groups of 9 (the holy 9) 'prisoners' are bound together around the neck by rope, but the ends of the rope terminate with lotus blossoms. (The lotus flower was a symbol of sun-worship shared by each of the sun-worshipping civilisations because it blossomed in the morning, worshipped the sun all day and closed its petals as the sun set.)

At the Mochica settlement of Huaca Cao Viejo, in the Chicama Valley of Peru *(plate 12c)*, the 'divine prisoners' again appear in wall paintings bound by the neck with rope. Each is shown with an erect penis. The message, like that given by the 1,137 ceramic pots at Sipan, is clear: procreation leads to reincarnation and human bondage on earth.

CHAPTER TWO

The Incas

Children of the Sun

At its height, in around AD 1500, the Inca empire covered the largest geographical area of any of the Amerindian cultures of South America, a distance of 5,230 kilometres (3,250 miles), from Purumauca on the north bank of the River Maule (35 degrees south, in southern Chile) to the River Ancasmayo (1 degree north, in modern-day Colombia). The empire was relatively short-lived compared with those of the Chavín and Mochica. Historical accounts say that the first lord (Inca) king Manco Capac appeared in around AD 1100 in the fertile Cuzco Valley in the highlands of Peru and that the reign of the thirteenth, Atahualpa, came to an end with the arrival of the Spaniard Francisco Pizarro in 1532. The highland settlement of Tiahuanaco, 4,000 metres (13,000 feet) high in the Peruvian (nowadays Bolivian) Altiplano, had been established, and abandoned, for around 200 years before the Incas arrived and settled there.

The origin of Tiahuanaco provokes more controversy among historians than probably any other topic. Some orthodox archaeologists believe that the first stage of Tiahuanaco development occurred during the Chavín period between AD 100 and 500, although they agree, somewhat enigmatically, that the Chavín could never have constructed the sophisticated monuments that survive to this day. Others maintain that Tiahuanaco predates the Chavín civilisation by around 15,000 years (more on this later).

Most agree that early Tiahuanaco, the first epoch, perished in around AD 500 for reasons unknown. It then received an influx of settlers, in around AD 600, from the southern coastal region of Nazca who revitalised the city for around 300 years before it again fell into decay in around AD 900. The Incas, when they 'arrived' (taking the city by force) in 1463, re-named the empty place 'the city of the dead', *Tiahuanaco*.

Again, controversy surrounds the demarcation of the epochs; the official site notice at Tiahuanaco today sets the chronology of the site at:

Epoch I and II	Andean epochs	1580 BC–AD 133
Epoch III	Urban epoch	AD 133–374
Epoch IV	Classic epoch	AD 374–900
Epoch V	Imperial epoch	AD 900–1200

William Prescott (in his *History of the Conquest of Peru*, pp. 8–9) comments:

> We may reasonably conclude that there existed in the country a race advanced in civilization before the time of the Incas and in conformity with nearly every tradition, we may derive this race from the neighbourhood of Lake Titicaca; a conclusion strongly confirmed by the imposing architectural remains which still endure after the lapse of so many years on its borders. Who this race were and whence they came may afford a tempting theme for enquiry to the speculative antiquarian, it is a land of darkness that lies far beyond the domains of history.
>
> The same mist that hangs around the origin of the Incas continues to settle on subsequent annals; so imperfect were the records employed by the Peruvians, and so confused and contradictory their traditions, that the historian finds no firm footing on which to stand till within a century of the Spanish conquest.

The first Inca, Manco Capac, may have been a mythological figure, a culture hero, or a living leader of some genius. The earliest historical Inca chief was his successor, Sinchi *(strong man)* Roca, whose rule commenced in around AD 1105 (although again few scholars agree; some say he ruled 100 years later) at Cuzco. The line of Inca succession then extended to: Lloque Yupanqui, Mayta Capac, Capac Yupanque, Inca Roca, Yahuar Huacac, Viracocha Inca, Pachacuti Inca Yupanqui,

Plate 1. The Long-Lost Pyramids of Peru

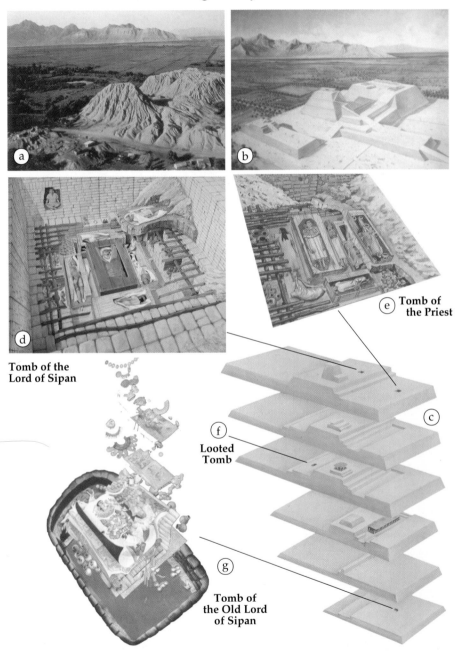

Tomb of the Priest

Tomb of the Lord of Sipan

Looted Tomb

Tomb of the Old Lord of Sipan

(a) Huaca Rajada, the water-weathered mud-brick pyramid complex of Sipan.
(b) Archaeological reconstruction of the pyramid complex. (c) Layered schematic showing different stages of construction. (d) Tomb of the Lord of Sipan, c. AD 290. (e) Tomb of the Priest. (I) Looted tomb. (g) Tomb of the Old Lord of Sipan, c. AD 100.

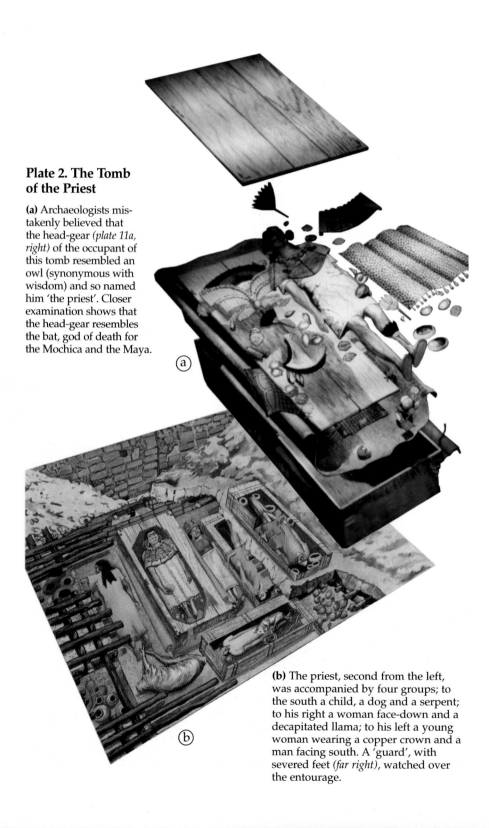

Plate 2. The Tomb of the Priest

(a) Archaeologists mistakenly believed that the head-gear *(plate 11a, right)* of the occupant of this tomb resembled an owl (synonymous with wisdom) and so named him 'the priest'. Closer examination shows that the head-gear resembles the bat, god of death for the Mochica and the Maya.

(b) The priest, second from the left, was accompanied by four groups; to the south a child, a dog and a serpent; to his right a woman face-down and a decapitated llama; to his left a young woman wearing a copper crown and a man facing south. A 'guard', with severed feet *(far right)*, watched over the entourage.

Plate 3. The Tomb of the Old Lord of Sipan (Viracocha, 'Foam of the Sea')

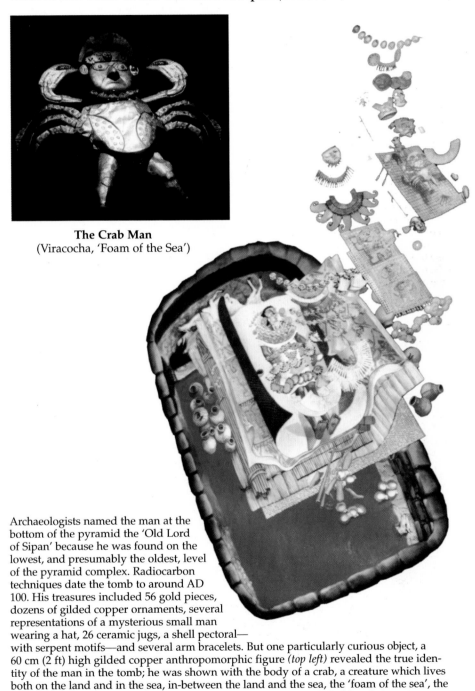

The Crab Man
(Viracocha, 'Foam of the Sea')

Archaeologists named the man at the bottom of the pyramid the 'Old Lord of Sipan' because he was found on the lowest, and presumably the oldest, level of the pyramid complex. Radiocarbon techniques date the tomb to around AD 100. His treasures included 56 gold pieces, dozens of gilded copper ornaments, several representations of a mysterious small man wearing a hat, 26 ceramic jugs, a shell pectoral—with serpent motifs—and several arm bracelets. But one particularly curious object, a 60 cm (2 ft) high gilded copper anthropomorphic figure *(top left)* revealed the true identity of the man in the tomb; he was shown with the body of a crab, a creature which lives both on the land and in the sea, in-between the land and the sea, the 'foam of the sea', the literal translation of the name Viracocha, the legendary white god of South America.

Plate 4. The Tomb of the Lord of Sipan

The sarcophagus of the Sipan sun-king differed from others at the complex. The lid was tied down by nine copper straps along each edge (9, 9, 9, 9), a number unique to the Supergods. The vertical edges, down each corner, likewise carried the same number of straps (9, 9, 9, 9). He was accompanied by eight others, nine (9) in all. This was no ordinary man. Like the other two sunkings, Lord Pacal of Mexico (9, 9, 9, 9) and Tutankhamun (9, 9, 9, 9) of Egypt (*see main text*), this man was a Supergod, later revered by the Incas (*see plate 5*).

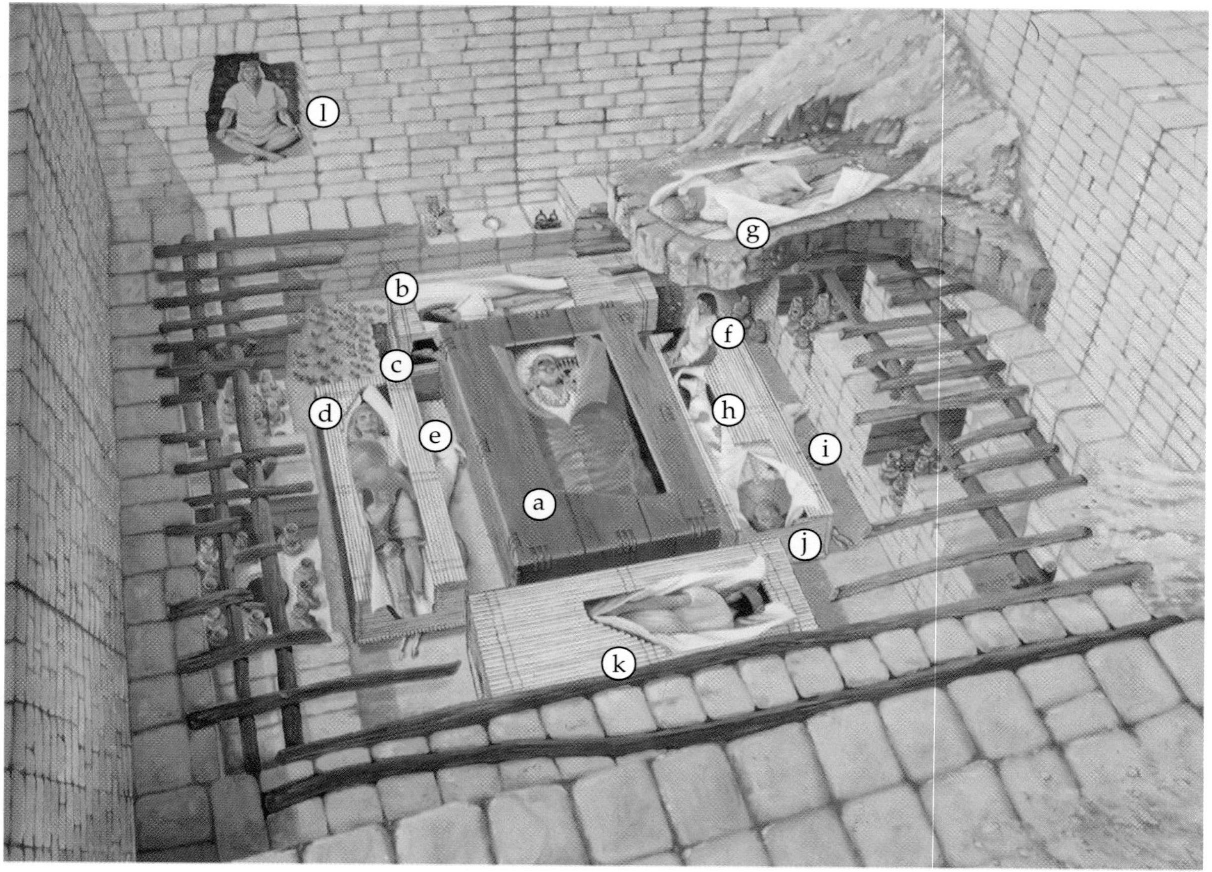

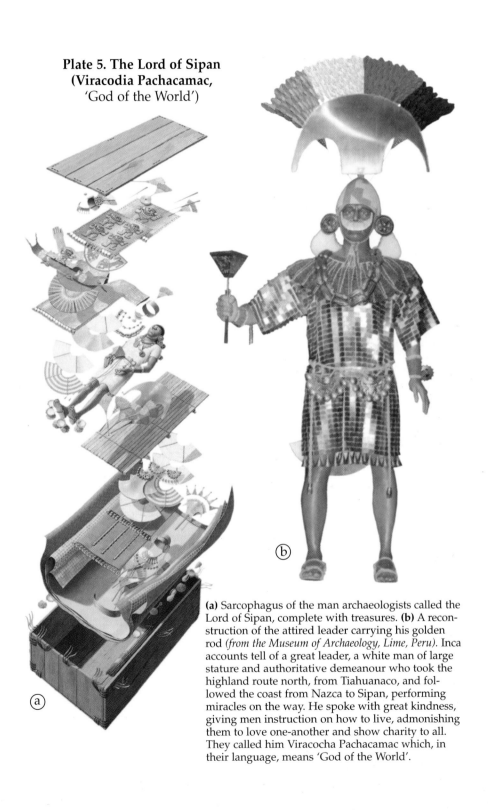

Plate 5. The Lord of Sipan
(Viracodia Pachacamac,
'God of the World')

(a) Sarcophagus of the man archaeologists called the Lord of Sipan, complete with treasures. (b) A reconstruction of the attired leader carrying his golden rod *(from the Museum of Archaeology, Lime, Peru)*. Inca accounts tell of a great leader, a white man of large stature and authoritative demeanour who took the highland route north, from Tiahuanaco, and followed the coast from Nazca to Sipan, performing miracles on the way. He spoke with great kindness, giving men instruction on how to live, admonishing them to love one-another and show charity to all. They called him Viracocha Pachacamac which, in their language, means 'God of the World'.

Plate 6. The Amazing Lid of Palenque
Decoding the Border Code Pattern
Instruction: Look for the Picture of Lord Pacal Dying

Composite border code indicators

Ear position indicators

Tonatiuh the sun-god (in the sky)

Bird

Man in the tomb with eyes closed, fingertips touching on chest and bare feet

The border code pattern conceals instructions which can be followed once the decoding process is used. This coloured section reads: to see the man in the tomb (who carries the mark of the sun on his head - a sunspot loop), look for a bird on his head. The man with the bird on his head is the sun-god. To find the secret story (hidden in the main part of the carving), orientate the two ears, featured in two transparencies *(as shown in figure 7d)* so that they oppose each other - either side of the head. When these instructions are followed, a secret composite picture of Lord Pacal appears *(plate 7d)*. A baby bird sits on his head, carrying a chain in its beak from which hangs a conch shell, the mark of the wind and Quetzalcoatl who, to the Maya, was synonymous with the sun-god on earth, the highest of gods.

Plate 7. The Sun-Kings of Mexico and Peru

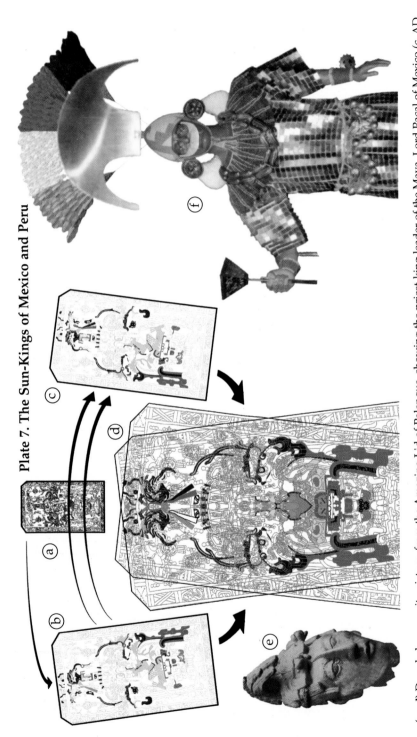

(a - d) Decoded composite picture, from the Amazing Lid of Palenque, showing the priest-king leader of the Maya, Lord Pacal of Mexico (c. AD 750), wearing the bat-mask of death over his head and the colours of the four corners (red, white, green and blue) above his head. **(e)** Stucco head of Lord Pacal from his tomb in Palenque. **(f)** The Lord of Sipan, Peru (c. AD 290), wearing the bat-mask of death across his mouth and the colours of the four corners above his head. It seems clear from the evidence that these two leaders were different incarnations of the same being.

Plate 8. The Mystery of the Man with the Hat

(a) Reconstruction showing the tomb of the Lord of Sipan, his cortege and treasures *(from the Museum of Archaeology, Lima, Peru)*. (b) Close-up of the trappings of the Lord of Sipan; his torso is covered by a mysterious small man wearing a hat. (c) and (d) Two different close-ups of the man wearing the hat. It seems likely that the hat represents the sun *(plate 11h)*, suggesting that the man in the tomb carried the sun (a halo) on his head.

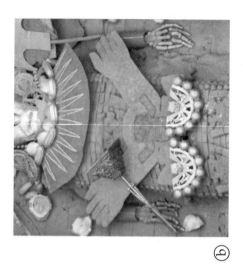

(a)

(b)

(c)

(d)

Plate 9. The Amazing Lid of Palenque
Story: The Death (and Rebirth) of Lord Pacal
Scene 4 *(scenes 1, 2 and 3 not shown here)*

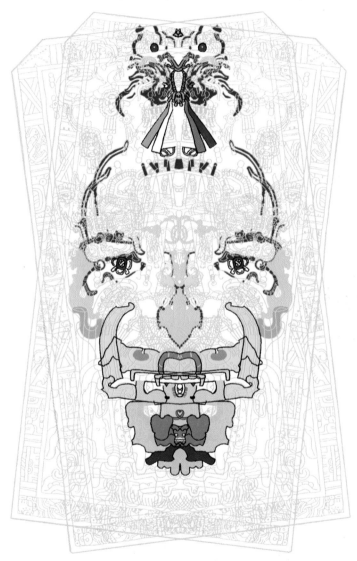

This composite picture, from the decoded Amazing Lid of Palenque, shows the head and face of Lord Pacal, of Mexico, in more detail. His mouth is covered by a bat-mask. A baby quetzal bird sits on his head. The bird carries a chain in its beak, from which hangs a conch shell, the mark of Quetzalcoatl. This scene therefore reads: Lord Pacal died (the bat-god, the god of death, took away his breath) he was reborn as (a baby quetzal bird) Quetzalcoatl *(see also figure 25)*. New discoveries, revealing the identity of the Lord of Sipan, of Peru, inspired a reexamination of the original decoded composite picture of Lord Pacal *(plate 7d)* which produced this more representative picture (above). Most important, the new decoding picked out a small man wearing a hat, similar to others that featured prolifically in the tombs at Sipan *(plate 10 b)*.

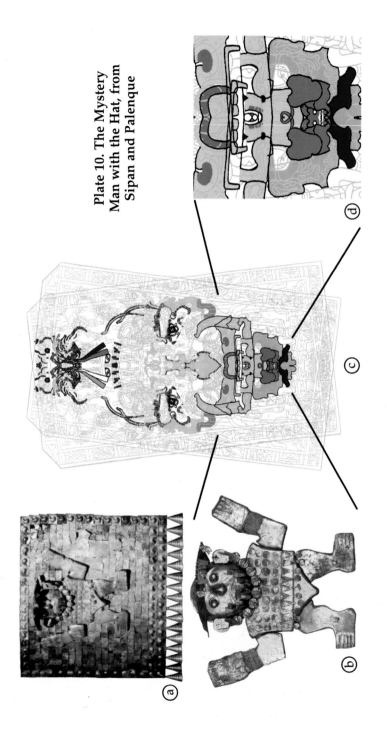

Plate 10. The Mystery Man with the Hat, from Sipan and Palenque

(a)

(b)

(c)

(d)

(a) and (b) Two more (of the many) representations featuring the mystery man with the hat, from the tomb of the Lord of Sipan. The man with the hat, covering Lord Pacals face, wears his heart on his chest, suggesting that the purified of heart become one of the 144,000 (*figure 25*-the spiritually purified who attain everlasting life). We also note the presence of the bat-god who covers the genital area of the man with the hat, suggesting that those who procreate find only death (through reincarnation in the physical world).

Plate 11. Sun-Worship and Bat-Worship

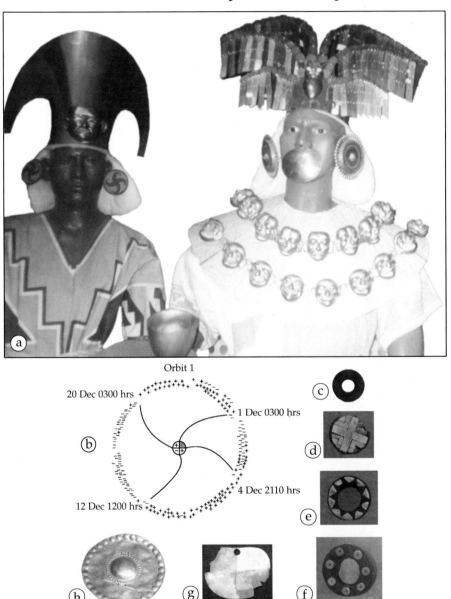

(a) Reconstruction of the Mochica priest *(right)* wearing the bat-god on his head and solar-style earrings. The attendant *(left)* radiates the sun (halo) from his head and wears earrings depicting the radiating solar wind. (b) Schematic representation of solar wind particles that radiate from the sun and interact with the earths magnetosphere (as determined by interplanetary spacecraft No. I (IMP 1, 1963)). (c - h) A few of the many and various artefacts which depict the sun, the magnetic fields of the sun and the motion of the planets around the sun found in the Sipan tombs complex. Both the Maya and the Mochica worshipped the sun as the source of life and the bat-god as the epitome of death.

Plate 12. The Fertility Cult of the Andes

(a) and (b) Inca 'Temple of Erections' from the west bank of Lake Titicaca in (modern-day) Bolivia. Fertility cults, along with sun-worship and bat-worship, were a common feature of the civilisations of Mexico, Peru and Egypt. (c) Mochica stucco-relief of the prisoners' found on the northern wall of the platform on the first level at Huaca Cao Viejo in the Chicama Valley, on the north coast of Peru. The characters are bound by the neck with heavy rope and parade with erections. A similar depiction of bound captives can be seen in the tomb of Tutankhamun *(see main text)*. The message here reads: *procreation leads to captivity* (procreation leads to reincarnation and eternal imprisonment on earth), reaffirming the message carried by the man with the hat featured beneath Lord Pacal's mouth in the decoded Amazing Lid of Palenque *(plate 10)*; the pure of heart go to heaven while those who procreate find only death and reincarnation on earth.

Plate 13. The Secrets in the Sky

Machu Picchu, secret sanctuary of the Incas, 2,500 metres (8,300 feet) above sea-level in the Cordillera Vilcabamba, Peru. The centre flourished around AD 1450, the time of a sunspot minimum, and was abandoned around 70 years later as radiation from the sun returned to normal levels. This mountain-top retreat was the last refuge of the Virgins of the Sun, concubines of the Inca (emperor). Evidence from the site *(plates 14 and 15)* suggests that the Incas understood the super-science of the sun.

Plate 14. The Secrets of the Stones (I)

(a) Reconstruction of one of the many buildings at Machu Picchu which suggests that roof coverings were made of grass, over a timber frame. Closer examination **(b)**, **(c)**, **(d)** and **(e)** suggests that the heavy-duty cylindrical solid rock roof supports would be greatly oversized for such a scheme. It is more likely that the roofs were made from heavy sheets of precious copper, covered in timber and grass. The copper, used to shield electric fields from the sun, would have been salvaged when the site was abandoned in around AD 1520. The closely fitting stones would electrically bond the stone structure, short-circuiting electrical fields to earth. Copper straps *(figure 40 shows one example)* used widely by the Incas to connect the stones, would further improve electrical conductivity to earth.

Plate 15. The Secrets of the Stones (II)

(a - e) Most of the external ostensible windows at Machu Picchu are blocked with stone whereas windows between rooms within buildings are open (see-through), suggesting that the Incas understood on the one hand what windows were for, and yet, on the other hand, that they went to extraordinary lengths to prevent light from entering buildings. The perfectly fitting stones and absence of windows together prevented ingress of external light, a known suppressant of the timing hormone melatonin in females; melatonin fluctuations stimulate the pituitary gland and in turn the production of fertility hormones oestrogen and progesterone in females. As a result fertility levels of the Virgins of the Sun were greatly improved during a period of sunspot minimum.

Plate 16. Tiahuanaco, Bolivia

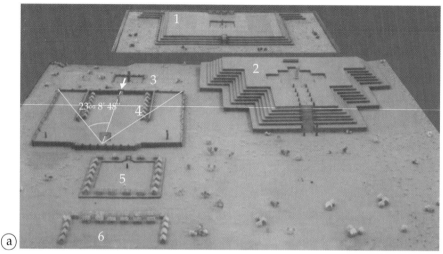

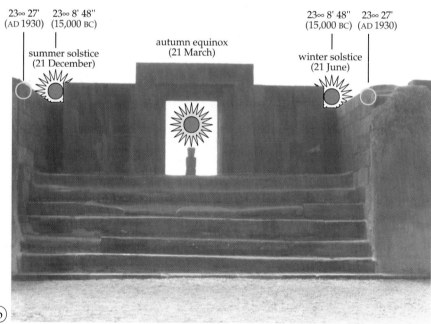

(a) Aerial view of Tiahuanaco, Bolivia *(reconstruction)*; 1. Kanta, 2. Akapana, 3. Temple of Stone Heads, 4. Kalasasaya, Temple of the Standing Stones; the lateral angles shown, according to Professor Arthur Posnansky in 1914 (re-measured more accurately in 1930), correspond to the tilt of the earth in around 15,000 BC *(see main text)*, 5. Putuni, 6. Kerikala. (b) Kalasasaya stairway (viewed from the direction of the white arrow in (a)); Posnansky also noticed that the sun would rise above the statue of Viracocha in the centre of the Kalasasaya stairway at the time of the autumn equinox and rise above the corners of the stairway at the times of the solstices, providing that the tilt of the earth on its axis (the obliquity of the ecliptic) corresponded to 23°8'48" (as he believed it did in around 15,000 BC).

Topa Inca Yupanqui and Huayna Capac, who was the last to rule over a united empire that was divided between his sons, Huascar and Atahualpa, shortly before his death.

A civil war ensued, and in 1532 Atahualpa's troops captured Huascar and his followers. But events were overtaken by the arrival of the Spaniards under the leadership of Francisco Pizarro, who in 1532 arranged a fateful meeting with Atahualpa. He was ambushed by a handful of conquistadores, captured, held for ransom and executed by the Spanish, thus extinguishing Inca rule in Spanish-occupied Peru.

It was in around 1350 that the Incas, still an insignificant tribe occupying only a small part of the Cuzco Valley under sixth Inca Roca, built a bridge across the River Apurimac. This allowed a gradual period of territorial expansion until 1437 when, under the eighth Inca, Viracocha, their plans suffered a setback: they were attacked and almost overwhelmed by a neighbouring tribe, the Chancas. Defending under siege, they turned the war within a year to their own favour under ninth Inca Pachacuti Inca Yupanqui, consolidating their gains on the plain around Cuzco. This gave the impetus to a more ambitious programme of expansion under Pachacuti Inca Yupanqui, who for the next 25 years enlarged the empire through a series of wars facilitated by a programme of development which embraced the armed forces, roads, bridges and communications. Quechua was declared the national language and sun-worship the official religion. In 1463 Pachacuti's troops defeated the Lupaca and Colla tribes based at Tiahuanaco, on Lake Titicaca, and in 1466 conquered their own coastal adversaries, the Chimu.

The Inca sun-worshipping religion was central to its control over the people. The word Inca means 'sun'; hence the Inca monarch represented the sun incarnate on earth. Immortality awaited those who subscribed to the strict Inca moral code; the pure would enjoy heavenly bliss whereas the wicked would journey to the centre of the earth agonisingly to expiate their crimes in the underworld.

Mummification preserved the bodies of the dead. These were often hunched in the foetal position in preparation for rebirth in the heavens. Many covered their eyes in the expectation of entering the house of their father, the sun, with its blinding radiance.

Following the conquest, several Inca mummies were hidden and worshipped by the Indians, much to the disdain of the Spanish authorities. Gonzalo Pizarro discovered and burned the mummy of

Viracocha Inca at the village of Jaquijahuana, where he himself was later hanged. In 1559 Juan Polo de Ondegardo, the corregidor (chief magistrate) of Cuzco, discovered that the ashes of the Viracocha Inca were even more venerated by the Indians than the mummy had been earlier. Polo later came across another cache of three Inca mummies and four coyas (Inca queens), among them Pachacuti Inca, Huayna Capac and his mother Mama-Ocllo. Historian Garcilasso Inca de la Vega was shown the seven bodies just before his departure for Spain in 1560 and remarked on their state of preservation:

> ... the bodies were so perfect that they lacked neither hair, eyebrows nor eyelashes. They were in clothes such as they would have worn when alive, with llautus on their heads but no other sign of royalty. They were seated in the way Indian men and women usually sit, with their arms crossed over their chests, the right over the left and their eyes cast down ... I remember touching the finger of the hand of Huayna-Capac, It was hard and rigid, like that of a wooden statue. The bodies weighed so little that any Indian could carry them from house to house in his arms or on his shoulders. They carried them wrapped in white sheets through the streets and squares, the Indians falling to their knees and making reverences with groans and tears, and many Spaniards taking off their caps ... (Hemming, p. 298).

At the age of 10 the most beautiful daughters of noblemen were chosen as 'virgins of the sun'. These novices, adherents of the holy order of sun-worship, spent their youth hidden away in sun-temples out of the sight of men. Placed under the supervision of elderly matrons (*mamaconas*), they spent their days receiving instructions on chaste religious duties and acquiring the skills of embroidery and spinning used in the manufacture of tapestries for the temples and clothing, for the Inca never wore the same garment twice. The great sun-temple, the Coricancha ('place of gold') at Cuzco, was said to house 1,500 virgins. At the age of 18 or 20 the most suitable became wives of the Inca, who might, at any one time, have as few as 100, or as many as 1,000 of the girls domiciled in palaces throughout the kingdom. Although these daughters of noblemen became concubines of the Inca, the rank of *coya* (queen) was, generally, reserved for the blood-sister/wife of the Inca, ensuring the unadulterated continuation of the heaven-sent royal Inca lineage.

Cuzco was the 'holy city' of the Incas and the Coricancha the most magnificent structure in the New World. The north of the town, at one end of the valley, was protected by a natural prominence in the Andes cordillera and a strong fortress defended by a stone wall 365 metres (1,200 feet) long facing the city. On the other side of the plain, two other semicircular walls provided fortification for the city. The quality, sophistication and sheer size of the ashlars (building-blocks) used in construction of the walls of the city astonished the Spaniards when they arrived.

Prescott comments (p. 10):

> The fortress walls and the galleries were all built of stone, the heavy blocks of which were not laid in regular courses, but so disposed that the small ones might fill up the interstices between the great. They formed a sort of rustic work, being rough-hewn except towards the edge, which were finely wrought; and, though no cement was used, the several blocks were adjusted with so much exactness and united so closely that it was impossible to insert the blade of a knife between them. Many of these stones were of vast size; some of them being thirty-eight feet long, by eighteen broad, and six feet thick (*figures 33–38*).
>
> We are filled with astonishment when we consider that these enormous masses were hewn from their native bed and fashioned into shape by a people ignorant of the use of iron; that they were brought from quarries, from four to fifteen leagues distant, without the aid of beasts of burden; were transported across rivers and ravines, raised to their elevated positions on the sierra, and finally adjusted there with the nicest accuracy, without the knowledge of tools and machinery familiar to the European.

It is indeed curious that the Inca did not use iron, as Prescott further notes (p. 68): 'the natives were unacquainted with iron although the soil was largely impregnated with it'. They preferred instead, it seems, either stone tools or ones made from copper that had been doped with six per cent tin, to produce a hardness comparable to steel.

There is a great difference between the properties of iron and copper; iron is magnetic and can be used to store (or deflect, *short-circuit*) magnetic fields, whereas copper is non-magnetic but a good electrical conductor and as such can be used to store (or deflect, *short-circuit*) electric fields.

When the Spaniards arrived in Peru they questioned the Incas about the perfectly fitting stone blocks found throughout the kingdom *(figures 33–38)*. They shrugged their shoulders and extended their arms, saying only that their ancestors had made them; but they knew not when or how.

They knew of the sophisticated ashlars used in the construction of the temples at Tiahuanaco, Bolivia, and assumed that their forebears must have learned their stonemason skills from the Tiahuanacos far back in antiquity. Stories told of a race of bearded white men who settled on the shores of Lake Titicaca and taught the natives the higher sciences of civilisation. As Prescott says (pp. 6 and 7):

> It may remind us of the tradition existing among the Aztecs in respect of Quetzalcoatl . . . *(who was thought to be one and the same as Lord Pacal of the Maya* [author's italics]) . . . who with a similar garb and aspect came up the great plateau from the east on a like benevolent mission to save the natives. The analogy is all the more remarkable as there is no trace of any communication with, or even knowledge of, each other to be found in the two nations.

The accounts may have become embellished over time, from at first one white man with a beard, to several. Prescott goes on to say:

> The date usually assigned to these 'extraordinary events' was about four hundred years before the coming of the Spanish . . . but however popular the legend . . . on the shores of Lake Titicaca extensive ruins exist at the present day which the Peruvians themselves acknowledge to be of older date than the pretended advent of the Incas who were thought to have furnished them with models of their architecture . . .

In an accompanying footnote Prescott adds: 'McCulloh cites the famous temple at Pachacamac, four leagues south of Lima, as an example of architecture more ancient than that of the Incas.' He also gives his source: *Researches Philosophical and Antiquarian concerning the Aboriginal History of America* (Baltimore, 1829), p. 405.

At Ollantaytambo, other Inca sites *(figures 34–38)* and Tiahuanaco, ancient stone blocks have been found strapped together with copper links *(figures 39–40)* which today continue to perplex historians and engineers alike. Why use soft copper straps to hold together enormous blocks of stone, some weighing 10 tonnes and more? The stability of

Figure 33. The Stones of Cuzco

(a) An entrance-way, not far from the Coricancha, in the backstreets of Cuzco. The lintel above the doorway carries two serpents (solar symbols). The surrounding stonework is built of perfectly fitting Inca stone blocks held together without any mortar whatsoever. The joints between the stones are so perfect a fit that it is impossible to insert the blade of a knife between them. (b) close-up of one section of wall showing the stones in more detail. The centre block, of the three polygonal blocks, has no fewer than 14 corners. The exposed surface of the stones is smoothed as though the blocks were once liquid, or in someway softened and then bagged into position.

Figure 34. The Stones of Ollantaytambo (I)

Examples of stonework from the Inca temple-fortress at Ollantaytambo, in the Sacred Valley of the Incas, near Pisac, which is 32 kilometres (20 miles) from Cuzco. (a) This enormous (20 tonnes) block of natural stone, which was quarried from a mountain-side 6 kilometres (3.7 miles) away, high above the opposite bank of the River Urubamba, shows another method of Inca stone-working; one side has been cleanly cut, as though sliced with a fine cutting tool. A taut length of cotton thread, or fine string, can be slid between the crack, so perfect is the cut. How the cut was made remains a mystery. (b) Walls built into the rock face at the foot of the temple. The walls perfectly fit the mountain to which they are attached. Just how they carved the architrave around the windows is unknown. (c) Aqueduct stone pipework, from the valley below, carved in the same mysterious way as the window architrave.

Figure 35. The Stones of Ollantaytambo (II)

Two more examples of stoneworking techniques found at Ollantaytambo. *(a)* Perfectly fitting stones from the temple at the top of the fortress show a similar pattern to those in Cuzco and other Inca towns. *(b)* Niches carved into the solid rock of the mountainside, as though the mountain was made of soft clay.

Figure 36. The Stones of Tambomachay

(a) The temple at Tambomachay in the Sacred Valley, about 5 kilometres (3 miles) from Cuzco. (b) Carved ceremonial stone bath, 'the bath of the Inca', from the temple.

Figure 37. The Stones of Qenko

(*a*) Qenko is located in the Sacred Valley, around 4 kilometres (2.5 miles) from Cuzco. The name means 'zigzag'. The limestone rock is particularly interesting and unusual. (*b*) It is as if the zigzag serpents and pools carved in the rock have been *poured* into position, like liquid lava, rather than carved or cut. Several tunnels are carved beneath the large boulder (*shown in a*) along with (*c*) a cave and an altar carved from solid bedrock.

Figure 38. The Stones of Machu Picchu

(a) The observatory at Machu Picchu. *(b)* Cave containing the so-called 'sacred shrine', an altar-like edifice located directly beneath the observatory; note the incredible way the stone blocks hug the rock face, like sandbags thrown into position, as though the stone may once have been pliable. *(c)* So-called Intiwatana, 'hitching post of the sun', carved from a solid piece of bedrock. According to Cuzco legend the Inca would ritually tie the sun, to the post on the day of the winter solstice to bring it back in the opposite direction.

the blocks and the integrity of construction, as time has shown, is fulfilled by the interlocking precision of the blocks, not by the soft copper straps. If this integrity was ever to be undermined, then the blocks would topple and the straps would rip apart, as though they were made of paper.

Many scholars believe the straps were smelted locally and then poured into grooves in the stone, because microscopic marks embedded in the straps can be seen to imitate corollary marks found in the stone. But as figures 39 and 40 explain, if the straps had been poured in situ then the surface of each strap would be expected to be slightly convex, due to the influence of surface tension experienced in the casting process. Secondly, the straps themselves would have adopted a cast line caused by the crack between the stone blocks, but the straps do not feature such a mark. A closer look at one of the blocks *(plate 25a)* shows a discoloured outer layer of stone. It is as though the surface of the stone has been somehow 'softened' and later hardened, permitting the introduction of the ready-formed copper strip. This would explain away the flat-topped nature of the straps and the absence of the inter-block cast line. So what was the purpose of the straps? We shall see later that they were for electrically earth-bonding the stones.

This provides a clue as to how pre-Inca (and Inca) stonemasons fashioned their stone blocks. It seems likely that, whoever these people were, they possessed the technology to soften and pour stone. We can do this today but only in one direction, from soft to hard; we call it concrete. It seems that the Incas and the Tiahuanacos could take the process one step further, from hard to soft again, using igneous rocks. At first this seems incomprehensible, but given the molecular structure of matter it is simply a question of overcoming the covalent bonds that bind atoms together. We can do this to ice, when we turn it to water, and we do it again when we turn water into steam. This explains how the Incas and Tiahuanacos assembled stones with such perfect precision. Close examination of the rounded edges of the stones *(figures 33–38)* suggests that the stone material has been 'poured', as though it were once contained within a sack or bag which has long since rotted and disappeared. This, perhaps, explains *how* the polygonal blocks of the Inca were made, but not *why*.

Why would any builder invest so much time and effort manufacturing blocks of stone that fit together *perfectly*? The laws of diminish-

Figure 39. The Mystery of the Copper Straps

(a) Copper strap from Ollan-taytambo, one of many found on the site together with (b) and (c), stone building-blocks showing groove to accommodate the copper strap. Archaeologists believe that the straps were used to hold the building-blocks together, but this could not have been the case; many of the blocks weigh ten tonnes or more. Earthquake-inspired movements could be expected to rip the soft copper strips apart. So what was the real purpose of the straps?

Figure 40. Schematics of the Copper Straps

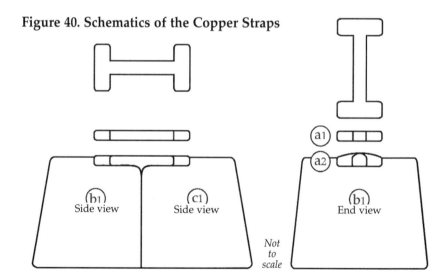

Figure 40. Researchers suggest that the copper straps (above) were smelted locally and poured into ready-made grooves in the stone blocks. However, the observed surface profile of the straps (shown in (a1)) suggests that this was not the case. (a2) shows the expected profile of a copper strap poured in situ; the top of the strap would be convex due to surface tension experienced in the pouring of the molten copper, and, moreover, the underside of the strap between (b1) and (c1) would have adopted the contours of the fissure between the two stone blocks. This suggests that the Incas (and Tiahuanacos) *somehow* softened (see main text) the outside layer of the stones (plate 25a) and then immersed the ready-made connecting straps. The copper straps would electrically earth-bond (ground) every stone block.

ing marginal returns favour imperfect, approximate or imprecise production methods over exact tolerances available from costly state-of-the-art precision engineering. Subsequent remedial solutions are often more acceptable, more cost-effective and sometimes more appropriate; draught excluders not only fill in gaps but also allow for flexible expansion and contraction of components over time. In the same way, there must have been an *easier*, more *cost-effective* way of filling cracks between stone blocks, perhaps by using pitch or resin rather than making the pieces fit perfectly. And therein lies the clue to the mystery: if cracks between stones were filled with pitch or resin the stones would be electrically insulated from each other, not electrically bonded to earth.

The absence of gaps between stones, moreover, precludes the ingress of daylight into buildings. In humans a light-sensitive area in the retina of the eye converts light into electrical signals which travel down the optic nerve into the hypothalamus gland (which is known to be associated with the body's biological clock). Each day, light signals enter the brain, and each night the hypothalamus sends signals to the pineal gland. The amount of light which strikes the eyes inversely determines the amount of melatonin production.

Melatonin was first isolated in 1958 by researchers A. B. Lerner and J. D. Case, who gave it the name after the substance was found to activate melanophores, pigment cells in frogs that turned the skin lighter or darker. Secretions of melatonin from the pineal gland are known to change skin colour of certain reptiles for camouflage, like the chameleon, and this is why the light receptor of some reptiles is positioned on top of the head, exposed to daylight, on the outside. In 1963 melatonin was recognised as a sex hormone following experiments on rats. Soon after this it became clear that melatonin production in humans was *inhibited* by light and, later still, that blood levels of the hormone are 10 times higher at night than during the day. Levels among men and women were also found to differ; the slightly larger female pineal gland was subject to seasonal cyclicity, producing *less* melatonin in summer when the hours of daylight are longer. Melatonin stimulates the pituitary, which in turn affects the production of the luteinizing hormone and the follicle-stimulating hormones. These affect the manufacture of the fertility hormones oestrogen and progesterone.

In 1995 two US-based doctors, Walter Pierpaoli and William

Regelson, published a book entitled *The Melatonin Miracle*. They carried out a series of experiments on mice, the results of which suggested that a daily dose of melatonin could halt, if not reverse, the ageing process in mice and humans. They also point out (p. 67) that melatonin enhances the sexual function and that 'several studies show that exposure to *electro*magnetic fields can interfere with the evening production of melatonin'.

We already know that *magnetic* fields *enhance* the production of fertility hormones in fe*males (Appendix 2)*. Here Pierpaoli and Regelson are saying that *electro*magnetic fields have the opposite effect, that they *diminish* production of fertility hormones. Electromagnetic fields comprise both *electric* and *magnetic* field components.

Figure 32 explained how the earth's magnetic field is affected by solar particle bombardment. During sunspot minima, fewer particles impinge on the Van Allen belts, resulting in lower levels of magnetic variations on the earth's surface. This is what happened between AD 1450 and 1520, during which time the world (and the Incas) suffered a sunspot cycle minimum *(figure 41)* together with a concomitant decline in fertility associated with the event.

At the same time the mini-ice age that accompanied the sunspot minimum *(figure 41)* caused less evaporation of water from the oceans, less rainfall, and drought. The Inca population began to decline. If the 'children of the sun' were to survive, they would have to manipulate the forces of nature to *increase* exposure to solar-inspired magnetic fields and *decrease* exposure to electrical fields. They would need to build a sanctuary for their virgins, in the sky.

The Secrets of Machu Picchu

Machu Picchu *(plate 13)* sits between the mountains of Machu Picchu (the 'old peak') and Huayna Picchu (the 'new peak') on the edge of the Peruvian jungle. When the American historian Hiram Bingham discovered the site, on 24 July 1911, he could scarcely believe his eyes.

Who could have built this city of stone in such a remote and inaccessible place, 2,500 metres (8,300 feet) high in the Cordillera Vilcabamba, 700 metres (2,300 feet) above the Urubamba River that flowed through the valley below? How did the Incas achieve their mastery in stonemasonry? From whom did they acquire their sophisticated knowledge of astronomy exemplified in many of the buildings

Figure 41. Sunspots and the Rise and Fall of Civilisations

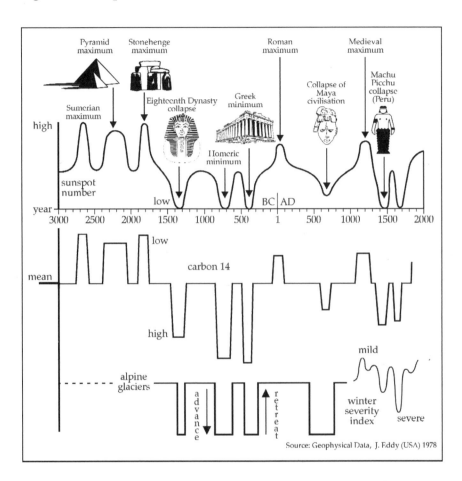

A series of graphs showing that the rise and fall of civilisations corresponds with the rise and fall of radiation from the sun. The top graph shows a long-term envelope of sunspot activity derived from the centre graph of carbon 14. More carbon 14 is absorbed in the growth rings of trees during sunspot minima. Sunspot minima also correlate with mini-ice ages (lower graph) and a winter severity index (based on a mean for Paris and London for the period shown). Reduced radiation results in reduced fertility on earth (*figure 32*) . The eighteenth dynasty of Tutankhamun collapsed during a massive mini-mum, as did the civilisation of the Maya 2,000 years later. The Inca city of Machu Picchu, occupied by the virgins of the sun from around AD 1450, was abandoned when the sun's radiation returned to normal levels in around AD 1520, long before the conquest.

at the site? Why did they worship the sun? Why were the bones (excavated by Bingham at the site) mainly female? And why was it so suddenly abandoned after a period of around only 70 years' occupation? He could never have imagined that the answers to his questions would have to wait until the end of the twentieth century, for the age of space exploration, to explain how the sun influences life on earth.

The site, which escaped detection by the Spaniards, was built during the reign of the great expansionist and urban developer, the ninth Inca Pachacuti, in around 1450. If the engineering skills of the Inca were ever in question, then the city of Machu Picchu must surely dispel any doubt. Here the finest examples of stoneworking were paralleled only by the remarkable technology which allowed the construction of wells and irrigation networks that feed the site. And, curiously, it is to the water supplies that we turn when seeking answers to Bingham's questions; studies of the nearby Quelccaya mountain icecap, south-east of Cuzco, by Lonnie Thompson of Ohio State University, confirm that severe drought affected the region during the Machu Picchu period of occupation (AD 1450–1520). So why build a sanctuary on top of a mountain, in solid stone, far from the only source of water (the river below) during a time of drought? Indeed, why carry building-stones, some weighing 100 tonnes or more, up the 3,000 steps of the 109 staircases that lead to the city from the valley below? And why walk the 700 metres (2,300 feet) up and down the mountain peaks to bathe in the river below? It seems clear that the Inca possessed knowledge superior to our own of today, a knowledge that embraced the softening, pouring and transportation of rock which thrived alongside an understanding of the super-science of the sun.

Earlier, the picture of the jigsaw puzzle demonstrated how the brain prefers to see information which *does not exist* in preference to that which does exist. The idiosyncrasies of the brain do not stop there. The brain also prefers to reject information it *cannot* understand, and it does this by calling on neural defence mechanisms that cause 'reasoning ability' to enter a programmable loop that I have termed 'loop-think'. This can be demonstrated as follows:

Consider the following information:

(i)   When I shout I can be heard across the street.
(ii)   I know a man who, when he shouts, can be heard a mile away.

(iii) I know a man who, when he shouts, can be heard on the moon.

Statements (i) and (ii) do not present the brain with any difficulty, but statement (iii) causes the brain to enter 'loop-think' in several easily defined steps:

Step 1 *Confusion*. The brain questions the validity of the information. How can the shout of a man be heard on the moon? It cannot.

Step 2 *Indignation*. It is not possible for the man to be heard on the moon, so either the information is incorrect or the person presenting the information thinks I am stupid. This is an insult to my intelligence. I am not stupid.

Step 3 *Hatred*. I don't *like* people who think I am stupid. Go away and leave me alone.

Adding more information:

(iv) The man who can be heard on the moon works at the BBC in London.

Which gives rise to:

Step 4 *Frustration*. Why didn't you tell me that he had access to technologies that involve radio wave transmissions and loudspeakers?

Step 5 *Reconciliation and acceptance*. It's not my fault that I didn't understand.

And a second example:

(i) I know a man who enjoys throwing sticks, but he does not like to retrieve the sticks.

(ii) I know a man who is cleverer than the first. He has trained a dog to retrieve the sticks.

(iii) I know a man who is cleverer than the second. His sticks return by themselves.

Again, the brain enters 'loop-think': how can a stick return by itself?

(iv) His stick is called a boomerang.

Step 4   Of course the stick comes back by itself because the edge of the stick is aerodynamically shaped in such a way that, when thrown into the wind, the wind forces the stick back to the place where its journey began, in the hand of the thrower.

Interestingly, this second example involves technologies more *ancient* than our own, those of the Australian Aborigines. Despite this, the information still caused 'loop-think'.

Loop-think, together with confusion, indignation, hatred and frustration, therefore protects individuals from an otherwise inevitable logic that would eventually convince us that we were all stupid, perhaps even useless and worthless, which might lead to depression and suicide.

We can now understand why archaeologists fail to see the decoded stories contained in the Lid of Palenque and why, despite the evidence before them, they fail to accept that large stones which fit perfectly *must* have either been cut, poured or softened; that large rocks found at the top of the mountains, quarried far away, *must* have been transported to their final resting place; and that cities built on mountain-tops were sited there for good reasons.

According to Dr George F. Eaton, an osteologist working with Hiram Bingham, most of the skeletons found buried at Machu Picchu were aged between 31 and 35. Of the 164 examined by Eaton, 102 were adult female, 7 young female, 22 adult men and 4 male children; the remaining 29 were unidentifiable or infants. The figures persuaded Bingham that the mountain-top retreat must have been a sanctuary for the virgins of the sun.

The architecture at Machu Picchu *(plates 14 and 15)* follows the highly advanced style of the Incas with walls constructed of perfectly fitting stone blocks precluding the ingress of light to the interiors. The windows of the houses are likewise blocked up, again with perfectly fitting stone blocks to the same effect. This is the case for most of the houses (but not for the observatories, which required observational access to the skies above). The absence of windows again suggests that the Inca went to great lengths to keep out daylight.

We also note the solid stone cylindrical roof supports that protrude, incongruously, without the grass canopy, from the sides of the stone walls. The reconstruction by archaeologists *(plate 14a)* attempts to persuade us that roof coverings were made simply, of grass or reed thatch over a timber frame. But the cylindrical stone roof supports *(plates 14a–e)* would be greatly oversized for such a scheme. It seems more likely that the roofs were covered first with a sheet of copper, similar to the sheet found in the tomb of the Lord of Sipan, or an even heavier one, and then covered in thatch. The closely fitting stones would not only keep out daylight but, like the copper sheet, electrically bond the entire edifice, together short-circuiting fertility-impeding electrical fields to earth. Conversely, the topological position of the site, on the mountain-top, would give access to stronger solar-inspired magnetic fields, unaffected by geographical magnetic anomalies prevalent in the valleys. These factors would stimulate the production of melatonin among the virgins of the sun, which would in turn inspire greater production of fertility hormones oestrogen and progesterone negating the solar-inspired decreases in fertility. The precious copper sheets would have been removed when the site was abandoned following a return to normal sunspot activity, and fertility behaviour *(figure 41)* in around AD 1520.

It is clear that the remarkable stonemasonry skills of the Inca were employed throughout the empire, from Tiahuanaco in the Bolivian highlands, the Cuzco Valley and between Pisac and Ollantaytambo in the Sacred Valley as well as the peaks of Machu Picchu. Likewise, the copper-strap earth-bonding practice is also widespread, suggesting that although Machu Picchu may have been the near-perfect location in which to site a sanctuary for the virgins of the sun, the rest of the populace also benefited, to some extent, by the same techniques used in buildings throughout Peru.

Which leaves just one crucial question: where did the Incas acquire their knowledge of the super-science of the sun and the advanced technologies that facilitated stone cutting, pouring, softening and lifting?

The Legends of Peru

The best accounts of Peruvian mythology were compiled by Spanish chroniclers at around the time of the conquest in 1532. One of these was the (already mentioned) Garcilasso Inca de la Vega, who was born in Cuzco in 1540. He was the son of the Spaniard Garcilasso de la Vega who arrived in 1534 from Spain in the company of Commander Pedro de Alvarado. His mother was a Peruvian royal princess, niece of the eleventh Inca Huayna Capac. Proud of his Inca lineage, he adopted the title Garcilasso *Inca* de la Vega and was raised a Roman Catholic with a sound education, despite the turmoil which accompanied colonial acquisition.

At the age of 20 he sailed to Spain and enlisted for military service, quickly rising to the rank of captain. But all was not well. Skeletons in the family closet overshadowed his achievements; the family name, stained by an alleged episode of disloyalty by his father to the Crown, eventually led to the son's shameful withdrawal from society. The stigma from that episode hung like a cloud above his head and later defeated recovery of the inheritance due from his mother's family. He left the army poor and in debt, retreated into isolation in Cordova and began to write about what he loved best, the days of his childhood in the land of the Inca.

His 'misfortune' gave way to a brilliant literary career that, in 1609, saw the publication of Part 1 of his *Commentarios Reales* (first published as *Primera parte dos los comentarios reales de los Incas*: Lisbon, 1609, translated by Harold V. Livermore, London and Austin, 1966), a comprehensive history of Peru under the Incas. Part 2, which covered the story of the conquest, appeared in 1616, shortly before he died a wealthy man at the age of 76. No one could compete with Garcilasso's pedigree as correspondent to the Inca. Only he, with Inca blood in his veins, could do these people justice, recount the stories he had heard at his mother's knees, by the fireside, in the valleys and the mountains, during the golden age of Inca splendour.

Cieza de León, a Peruvian from the age of 13 completed Part 1 of his *Crónica del Perú* in 1550 (first published as *Parte Primera de la chronica del Perú* in 1553) aged 32. Parts 2, 3 and 4 were either not fully completed or unpublished. His accounts for the main part provide a snapshot of the geography and topography of the region, but while compiling these, over a 10-year period, he seized the opportunity to talk to indigenous Indians about their history and traditions. The book was not published until 1553 in Seville, Spain. Publication in Italian, in Rome, two years later brought him to the attention of a wider international audience.

Historian Juan de Sarmiento visited Peru in the early 1550s, as President of the Council of the Indies – a post of high authority –

eager to compile a history of the new colony. His position allowed access to the Inca nobility, who revealed to him the secrets of their legends. The result was a 400-page unpublished manuscript entitled *Relación de la sucesion y govierno de las Yngas Señores naturales que fueron de la Provincias del Perú y Otras cosas tocantes á aquel Reyno, para el Iltmo.*

Another Spaniard, Juan de Santa Cruz Pachacuti-Yamqui Salcamayhua, spent years of discourse among the Inca which led to the publication of his *Account of the Antiquities of Peru* (first published as *Relación de antigüedades deste reyno del Pirú*, c. 1615, ed. M. Jiménez de la Espada in *Tres relaciónes de antigüedadas peruanas*, Madrid, 1879, translated by C. R. Markham, Hakluyt Society, 1873), a document of ancient folklore and myth attached to the ancient civilisations of Peru.

Other notable writers, and publications, include Fray Martín de Morúa, *Historia del origen y geneología real de los reyes Incas del Perú* (Madrid, 1946); Father José de Acosta, *The Natural and Moral History of the Incas* (Seville, 1590); Cristóbal de Molina of Cuzco, *The Fables and Rites of the Yncas* (translated and edited by C. R. Markham, in *Rites and Laws of the Yncas*, Hakluyt Society, London, 1873, Paris, 1573) and Father Bernabé Cobo's *Historia del Nuevo Mundo* (Cuzco, 1653). The most authoritative Western accounts were compiled by William H. Prescott, *History of the Conquest of Peru*, Routledge and Sons, 1893), John Flemming (*The Conquest of the Incas*, Macmillan, 1970) and Wolfgang Von Hagen (*The Ancient Sun Kingdoms of the Americas*, Thames and Hudson, 1962).

When referring to the mythological accounts, we are mindful that the myth is of the accident and not of the essence, that the historical background lies hidden between the lines. As Prescott says (pp. 6 and 7):

> Such legends will not be considered puerile nor will their similarity with those of remote races seem inexplicable, when they are viewed in their true light ... Thus considered, the very 'myths' ... that were discarded as 'lying fables' prove to be sources of history in ways that their makers and transmitters little dreamed of.

What better example do we have of this than that of Lord Pacal, when he encoded his secrets into the architecture, jewellery and carvings of his people; he called on the ostensibly 'mythological' pantheon of Maya gods, knowing that these could be used, like actors in a play, to release his secret knowledge to mankind when the time was right and the code was broken. Then and only then would the plot, concealed in the 'myth', be revealed as the actors emerged, in full costume, to perform the grand theatre production of *The Amazing Lid of Palenque*.

And common sense tells us that there has to be some kind of logic, rationale or truth associated with myth, some possibility that the story may be plausible, otherwise it would have failed to fascinate and, likewise, have failed to propagate through the ages.

If, therefore, we wish to learn more of the history of Peru we need only refer to the mythological accounts set down in that history; how the first Peruvians were brought forth from the darkness into the light; how they found their homeland with a rod of gold; and how a white man walked among them performing miracles and left:

> Our Father, the sun, seeing men live like wild animals, was moved to pity and sent from the sky to the earth one of his sons and daughters to instruct them in the knowledge of our Father the sun, that they might adore him and have him as their God, and to give them laws and prescriptions whereby they might live as men in reason and comity.
>
> With this injunction and mandate our Father the sun sent down his two children to Lake Titicaca, eighty leagues from Cuzco, and told them to pass where they would and wherever they stayed to eat or to sleep they should sink in the soil a rod of gold, which he gave to them. This rod was half a yard long and was to serve as a sign, for where it sank in the earth with a single blow, there they were to stop and found the sacred city of the sun (Garcilasso Inca de la Vega, *Commentarios Reales*, Part 1, Ch. 15).

The Indians say that all men were drowned in the deluge and they report that out of the great Lake Titicaca came one Viracocha, who stayed in Tiahuanaco, where at this day there is to be seen the ruins of ancient and very strange buildings, and from there came to Cuzco, and so began mankind to multiply (Father José de Acosta, *The Natural and Moral History of the Incas*, Book 1, Ch. 25).

The Indians also have another myth in which they say that the creator had two sons, Imaymana Viracocha and Tocapo Viracocha.

When the creator had fashioned the peoples and nations, giving to each their appropriate language, and had sent the sun, the moon and the stars to their place in the sky from Tiahuanaco, the creator, whom the Indians call Pachaychachic (teacher of the world) or Ticci Viracocha, which means the unknowable God, went along the highland road and visited the tribes to see how they had begun to multiply and to fulfil the commandments he had given them. Finding that some tribes had rebelled against his commandments, he changed a large part of them into stones in the shape of men and women with the same costume that they had worn. The changing into stone occurred at the following places: in Tiahuanaco, in Pucara and in Jauja, where they say he turned the huaca called Huarivilca into stone and in Pachacamac, in Cajamarca and in other regions. Indeed today there are huge figures of stone in these places, some of them almost the size of giants, which must have been fashioned by human hands in times of great antiquity, and as the memory failed and in the absence of writing they invented this legend saying that the people were turned into stones by command of the creator on account of disobeying his commands. They also say that at Pucara, which is forty leagues from Cuzco on the Collao road, fire came down from the heavens and burned a great part of them, while those who tried to escape were turned to stone. The creator, who they say was the father of Imaymana Viracocha and Tocapo Viracocha, commanded Imaymana Viracocha, the elder of his two sons, in whose power all things were placed, to set out from that place and traverse all the world by the road of the mountains and forested valleys. As he went he was to give names to all the trees large and small, to the flowers and fruit they were to bear, and to indicate to the people which were edible and which were not and which had medicinal properties. He also gave names to the herbs and flowers, and the time when they were to produce flowers and fruit and taught people which could cure and which could not. His other son, named Tocapo Viracocha, which in their language means 'the maker', he ordered to go by road of the plains, visiting people and giving names to the rivers and trees and instructing them as to the fruits and flowers. And thus they went to the lowest parts of this land until they came to the sea where they ascended into the sky after having finished making all that there is in the land. In the same myth they also say that at Tiahuanaco, where he created the tribes of men, he created all the different kinds of birds, male and female of each, giving them the songs which each kind was to sing. Those that were to inhabit the forests he sent to the forests and those that were to inhabit the highlands to the highlands, each to the region proper to its kind. He also created all the different species of animals, male and female of each, and all the snakes and creeping things there are in the land and commanded each to its proper habitat. And he taught the people the names and properties of the birds and snakes and other reptiles. These Indians also believed that neither the creator nor his sons were born of woman and that they were unchanging and eternal (Cristóbal de Molina of Cuzco, *The Fables and Rites of the Yncas*).

Before the Incas ruled or had even been heard of in these kingdoms these Indians relate a thing more noteworthy than anything else they say. They assert that they were a long time without seeing the sun and, suffering much hardship from this, they offered prayers and vows to those whom they beheld as gods, beseeching of them the light they lacked. At this the sun, very brilliant, rose from the island of Titicaca in the great lake of the Collao, and all were rejoiced. After this had happened they say that there suddenly appeared, coming from the south, a white man of large stature and authoritative demeanour. This man had such great power that he changed the hills into valleys and from the valleys made great hills, causing streams to flow from the living stone. When they saw his power they called him Maker of all things created and Prince of all things, Father of the sun. For he did other still more wonderful things, giving being to men and animals; by his hand very great benefits accrued to them. This is the story that the Indians themselves told me and they heard it from their fathers who in turn heard it from the old songs which were handed down from very ancient times.

They say that this man travelled along the highland route to the north, working marvels as he went, and they say they never saw him again. They say that in many places he gave men instructions on how they should live, speaking to them with great love and kindness and admonishing them to be good and to do no damage or injury one to another, but to love one another and show charity to all. In most places they call him Ticci Viracocha. In many places they built temples to him and in them they set up statues in his likeness and offered sacrifices before them. The huge statues in the village of Tiahuanaco are held to be from those times.

After much time had passed they saw another man like in appearance to the first but they do not mention his name. They have it from forebears that wherever he passed he healed all that were sick and restored sight to the blind by words alone. Thus he was beloved by all. So, working great miracles, by his words, he came to the district of Canas and there, near the village of Cacha, the people rose up against him and threatened to stone him. They saw him sink to his knees and raise his hands to heaven, as if beseeching aid in the peril which beset him. The Indians declare that thereupon they saw fire in the sky which seemed all around them. Full of fear they approached him whom they had intended to kill and besought him to forgive them; for they regarded this as a punishment for their sin in seeking to stone a stranger. Presently they saw that the fire was extinguished at his command, though the stones were consumed by fire in such wise that large blocks could be lifted by hand, as if they were cork. They narrate further that, leaving the place where this occurred, he came to the coast and there, holding his mantle, he went forth amidst the waves of the sea and was seen no more. And as he went they gave him the name Viracocha, which means 'foam of the sea' (Cieza de León, *Crónica del Perú*, Part II, Chs. 4 and 5).

I asked them what their tradition had to tell about the appearance of Viracocha when he was seen by the first men of their race and they told me he was a man of tall stature clothed in a white robe which came down to his feet and which he wore belted at the waist. He had short hair and tonsure like a priest. He went unshod and carried in his hands a thing which, in the light of what they know today, they liken to the breviaries which priests carry. And I asked them what was the name of the person in whose honour that stone was set up and they told me it was Con Tiki Viracocha Pachacamac, which means in their language 'God of the World' (Juan de Santa Cruz Pachacuti-Yamqui Salcamayhua, *Account of the Antiquities of Peru*).

Who Were the Lords of Sipan?

When we examine the various stories, synthesise the diverse accounts and allow for adulteration of the message over vast periods of time, a general picture begins to emerge: the creator of the universe, seeing his people suffer, sent two people down to earth to teach them the higher orders of science and spirituality. These two, who had no mother (born of immaculate conceptions), seem to have originated in the region of Tiahuanaco and travelled the length of Peru performing miracles and preaching a doctrine of love and forgiveness, before walking to the coast. Both moved large blocks of stone, as though they were made of cork. Sometimes the stones 'caught fire'. Both were called Viracocha, 'foam of the sea', white men with beards (according to Prescott's *History of the Conquest of Peru*, pp. 6 and 7, mentioned earlier). They dressed like priests and carried a golden rod, following the instruction that wherever the rod sank into the ground they were to settle. The second one, like in appearance to the first, appeared much later.

The treasures found in the tombs at Sipan suggest that these two living gods were one and the same as the Lords of Sipan. The Old Lord of Sipan (the crab man), foam of the sea, must surely have been Viracocha, and the Lord of Sipan, in his Supergod coffin of 9s and his 96 (sunspot cycle) roof timbers, has to be Viracocha Pachacamac, god of the world.

CHAPTER THREE

The Tiahuanacos

The Secrets of Viracocha

This is the land of the Aymara Indians high in the Andes altiplano (the high plain) 4,000 metres (13,000 feet) above sea-level. The air is thin and crisp, the sky blue and the cheeks of the Aymara bright red. They say it takes six months for the body to adjust to the altitude, to manufacture more red haemoglobin (blood cells) which help the lungs suck out what few oxygen molecules exist in the rarefied air. And they don't smile much either, unlike their neighbours the Quechua from the fertile valleys of the Incas. This is a different world. At this altitude the decreased barometric pressure allows the air within the body to expand. The head feels as though it will explode. The nose feels as though it will cascade with blood at a moment's notice. And the eyes, scratched by the wind and the sand, burn in the sun.

Tiahuanaco, under Inca rule, was conquered by the Spanish in 1538, 6 years after Peru and, apart from around 30 years of turmoil which accompanied the acquisition, the 200 years that followed were relatively peaceful. Revolutionary unease against Spanish colonial rule first began in La Paz in 1661 and was followed by unrest in Cochabamba in 1730, spreading further afield in a second wave from 1776 to 1780. In 1809 calls for independence came from the University of San Francisco Xavier, at Sucre. On 9 December 1824 Simón Bolívar's general, Gral Antonio José de Sucre, won the decisive battle of Ayacucho in Peru and marched on to fight the Spaniards at the battle of Tumulsa, in the altiplano. On 2 April 1825, Bolivia was declared an independent state.

In 1892, following surveys of the site, German archaeologists Max Uhle and Alphons Stübel published scientific papers describing the ruins at Tiahuanaco. Uhle returned two years later to study the cultures of the region, which he classified according to pottery styles. In 1903 a French scientific expedition under the leadership of Count Créqui de Montfort carried out excavations which located a buried temple *(plate 16, temple 3)* adorned with hundreds of red sandstone heads around the walls. In the centre stood three stone statues *(plate 22a)*, one of a man with a beard whom the Indians named Viracocha and just next to him two shorter ones, nowadays referred to as 'the children of Viracocha' *(plate 22b)*.

Bolivian archaeologist Professor Arthur Posnansky was one of the first academics to address the question of the foundation date of Tiahuanaco. His book, *Una Metropoli Prehistorica en la America del Sud*, published in 1914, was the most comprehensive book on Tiahuanaco and Lake Titicaca to appear at the time. The bilingual, single bound volume, republished in 1945 in both Spanish and English under the title of *Tihuanacu, The Cradle of American Man*, was used as a reference in *The Lost Tomb of Viracocha*.

At first Posnansky set down his own periods of development at Tiahuanaco into three periods based on sedimentation samples and lake levels of nearby Lake Titicaca; the First Period corresponded to the geological upheaval that elevated the altiplano from the ocean floor. The Second Period corresponded to the melting of the glaciers, the consequential overfilling of Lake Titicaca (with glacial meltdown) and then the subsequent partial emptying caused by tectonic movement. These were followed by a Third Period that saw the advent of polygonal, stone blocks, similar to those used by the later Incas; a Fourth Period, exemplified by the use of dried-mud brick, and finally a Fifth, and final Period, that of the Incas (Posnansky, pp. 48 and 49). (The specific dates demarcating these periods are not defined in Posnansky's book; more on this later.)

Perhaps because of his uncertainty surrounding the definitive dating of the periods of development, Posnansky continued his research at Tiahuanaco. After surveying and mapping the site in considerable detail *(plate 16a)* he noticed that the lateral angles between the cornerstones of one of the temples, the Kalasasaya (the

Figure 42. Astronomical Alignments at Tiahuanaco

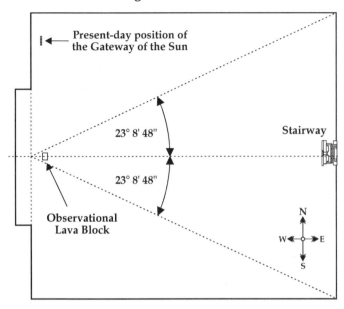

Posnansky noticed that the angle from the observational lava block to each of the corner-stones measured 23° 8' 48" *(see also plate 16)*.

Figure 43. The Dating of Tiahuanaco according to Posnansky

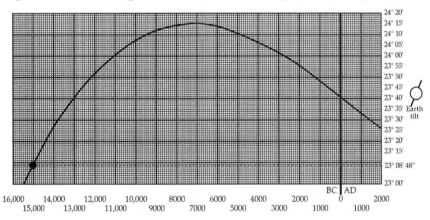

Posnansky's method of calculating the age of Tiahuanaco is based on a formula of extrapolation recommended by the ephemeris conference of Paris (1911). This method was used by Sir Norman Lockyer, President of the Physical Solar Observatory of London, who in 1909 was the first to use it while undertaking calculations in his work 'Stonehenge and other British Stone Monuments'. Posnansky's measurements date the foundation period of Tiahuanaco at around 15,000 BC, thus making it the oldest site of antiquity on earth.

Temple of Standing Stones), and a partially buried *observational* lava block (that once marked the location of the monolithic stone Gateway of the Sun *(figure 42)* measured 23° 8' 48", a figure very close to the present-day angle of the tilt of the earth on its axis (the obliquity of the earth).

Further surveys revealed that the sun would rise directly above a statue of Viracocha at the time of the autumn equinox (21 March), when viewed from the stone steps of the main entrance-way to the Kalasasaya *(plate 16b)*, persuading him that those who built the site had intentionally encoded astronomical alignments into the monuments.

Further investigation showed that the sun would rise above each corner of the Kalasasaya entrance-way at the time of the solstices, 21 December and 21 June, were it not for a slight discrepancy; the sun *would* have risen exactly above the corners had the tilt of the earth amounted to 23° 8' 48" *(which it did not*; the tilt of the earth when he measured it was 23° 27", much the same as it is today). At around the same time (1909) a British astronomer, Sir Norman Lockyer, President of the Physical Solar Observatory of London, had made a name for himself using a novel method to ascertain the foundation date of Stonehenge in England, pointing out that some of the stones would align perfectly with astronomical reference points were it not for the fact that the earth appears to have tilted, very slightly, on its axis since the monument was built.

Posnansky then researched the possibility that the earth had shifted on its axis over the past few thousand years (the proposed shift being above and beyond any movement due to astronomical cycles already recognised at that time by the astronomical fraternity, including precession – the slow backwards shift of the equinoctial points on the sun's path through the sky). In 1911, following representations from Lockyer, he and others succeeded in gaining acceptance for the notion that the earth had indeed shifted very slightly over the years and that the amount of shift was quantifiable. The date of foundation for a monument could be obtained, they said, by referring the figure of obliquity, obtained from empirical measurement of the monument, to a curve derived from a special formula. The method was ratified by astronomers who attended the astronomical ephemeris conference held in Paris in 1911.

Posnansky, using Lockyer's method *(figure 43)*, determined the age of Tiahuanaco at 15,000 BC. This set the archaeological community on fire. If this were true, then Tiahuanaco had to be the oldest site of antiquity on earth; whoever established the site must, therefore, have possessed a highly advanced knowledge of astronomy which they set down in their monuments. Moreover, the Tiahuanacos were masters of stonemasonry and must have possessed some kind of under-standing of anti-gravity to enable the movement of such colossal stone blocks, some weighing 100 tonnes or more. Examination of the stones, used in the buildings, confirms that the basalt, andesite, limestone, red sandstone and volcanic tuff were quarried from as near as 96.5 kilometres (60 miles) and as far afield as 322 kilometres (200 miles).

This was all very well except for a few loose ends; clearly Posnan-sky's date depends on the efficacy of Lockyer's formula, from which the curve was determined. As Posnansky himself pointed out (p. 90):

... if the curve should vary with future studies and trials in the coming centuries of exact astronomy, then the calculation in regard to the age of Tihuanacu would also vary.

I have been unable to find any astronomical information to substanti-ate Lockyer's claims that the earth has tilted *gradually* (linearly and consistently) over periods embracing thousands of years (that might enable the construction of the ephemeris graph). Moreover, the notion of a gradual tilt flies in the face of common sense. In the 1950s the scientist Immanuel Velikovsky pointed out that science was at a loss to explain how coal deposits could have developed in the ice-cold tundra of the Antarctic where no trees grow, how fossilised palm trees could have established themselves at Spitzbergen in the Arctic Circle, which for months of the year is deprived of daylight, and how perfectly preserved long-haired woolly mammoths, discovered under layers of Siberian permafrost with buttercups clenched between their teeth and undigested food in their stomachs, could possibly have survived in an area where no food grows.

Velikovsky was convinced that the earth at some time in the past must have tilted on its axis, not gradually but instantly, each time by a massive amount, causing catastrophic calamity across the globe. Areas once positioned at the poles would have been repositioned at the equator and, at the same time, the hot equatorial regions would have flipped over into the polar regions, instantly freezing mammoths.

Massive tidal waves would have swept across continents, burying forests under miles of mud, inertial forces would shift and crash and smash together the earth's tectonic plates, levelling mountains and at the same time raising sea-level plains high into the skies, accounting for the presence of large quantities of seashells in places like Tiahuanaco, 4,000 metres (13,000 feet) above sea-level.

We know, from studying the treasures of the Maya and the super-science of the sun, that massive earth-tilts (commonly referred to as pole-shifts) are caused by the sun's twisting magnetic field (*figures 44 and 45*). The inference, from Lockyer's model, suggests that massive pole-shifts do not occur, which flies in the face of the geophysical evidence, Velikovsky's hypothesis and common sense.

Posnansky goes on to say (p. 90), hedging his bets, that (as far as he is concerned):

> ... in any event, leaving aside the calculation by astronomical methods, the age of Tihuanacu, a figure somewhere beyond ten thousand years (the age of the second and third periods), will always be on the basis of geology and paleontology and anthropology very great, no matter by what method or standard it is judged.

So even Posnansky had his doubts about Lockyer's method of calculation.

Today, orthodox archaeologists dismiss Posnansky's dating methods, preferring instead those set out in the official site notice at Tiahuanaco (see p. 56).

Posnansky was an Austrian by birth who emigrated to Bolivia at the end of the nineteenth century. He was a civil and geodetic engineer, archaeologist, anthropologist, and a lecturer at the University of La Paz. He rejected, outright, the orthodox view that settlers had populated the Americas after crossing the Bering Strait from Asia at the end of the last glacial period. He was also among the first to propose, controversially, that civilisations existed in the polar regions on earth before climatological changes sent them packing to South America and elsewhere.

The Prologue to his book, the 1945 version, begins:

> ... Posnansky envisions the geological development, especially of the western hemispheres, under the influence of cosmogonal stress

Figure 44. How the Sun's Twisting Magnetic Fields Destroy Life on Earth

(a) The sun and earth's magnetic fields are mutually coupled. (b) analysis of sunspot activity *(see The Tutankhamun Prophecies, Appendix 1, ix)* shows that the sun's magnetic field shifts direction after 3,740 years (1,366,040 days). Magnetic shifts always bring infertility cycles through variation in the production of oestrogen and progesterone in females. The concomitant shifting of the earth's magnetic field allows an increase in harmful ionising radiation from the sun to enter the earth's atmosphere causing increased spontaneous foetal abortion (miscarriages) and hence higher infant mortality. Sometimes, in a worst-case scenario, the earth flips on its axis, realigning its magnetic field to that of the sun. When this happens, catastrophic destruction frequents earth.

Figure 45. How the Maya Understood the Super-Science of the Sun

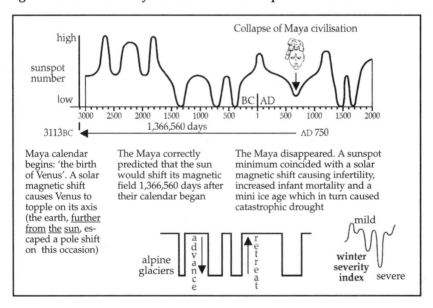

The Maya worshipped the sun as the god of astrology (personality determination) and the god of fertility. They worshipped the number 1,366,560 as the mythological birthdate of the planet Venus, correctly predicting that their own civilisation would decline 1,366,560 days (one solar magnetic reversal) after their calendar began in 3113BC. *(The Mayan figure of 1,366,560 differs slightly from the computer calculated value of 1,366,040 days.They used observations of the planet Venus to monitor the cycle; 2,340 revolutions of the Venus interval (figure 31), as seen from earth, amounts to 1,366,560 days).*

89

that caused the mountains to rise, the seas to recede and the polar regions to cool first under changing spectral conditions, so that organic life could develop there. Such a concept is not entirely new and has been held by others (Biedenkapp, Hörbiger, Ludendorf et al).

It is interesting to note Posnansky's choice of the word 'cosmogonal', meaning 'solar-inspired', as used frequently throughout this book. He could not simply have been referring to cosmic rays (sunshine), which would hardly cause mountains to rise. He must have therefore acquired some kind of appreciation of the super-science of the sun from his researches into Tiahuanaco. Chapter One of the book continues:

> The face of the earth has, with the passage of time, undergone great transformations. Where today we find the arctic region covered with a vast tunic of ice, there lies hidden, perhaps in an impenetrable silence, the ground which in very remote epochs was the dwelling place of great concentrated masses of human beings . . . The theory that man may logically have had his origin in the polar regions is gaining ground anew since, when the climate in arctic territories was relatively modest, life in the remainder of the terraqueous globe was in all probability impossible, due to the intense heat which did not permit development of human beings, or rather pre-human beings.

Many, like J. M. Allen, author of the book *Atlantis, The Andes Solution*, believe Tiahuanaco to be the oldest archaeological site on earth and therefore the birthplace of mankind. He, along with a growing band of followers, feels certain that this was the lost city of Atlantis, as romanticised and chronicled by the philosopher Plato.

Posnansky's claim that Antarctica was the home of a pre-Andean civilisation implies it could well have been home to the Atlanteans, purveyors of the super-science of the sun. The Maya, who also understood the super-science of the sun *(figure 45)*, predicted their own demise around AD 750. The same prognosis, in an earlier epoch, may have alerted the Atlanteans to seek refuge in the nearby highest plateau on earth, one that had a plentiful supply of freshwater (Lake Titicaca) to avoid the expected tidal waves and deluge brought about by a solar-inspired pole-shift.

Thus, Posnansky believed Tiahuanaco to be the cradle of civilisation

in the present interglacial epoch, his archaeological and anthropo-
logical researches persuading him that two races had established
themselves there in ancient times. Geological and climatological
changes then forced these peoples to migrate to other countries: Brazil,
Argentina, Chile, Peru, Ecuador, Colombia, Mexico and to Arizona.
(It should be noted that Posnansky believed the equatorial regions
did not suffer the same glaciation periods as elsewhere on the globe,
thereby permitting his foundation date for Tiahuanaco of 15,000 BC to
stand – irrespective of the fact that the last glaciers did not recede
until around 12,000 years ago.)

In time, Posnansky's ego, inflated by his good works and discoveries,
gave way to some tenuous ideas in regard to the meaning (decoding) of
the many inscriptions at the site. In other places in the book, he races
forward with an easy-to-detect deliberate vagueness, particularly in
regard to the dates of the phases of development (previously
mentioned) which undoubtedly occurred at Tiahuanaco. The
astronomically obtained foundation date, of 15,000 BC, is the only
absolute date he puts forward during the entire development period:

> When we consider the amount of building carried on during the
> First Period of development at Tihuanacu and when we think of
> their having to use tools as primitive as those at their disposal, it is to
> be presumed that this epoch lasted a *considerable length of time* . . . It is
> also possible that, precisely in that period, *great geotectonic movements*
> *occurred which in some way or another changed the physical aspect of the*
> *continent* [author's italics]. These alterations on the Altiplano were
> perhaps the repercussions of great cataclysms and evolutions which
> were taking place in other locations. Moreover, the latter were the
> cause for the migration to the Altiplano of many tribes of the Arawaks
> from the east, terrified and fleeing from the places where these
> phenomena were being produced in all their vigour. On that account
> it is probable that in this current of immigration there came to the
> Andean upland those numerous groups of Arawaks who, later as
> servile peoples, furnished helots – a tremendous impulse for the
> cultures of the Second and Third Periods.

> In the Second Period of Tihuanacu such a surprising soaring of
> culture is observed that one is immediately struck by it. This
> flowering demonstrates that the builders of the primitive epoch
> would never have been able to create the monuments of the Second

Period had they not received a remarkable incentive from the most highly developed tribes of South America, the Khollas ... art and science developed from a relatively low state to a height evinced by the megalithic monuments which are still to be found ... sciences, arts and ceramics and sculpture reached such a degree of perfection that these were not surpassed by any American people until the conquest ... that the premature ruin of Tihuanacu in the Third Period was the result of a cataclysm, is a fact proved beyond all doubt by the latest excavation. This catastrophe was caused by seismic movements which resulted in an overflow of the waters of Lake Titicaca and in volcanic eruptions. The latter came without doubt from the mud volcano Kjaphia situated some fifty kilometres in a straight line from the ruins (p. 54).

... with regard to questions concerning the epochs which followed those of Tihuanacu ... after three periods of Tihuanacu the culture of the Altiplano did not attain a high point of development but fell rather into a total and definitive decadence. The three periods were followed by a fourth ... a period of monumental adobe construction, and finally that of the Incas (p. 57).

In 1958 Bolivian archaeologist Carlo Ponce Sangines sank more than 500 shafts into the ground around Lake Titicaca searching for more clues buried in the layers of strata. Using the latest (1940s) carbon-14 dating methods, he divided the development of Tiahuanaco into three phases through the dating of timbers, charcoals and fabric remnants found in the area, these being the 'Formative', 200–1 BC, the 'Urban', 1 BC–AD 400, and the 'Imperial', AD 400–1300. Sangines' excavations uncovered five separate towns each on top of the other, successively destroyed by earthquakes and volcanic eruptions.

Here again we see a reluctance to tighten up on dating, especially during the golden age of Tiahuanaco that saw the extraordinary manipulation of both igneous and sedimentary rocks (ostensibly copied by the later Incas), the rise of the great buildings, the smelting of gold and the production of bronze and the preoccupation, understanding and awareness of astronomical and geophysical mechanisms which, according to Sangines, fell somewhere within his third period. Notwithstanding, his carbon-14 dates are now known to be inaccurate owing to past fluctuations in cosmic-ray activity. (A calibration procedure is now applied using reliable dendrochronological data from the bristlecone pine *(figure 41)* to correct the radiocarbon dates. From these the official dates of development periods (see p. 56) were interpolated).

Most popular 'mystery' books, perplexed by the enigmas of Tiahuanaco, ask the same old questions. None, to my knowledge, has come any closer to providing any answers. Some go further, saying:

> . . . the people of Tiahuanaco seem to have left no written records. Grooves on the statues could be some sort of picture-writing. But as yet no one knows how to decipher them (Reader's Digest, *The World's Last Mysteries*).

Others go even further by saying '. . . and probably never will'.

Decoding the Stones of Tiahuanaco

Our investigation begins with the giant block of andesite carved into the Gateway of the Sun *(plate 17a and b)* which today stands at the northwest corner of the Kalasasaya *(figure 42)*. Posnansky accepted that the gateway, thought to have been erected in around AD 500, once stood on the centre line of the temple above the observational lava block, from where the angles of obliquity were measured. No one seems to know why the gateway was moved. It was hit by lightning, in antiquity, which split the structure from lintel to jamb *(plate 17c)*, causing the archway to explode and collapse. Perhaps the fallen pieces were simply dragged clear of the measurement-point to await later restoration, which was not undertaken until much later, by archaeologists unaware of where its true location should have been.

The lintel, on the east-facing side, is ornately carved with 'symbols and hieroglyphs' that Posnansky believed describe astronomical and calendrical events. In the centre stands a bas-relief carving of what most scholars agree depicts an iconographic representation of Viracocha, as the sun-god. In his right hand *(see plate 19g for greater detail)* he carries a 'staff', the lower end of which shows the profile head of a bird. The top of the staff shows a semicircle, an odd mark for the sun-god (normally associated with a full circle of the sun) to carry. The lintel is surrounded by 48 other iconographic figures *(plate 17f)* that resemble and adopt the stance of the Mexican god *(plate 17g)* of sacrifice, fire and rebirth, Xipe Totec (shy-pee-totec). The carved figure appears in two different types on the lintel, as illustrated *(plate 17f)* and again a skeletal version of the same figure (not illustrated). The story of the god Xipe Totec was encoded into one of the Maya paintings, now known to be a Maya Transformer *(figures 49–53)*. The Transformer, like other Transformers, contains only half of the information (to decode the stories a transparent facsimile of the picture is required).

But why show the sun-god carrying only *half* of the sun and why surround him with only 48 iconographic representations of the god of fire when the number 48 is not astronomically significant? If Viracocha carried a full circle and was surrounded by 96 *(figures 6–9)* figures, then that would be astronomically significant, and we could then say, with confidence, that whoever carved the monolith possessed a sophisticated understanding of the super-science of the sun. It seems, again, that *half* of the information is missing. We came across this earlier when attempting to decode the carvings of the Maya. In order to decode the pictures it was necessary to make a transparent copy of the carving and then, using the Maya Transformer decoding process, secret pictures were revealed.

But superimposing two transparencies of the Viracocha bas-relief carving *(figure 46)*, we immediately encounter a problem: the black areas of the bas-relief obscure the underlying drawing *(figure 46b)*. Examining the drawing again, we now note *(figure 46a)* that the staff Viracocha carries in his right hand differs from that carried in his left. The right-hand one carries 3 black (infilled) rectangular shapes and 3 white (infilled) rectangular shapes, whereas the left carries just 3 black rectangular shapes. Here the encoder is drawing attention to the rectangular shapes, which are important: 3 + 3 + 3 = 9 *(figures 10–12 and plate 4)*. The distinction is emphasised by the left-hand staff, which raises the question *'where are the missing white rectangles?'*. This tells us to turn the black rectangular shapes (on the right-hand staff) into white rectangular shapes, an instruction to convert the bas-relief format of the carving into an outline drawing *(figure 46c)*. Once this is done, the semicircles can once again be overlaid. This time the underlying pattern is not obscured and the composite picture of a feathered snake can be seen running vertically down between the Viracocha figures *(plate 18e)*. Beneath this, a composite representation of a snake's head, with wings, stares at the viewer. A similar snake's head with wings appears in one of the scenes *(plate 18f)* from the decoded Mosaic Mask of Palenque *(plate 29, boxed, top right)* which

Figure 46. Cracking the Code of the Viracocha Transformer

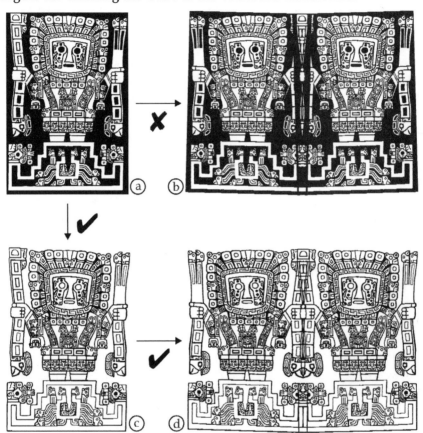

The top left-hand corner of the carving shows a semicircle (one *half* circle). The front side of the gateway also carries **48** other carvings. These clues are in themselves astronomically insignificant. However, we note that there are **96** microcycles of magnetic activity in one *whole* sunspot cycle *(figure 8)*. This suggests that half of the available information may be missing. By making a transparent facsimile of the Viracocha carving, the available information is doubled and now becomes astronomically significant (there are two semicircles in one sun, and 2 x 48 = 96 microcyles of magnetic activity in one sunspot cycle). The first step in the decoding process is to overlay one half semicircle on its transparent facsimile, as shown in *(b)*, above. However, this Peruvian 'Transformer', unlike the Maya Transformers, contains a built-in 'decoding inhibitor'. Attempts to decode the carving in this condition are defeated because the black areas obscure the underlying line patterns, as in *(b)*. We note, from *(a)*, that creatures with a long body and the profile of a bird's head hang upside-down from each of the hands of Viracocha. The body of each contains rectangles. Some of the rectangles are infilled with black, others infilled with white. This is an instruction which tells us to convert the black solid areas of the bas-relief carving into a line drawing; *'turn the black rectangles into white rectangles'*, as in *(c)*. Now when we attempt to decode the Transformer by overlaying the two semicircles, as in *(d)*, a composite design appears which shows that Viracocha is, like Lord Pacal of Mexico and Tutankhamun of Egypt, the feathered snake *(plate 18)*.

covered the face of Lord Pacal in his tomb *(plate 18f)*. This tells us that Viracocha was the feathered snake, like Lord Pacal. This is the first step in decoding the Viracocha 'Transformer', which is slightly more complex than those we know were created by Lord Pacal, due to the 'decoding inhibitor' which, as we have seen, must be overcome (by converting the bas-relief into a line drawing) before decoding can commence. This was clearly intended to prevent unauthorised decoding of the secret pictures. Only those with the knowledge of Maya Transformers could overcome this first line of defence and break the code of the Tiahuanacos.

Before we move on to the second level of decoding, we need to take a brief look at Xipe Totec, who was the first son of the original divine couple. His colour was red, and he represented the eastern sky. He was thus associated with the birth, and rebirth, of fire (sunrise) in the sky and, like Xiuhtechutli (shy-tee-coot-lee), an earlier god of the Maya who represented fire on earth, carried two sticks that he used to rub together to create fire. Xipe Totec was also associated with the snake that sheds its skin, symbolising rebirth, and so became known as the god of skin, or foreskin. The positive attributes of this benevolent god were lost to the Aztecs and later peoples, who instead interpreted his symbolism as the malevolent literal skinning or flaying of sacrificial victims.

The god Camaxtle (cam-ash-lee) was another emanation of Xipe Totec. He was 'lord of the stags', represented by two stags' heads, one fleshed, the other skeletal. The story of Camaxtle is similar to the story of Samson in the Bible, in that Camaxtle was given superhuman strength with which to fight his adversaries. Legend says that Camaxtle was walking down the road and heard a loud noise above, and a two-headed stag fell from the sky. Camaxtle caught it and gave it as a god to his people, who ate it, thereby acquiring superhuman strength to defend themselves against their adversaries. There is another interesting aspect to the Camaxtle story, concerning his wife, Chimalma, which we will consider shortly.

In 1946 American conscientious objector Carlos Frey fled to exile in the jungles of the Yucatán Peninsula, in Mexico, where he met and married one of the Lacondon Indians, modern-day survivors of the Maya. In time his position of privilege among them allowed him to join them on their annual pilgrimage to a secret holy temple *(figures 47 and 48)* built by their Mayan ancestors, in around AD 750, near

Figure 47. The Temple in the Jungle

The mysterious temple in the jungle discovered by Carlos Frey in 1946.

Figure 48. Elevations of the Temple in the Jungle

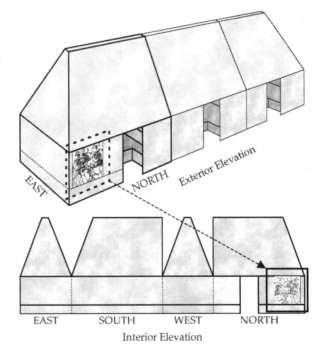

Every wall and ceiling in the temple is covered with strange and baffling murals. (The area box-framed is discussed in this chapter.)

Figure 49. The Mysteries of the Mural

Section of the mural from the first room of the temple showing the circle with a cross *(arrowed)* representing a cross-sectional schematic of the sun's magnetic structure. Archaeologists mistakingly believe that the scene shows a group of dancers dressed up as lobsters, crabs and sea-monsters.

Bonampak, about 160 kilometres (100 miles) south-east of Palenque. The walls and ceilings of the temple were covered in murals depicting battle scenes and other strange paintings obscured by the build-up of limestone scale. It was these more than anything, from 1946 onwards, that would, as we shall shortly see, mistakenly persuade archaeologists that the Maya were bloodthirsty and warlike.

One section of the painting *(box-framed in figure 48)* shows a circle divided into four parts, symbolising the cross-sectional schematic of the sun's magnetic fields *(figure 49, arrowed)*. Archaeologists maintain that the scene simply shows a group of dancers dressed up as lobsters, crabs and sea-monsters. But closer examination, using the Maya Transformer decoding process, reveals a picture of a man carrying two sticks *(figure 50)*. His chest is formed from the complementary heads of two stags. Above his head a poppy-headed chalice contains the seeds of renewal. A foreskin-covered penis hangs down between his legs. This is the story of Xipe Totec, god of rebirth, skin, foreskin and his other emanation, Camaxtle, the double-headed stag. This initial scene is located using the solar-cross mark as the first centre of transparency rotation.

Other decoded scenes appear when different areas of the picture are coloured in and other centres of rotation are used. Figure 51 shows the birth of Camaxtle. The baby – whose head carries two sets of horns – emerges from his mother's womb. The mother is restrained by two midwives and her head is licked by two stags' heads, one fleshed, the other skeletal, symbolising the *rebirth* of Camaxtle, born again from bones. Note that the scene shows the birth of Camaxtle among animals (in a stable?). Other pictures *(see The Supergods)* show the young Camaxtle in his emanation as Xipe Totec, growing up as a child and then a youth. Eventually *(figure 52)* we are told that Xipe Totec becomes a white man with a beard. This man carries two wooden sticks and stands crossed-legged, informing us that the white man with the beard died on a cross made of two wooden sticks, which, if this interpretation is reasonable, parallels the story of Christ, who was born in a stable and died through sacrifice on a cross made of two pieces of wood. The story in this section of the decoded mural, therefore, strongly links the belief of the Maya (inspired by Lord Pacal) to that of the Christian faith, implying that the Maya were aware of the paradigm of Christianity, and of the Christ-child born through an immaculate conception, in a stable, who grew up to be a white man with a beard who was sacrificed and died on the cross. Moreover, the significance of the two stags' heads, one skeletal, the other fleshed out, symbolising *rebirth*, suggests that Lord Pacal was the *rebirth* of Christ. This is the genius concealed in the myth and the encoding. At the end of the performance *(figure 53)*, Xipe Totec in his guise as Camaxtle, half-stag, half-man, bows to an audience of two stags, who applaud the end of the performance.

Mainstream scholars, for the most part, agree that Camaxtle married a girl called Chimalma, who reportedly swallowed a jade bead that impregnated her without even touching the insides of her body. Another account, by historian Ignacia Bernal, suggests that Chimalma was also the second wife of the warrior Mixcoatl who conquered the valley of Mexico after chancing upon her during one of his military sojourns into Morelos. He took her, lay with her and she later conceived, giving birth to Ce Acatl Topiltzin Quetzalcoatl, a legendary leader (ostensibly), who was believed to have become the king of the ancient Toltec city of Tula that flourished from around AD 750 to AD 1068, 74 kilometres (46 miles) northwest of today's Mexico City. In another scene from the mural *(see The Supergods)* Chimalma appears

Figure 50. The Story of Xipe Totec

When the solar-cross mark is overlayed, aligned, and the two transparencies rotated as shown, a picture of Xipe Totec appears. The striped skirt confirms his identity *(see main text and plate 17g)*. He carries two sticks which, as the god of fire, he used to rub together to make fire. His chest is formed from the complementary heads of two stags, confirming his association with Camaxtle. His penis hangs down between his legs, confirming his identity as the god of skin or foreskin. Above his head a poppy head associates him with the seeds of rebirth and renewal.

Figure 51. The Birth of Xipe Totec

Here, two midwives restrain the mother of Xipe Totec/Camaxtle as she gives birth to her son, Xipe Totec in his emanation as Camaxtle. The head of Camaxtle, the double-headed stag, is represented by the emerging head with two sets of complementary antlers, or horns, in the lower centre of the scene. A large stag's head, which carries another skeletal stag's head, fills the composite picture above. The stag licks the head of the female in labour, suckling and comforting the mother during the painful process of birth.

Figure 52. Xipe Totec, the white Man with a Beard

Here Xipe Totec, the god of sacrifice, appears as the white man with a beard. In his hands he carries two wooden sticks; the two seated stags pull back the skirt of Xipe Totec to reveal his crossed legs. This tells us that Xipe Totec, the white man with a beard, died on a wooden cross.

Figure 53. The Story of Xipe Totec — The End

In the final scene of this epicentre series, Camaxtle makes a bow (curtsy) to signify the end of the performance. The two stags in the audience offer rapturous applause.

swallowing a jade bead, and another (not shown here) shows her pregnant, with twins in her womb. These remarkable pictures, from Lord Pacal's Maya Transformer collection, seem to confim that a living woman, Chimalma, did indeed conceive through an immaculate conception, that she did give birth to Lord Pacal (the twins, the planet Venus, eponym of Quetzalcoatl), who was born through an immaculate conception who went on to rule at Tula, before his death in AD 750 at Palenque, and was remembered as the great Quetzalcoatl, the feathered-snake Supergod of the Mayas.

It was the scenes from the mural *(figures 51 and 52)* that first associated Lord Pacal (who commissioned the mural) with the Christian leader Jesus, and which later led to the development of the notion of Supergods. The presence of Xipe Totec on the lintel of the Gateway of the Sun now links Viracocha with Xipe Totec, meaning that Viracocha, in accordance with mythological belief, was also a white man with a beard who was born through an immaculate conception.

Returning to figure 46a, further examination of the Viracocha basrelief shows him with only three fingers and a thumb on each hand; one finger is missing from each hand. His face, which closely resembles a golden facsimile found in the tombs at Sipan *(plate 19f)*, is also unusual in that the sun-god, in both representations, is missing the extended tongue commonly featured in sun-god depictions *(see plate 19a,* showing the sun-god Tonatiuh from the Aztec calendar; *plate 19c,* showing the sun-god from a Peruvian Nazca textile; and *plate 19d,* showing the sun-god Tonatiuh from the Amazing Lid of Palenque). The missing fingers and tongue take us on to the next level of decoding of the lintel-Viracocha Transformer. However, we need, firstly, to examine the Viracocha statue which stands on the centre line of the temple of the Kalasasaya directly in front of the Gateway of the Sun *(plate 20).*

The huge statue carries one figure in each hand, a male in his right hand and a female (wearing a dress) upside-down in his left. Both hands carry the correct number of fingers.

The statue conveys the following message (instructions):

(i)   Take the *man* in one hand = make a drawing of lintel-Viracocha *(plate 21, a1).*

(ii) Take the opposite *(plate 21, b1)* of (i) (a *woman*) = make a mirror image of the first.

Figure 54. The Viracocha Transformer

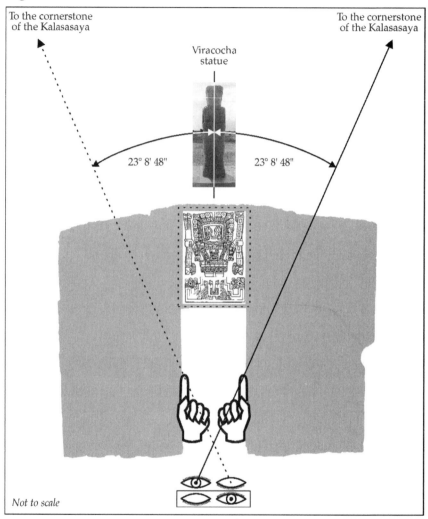

The Viracocha Transformer, when decoded *(plates 16 – 21)*, calls for the observer to stand behind the Gateway of the Sun in the Kalasasaya at Tiahuanaco. The lateral angle from the centre of the gateway to each of the cornerstones of the Kalasasaya can then be measured using parallax error derived from alternately opening and closing each eye (measured against raised index fingers) as shown above. This is the reason the Viracocha Transformer carries only three fingers and a thumb - the message being *'using one finger from each hand...'*. The measured angle of 23° 8' 48" corresponds to the tilt of the earth on its axis at the time Tiahuanaco was built. This angle varies from the tilt of the earth, measured as 23° 27' in 1930. In 1914 Professor Arthur Posnansky believed that the Kalasasaya contained astronomical alignments *(plate 16)* and obtained the same information using surveying instruments. He proposed consequently that Tiahuanaco dated as far back as 15,000 BC *(figure 43)*.

(iii) Turn the mirror image of (ii) upside-down *(plate 21, c1)*.

(iv) Lay the man on top of the woman (in the customary position) *(plate 21d)*.

A rotational 'epicentre' now becomes apparent, in the dead centre of the twin-transparency arrangement. At the same time the missing tongue of Viracocha appears in the mouth of Viracocha. When the transparencies are rotated, about the epicentre, the tongue of Viracocha waggles from left to right and, at the same time, Viracocha alternately opens and closes each eye in turn. Now we need to reconcile the meaning of the missing fingers on the Viracocha bas-relief; we are mindful of the location of the bas-relief Viracocha, standing as he does above the opening of the Gateway of the Sun looking towards the stairway of the Kalasasaya, beyond the Viracocha statue. This invites the observer to assume the same position; to stand beneath the carving of the bas-relief Viracocha and look through the Gateway of the Sun towards the stairway of the Kalasasaya, beyond the statue of Viracocha *(see figure 54)*.

Having assumed the position, the observer must now raise one *(missing)* finger from each hand, so that the fingers frame the door-jambs of the gateway. Following the instructions given in plate 21, the observer now alternately opens and closes each eye in turn, from left to right and back again (emulating the sideways wagging tongue of the sun-god featured in plates 21d and e). The lateral angles from the doorway to each of the cornerstones of the Kalasasaya can now be measured using parallax error derived from alternately opening and closing each eye in turn against each of the raised index fingers, as shown in figure 54.

The Viracocha statue, together with the bas-relief Viracocha, therefore invites the observer to measure the angles from the doorway of the Gateway of the Sun to the corners of the Kalasasaya, which is precisely what Posnansky did, without the help of the decoding instructions, to measure the obliquity of the ecliptic at that time.

But this does not necessarily mean that Posnansky was right about the foundation date of the temple; we cannot say with certainty that the Tiahuanacos were inviting us to ascertain the *age* of the site. All that we do know, for sure, is that they were drawing our attention to the *angle of tilt of the earth*. It seems more likely that they were simply drawing our attention to the tilt of the earth to explain that the five

Figure 55. Decoding the Second Level of the Viracocha Transformer

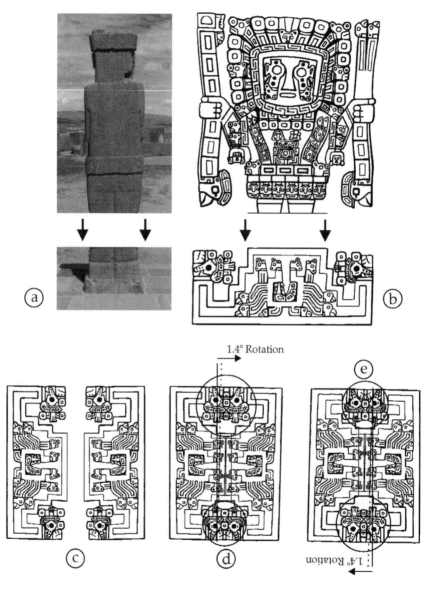

The statue of Viracocha (a) in the Kalasasaya is made of two separate pieces of stone (plate 20, c1 and c2). This tells us that the Viracocha Transformer, from the Gateway of the Sun, should be cut at the knees (b). The lower part of the Viracocha Transformer now becomes a self-contained Transformer in its own right (c). When the transparencies are juxtaposed by 1.4° (as shown), a second level of composite pictures, (d) and (e), appear when the decoding process is used.

periods of destruction, which accounted for the five successive rebuildings of Tiahuanaco, were brought about by solar-inspired magnetic shifts that caused the earth to tilt, or shake, on its axis, bringing catastrophic destruction to each epoch – which means that Posnansky *was* right, but for all the wrong reasons.

The Second Level of Decoding

Close inspection of the Viracocha statue shows the carving to be made of two separate blocks of stone; the statue is 'broken' at the knees *(figure 55 and plate 20c)*. Bas-relief Viracocha, when we examine him closely, is also 'broken' at the knees, as though he is kneeling on a platform *(figure 55b)*. These instructions tell us to cut the bas-relief Viracocha drawing at the knees. When we do, a separate drawing of the platform becomes available for use as a Transformer in its own right. Composite pictures immediately appear (circled in *figures 55d and e*) showing iconographic representations of Chaac Mool heads *(plate 22e and f)*. This style of figure was found widely throughout Mexico during the Maya-Toltec period. We now note that the Chaac Mool heads bear an uncanny resemblance to many of the hundreds of stone heads that protrude from the walls of the Temple of Stone Heads at Tiahuanaco *(plate 22c and d)*.

Returning to figures 55d and e, we now note that the composite picture becomes a schematic of a ground plan, that of a quadrangle, resembling a schematic of the Temple of Stone Heads, with miniature heads protruding from the walls. Other orientations (not shown here) reveal the location of a secret chamber hidden in the temple.

Before we leave the 'Temple of Stone Heads' we note that the positions of the statues *(figure 85)* standing in the centre of the quadrangle (previously referred to as Viracocha and the 'children of Viracocha') are juxtaposed in a similar way to the three stars in Orion's belt, suggesting that Viracocha, when he died, became a star in the heavens. His companions, the two smaller statues, the so-called 'children of Viracocha', tell us that not only was Viracocha reborn as a star but that he was reborn as the 'twins', the twin star Venus.

Inspection of the larger statue, on site, shows carved feathered serpents down each side. Taken together, the position and carving reveal the true nature of Viracocha: the feathered snake, the sun, the brightest and purest source of light in the heavens.

CHAPTER FOUR

The Sun-Kings

The Many Lives of the Feathered Snake

Two decoded scenes from the Amazing Lid of Palenque together show the birth of Quetzalcoatl; the top part of figure 56 shows an eagle with outstretched wings and a forked tongue flying towards the viewer. Two half conch shells hang from a chain draped around the eagle's neck. The lower part of the composite shows the head of a snake with an outstretched tongue. The Maya flower-like symbol for completion sits between the two representations. The whole picture therefore emphasises *completion*. The forked-tongued eagle is incomplete; it carries only two half conch shells and not the full single conch shell of Quetzalcoatl. The message seems to read: 'Quetzalcoatl is *not* complete; he is not a complete feathered snake.'

Figure 57 shows the second scene of the story: the eyes of Lord Pacal, in the top border (detailed in the right-hand circle), watch over events as they unfold. The feathered snake at the top is now shown with a very tiny head of Lord Pacal (detailed in the two circles), instead of an eagle head with a forked tongue. Closer inspection shows that one single *completed* conch shell hangs from the neck of a tiny miniature head. (The same face appears in another decoded picture from the Mosaic Mask of Palenque *(plate 18f, above the forehead of the feathered snake)*. The message here reads: 'Lord Pacal watched over the creation of himself' (watched over the transitional development from two half conch shells to one complete conch shell).

Figure 56. The Amazing Lid of Palenque
Story: The Birth of Quetzalcoatl
Scene 1

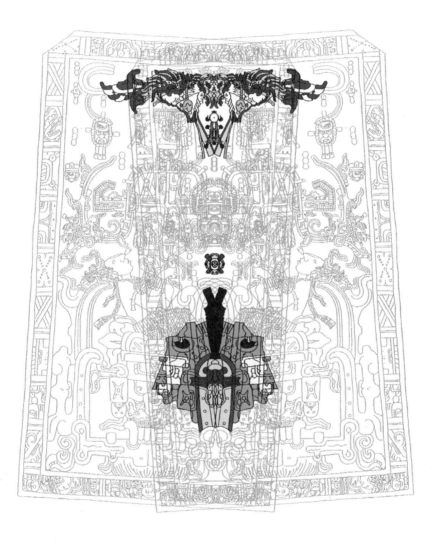

At the top of this composite picture the eagle with the forked tongue flies towards the viewer. Beneath, a snake rears its head, shooting forth its forked tongue. This snake tells us that the eagle above, with the forked tongue, is also a snake. The eagle with the forked tongue therefore depicts Quetzalcoatl, the feathered snake. Two half conch shells, symbol of the wind and the eagle, hang on a chain on either side of the eagle's neck. The flower shape in the centre of the composite picture represents the Maya symbol for completion.

Figure 57. The Amazing Lid of Palenque
Story: The Birth of Quetzalcoatl
Scene 2

Here the head of the eagle with the forked tongue *(figure 56)* is replaced with a very tiny head of Lord Pacal. Now the chain, which hangs from the neck of the eagle, hangs from this tiny head to suspend one single completed conch shell *(circled, left)*. Above the bird, in the border, the eyes of Lord Pacal *(detailed in the circle, right)* watch over the creation of Quetzalcoatl. This reveals that Lord Pacal created himself. Beneath the eagle, a large Olmec head carries a cross-sectioned conch shell on his forehead. The Olmec head is therefore also Quetzalcoatl. The lower part of the Olmec face is covered by an approaching bat. The bat, god of death, here carries away the 'dead' Olmec head, who is replaced by the new birth of Lord Pacal above. This shows Lord Pacal to be the reincarnation of the Olmec head.

The tiny head (detailed in the right-hand circle) carries two sets of horns, one set outstretched, like those of a buffalo, and another set crossed, above its head. These associate Lord Pacal with the man who had two sets of horns, Camaxtle, who died on the cross.

The bottom part of the picture features an iconographic representation of an Olmec head *(figure 58a)* that carries a completed cross-sectioned conch shell above his head (the mark of Quetzalcoatl). Many of these stone heads, some weighing as much as 40 tonnes, have been found in the La Venta and San Lorenzo regions of the Gulf Coast of Mexico. No one knows who the giant Olmec heads are meant to represent. Some archaeologists believe that he must have been an important leader in Central America during the Olmec period, between 1200 BC and AD 500. Scene 2 of the Birth of Quetzalcoatl composite *(figure 57)* sheds new light on this old mystery; Lord Pacal watches over the creation of both himself and the Olmec head featured in the same picture. Lord Pacal must therefore have created the Olmec head, as well as himself. The Olmec head must therefore have been an earlier incarnation of Lord Pacal, which in turn means that the black man, the Olmec head, must have reincarnated as a white man with a beard.

This interpretation of the evidence is supported by decoded pictures from other artefacts; figure 58b shows another decoded scene from the Mosaic Mask of Palenque. The large eyes of an Olmec head dominate the top of the picture. The head carries, on its forehead, a picture of a white man with a beard, confirming that the Olmec head was once the white man with a beard. We know that the image is meant to represent a white man with a beard because a miniature jade figurine *(figure 59b)* was found in the sarcophagus alongside Lord Pacal, providing an important clue to the interpretation of the decoded image.

The lower part of the picture shows a baby fruit bat with a bead in its open mouth, associating the bat with the Mosaic Mask of Lord Pacal that also carried a bead in its mouth. A white man with a beard, resembling the jade figurine, appears on the forehead of the bat. Here again we have Lord Pacal watching over his own creation.

This evidence tells us that the Olmec head, Lord Pacal and the white man with a beard were all one and the same – different incarnations of the same god. He created himself and was known as the feathered snake. Other decoded pictures from the Amazing Lid of

Figure 58. The Mosaic Mask of Palenque
Story: The Olmec Head and the Bearded White Man

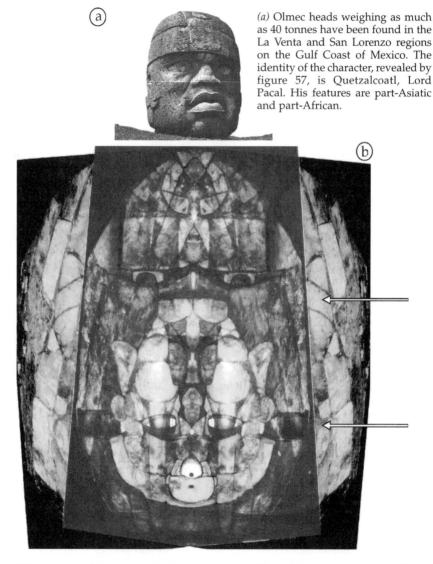

(a) Olmec heads weighing as much as 40 tonnes have been found in the La Venta and San Lorenzo regions on the Gulf Coast of Mexico. The identity of the character, revealed by figure 57, is Quetzalcoatl, Lord Pacal. His features are part-Asiatic and part-African.

(b) This composite scene, decoded from the Mosaic Mask of Palenque, shows an Olmec head looking down on a baby fruit bat. The bat carries a bead in its open mouth. The face of a bearded white man emerges from the bat's forehead. The scene is framed by feathers. The composition suggests that the man in the tomb, who also carried a bead in his mouth, is the bat, associated with the bearded white man and the Olmec head. The final inference is that the man in the tomb was both the bearded white man (Quetzalcoatl) and the Olmec head.

Palenque *(figure 25)* informed us that Lord Pacal was a perfectly purified being, one of the 144,000 who, when he died, became Venus, the brightest star (planet) in the heavens.

As we have seen, treasures from the tombs at Sipan unambiguously associate the Lords of Sipan with decoded pictures from the Amazing Lid of Palenque, and hence with Lord Pacal.

The Viracocha bas-relief carving, from the Gateway of the Sun at Tiahuanaco, together with the other clues at the site tell us that the

Figure 59. Schematic of the Olmec Head and the Bearded White Man

This jade figurine *(b)* of a bearded white man accompanied Lord Pacal in his tomb at Palenque. The extended tongue emulates that of Tonatiuh, the sun-god.

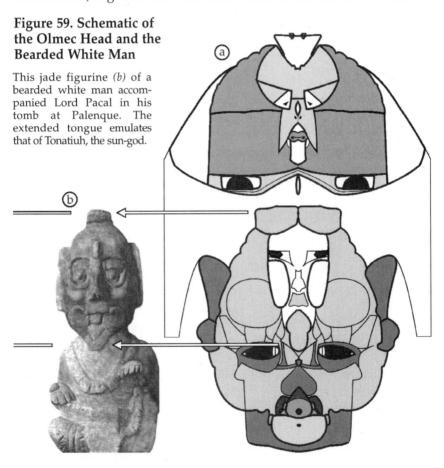

(a) This sketch shows a composite scene of the Olmec head overlooking the bat with the bead in its open mouth. The head of the white man with the beard *(b)* appears in the centre of the composition (between the tail-ends of the arrows). The helmet of the Olmec head features a face wearing a beard and moustache, extending from the forehead to the crown of the head, similar to the helmet marking on the stone head, suggesting the Olmec head is another representation of Quetzalcoatl.

feathered snake, known as Viracocha, lived again at Tiahuanaco, probably around AD 500. Viracocha, like Lord Pacal, taught his people the super-science of the sun.

The bas-relief was clearly fashioned along the lines of the earlier golden sun-face *(plate 19f)* found in the tombs at Sipan.

The associations do not end there. When searching for the mystery man with the hat, in the Amazing Lid of Palenque, another previously undiscovered composite picture came to light. One of the reasons it had been missed the first time around was because it was concealed beneath another composite picture already catalogued *(plate 30)* that showed the twins, Quetzalcoatl, being carried into the underworld by Lord and Lady Death. In this scene the twins, suckling the twin star Venus, tell us that Quetzalcoatl became Venus when he died. The scene serves a second purpose, introducing us to the characters Lord Death and Lady Death, who also appear in the new scene.

The second reason the undiscovered scene had been missed the first time around was due to the complexity of the information and unfamiliarity of the subject matter that, astonishingly, brings together the leaders of Palenque, Sipan and Tiahuanaco.

The lower part of the newly discovered composite *(plate 23)* again shows Lord (pink) and Lady (green) Death, but this time adopting the posture of the mystery man with the hat from Sipan. These two hold high the large (black outline) face of the man with the hat himself, the Lord of Sipan. On his forehead he carries (coloured in yellow) a picture of one of the long-toothed gilded copper jaguar-chambers from the tomb of the Old Lord of Sipan. This associates the man with the hat (the Old Lord) with the jaguar, the sun. At the top of the composite, the triangular face of the bearded Viracocha, resembling the statue of Viracocha in the Temple of the Stone Heads at Tiahuanaco, emerges from the forehead of the jaguar *(plate 24 features the same story using archaeological artefacts from the sites)*. Here is the evidence that proves, for the first time, that the same leader taught the Maya, the Mochica and the Tiahuanacos the same language, a language of pictures. His names were the Old Lord of Sipan, the Lord of Sipan, Viracocha and Lord Pacal, who together with Tutankhamun were the sun-kings.

These new discoveries call for a re-evaluation of Supergod selection criteria. Lord Krishna was an incarnation of the Indian god Vishnu, who came to earth twice, the last time in around 1700 BC. The scriptures say that he reincarnated as Buddha in around 500 BC.

Decoded stories from the Mosaic Mask of Palenque *(turn figure 58b upside-down)* show a seated Buddha on the Christ-like face of Xiuhtechutli, the Maya god of fire (on earth) who, like Xipe Totec (god of fire in the sky), was also a god of sacrifice; sacrificed victims were burned in the brazier that he carried on his back *(figure 77b, c and d).*

These scenes *(figure 58b, upside-down)* are superimposed on the forehead of a young boy who wears a feathered hat and extends a snake-like tongue; the young boy, Lord Pacal, was the feathered snake. Tutankhamun was another boy-king who was known to his people as the feathered snake; he, too, carried the bird and the snake on his forehead.

Earlier Supergod selection criteria recognised that each was born through an immaculate conception; each was associated with a bright star, either at birth or death, and each performed miracles. But as far as we know Krishna, Buddha and Jesus did not teach the super-science of the sun, which allows us to reclassify the Supergods into two separate schools: all of them taught the higher orders of spirituality, but only the sun-kings taught the super-science of the sun *(figure 60).*

The Mystery of the Missing Sun-King

But who taught the Incas the super-science of the sun? The best candidate must surely be the Inca who was named Viracocha Inca, and yet historical accounts have more to say of his successor, the expansionist Pachacuti Inca Yupanqui. Unfortunately, because Pizarro burned the mummy of Viracocha Inca and because historical records say little, virtually nothing remains that might justify the elevation of any Inca to the rank of Supergod. We can only recognise that the evidence shows, quite overwhelmingly, that a great sun-king walked among the Incas, the children of the sun. He taught them the super-science of the sun, taught them to fashion, and move, colossal stone blocks with a sophistication beyond the understanding of modern man and he taught them that heaven awaited the pure.

We will reconsider the dates and identities of the sun-kings shortly.

Figure 60. Supergods and Sun-Kings

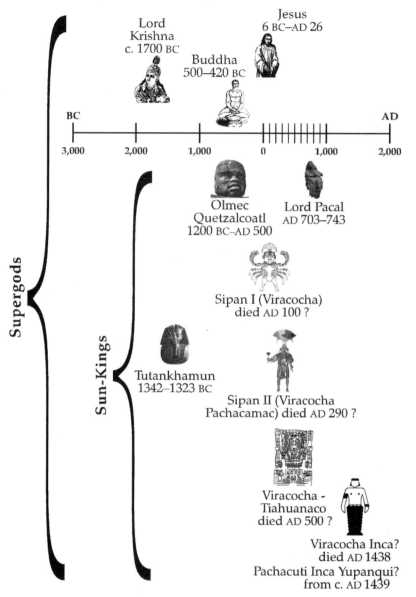

New discoveries from Peru and Bolivia tell us that the Lords of Sipan (Viracocha and Viracocha Pachacamac) together with Viracocha of Tiahuanaco, were the forerunners of Quetzalcoatl, (Lord Pacal) of Mexico (who was a reincarnation of Quetzalcoatl of the Olmecs, who lived during the Olmec period that spanned from around 1200 BC–AD 500). Evidence suggests that one of the Inca kings was also a sun-king. These sun-kings taught the super-science of the sun and the higher orders of spirituality.

CHAPTER FIVE

The Mysterious Lines of Nazca

The Secrets of the Sand

Closer examination of the Viracocha Transformer *(figure 61a)* reveals a picture of a stylised bird along the body of the feathered snake. Readers familiar with the lines of Nazca will recognise immediately that the outstretched wings and extended geometric tail-feathers closely resemble a line drawing of a bird *(figure 61b)* in the desert sand near Nazca, on Peru's southern coast.

The Nazca culture grew from the ashes of the earlier south Peruvian Paracas culture, around AD 200 to 500. Pottery, catalogued by archaeologist Max Uhle in 1901, identified a late period of development that followed between AD 500 and 700 and a terminal period from AD 700 to 800. Little remains of the once-great civilisation noted for its ceramics, weaving, wood carvings and gold work; what few buildings stood there have long since crumbled, levelled by earthquakes over the years.

The River Ingenio, 22 kilometres (13.6 miles) north of Nazca, is one of five rivers *(figure 3)* that drain to the River Grande that flows to the Pacific some 50 kilometres (30 miles) to the south-west. The town of Nazca sits on a plain 610 metres (2,000 feet) above sea-level, just higher than the coastal fog belt. The days are blazing hot and the nights cool and clear. It seldom rains; perhaps 1.25 centimetres (half an inch) might fall here over two years. This, together with the humidity-free climate, has allowed the near-perfect preservation of tapestries, cloth and mummies from the ransacked tombs at Chauch-

Figure 61. The Mysterious Markings of Nazca

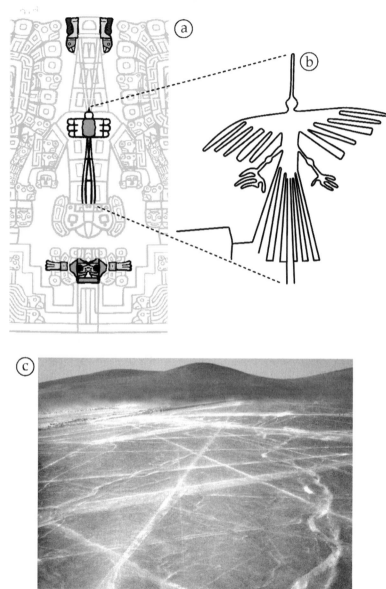

(a) Iconographic drawing of an open-winged bird from the Viracocha Transformer (*detail from plate 18e*). (b) Line drawing of an open-winged bird from the plains of Nazca, one of many representations of mysterious creatures drawn in the desert sands. These are accompanied by hundreds of straight symmetrical lines, featured in the aerial photograph (c), and figure 62.

illa 30 kilometres (18.6 miles) to the south.

Reports of strange lines in the desert first began to filter through following commencement of scheduled airline flights between Lima and Arequipa in the 1920s. Peruvian archaeologist Mejia Xesspe was the first to explore the deserts in the region in around 1927. His results, published in 1939, spoke of *ancient ceremonial roads and sacred pathways,* many of which followed perfectly straight trajectories over miles of desert.

News of the discoveries reached the American university lecturer Paul Kosok, in New York, who believed the lines might in fact be the remains of ancient man-made waterways. His earlier work on Egypt and Mesopotamia had already persuaded him that irrigation was the single most important factor that accompanied the rise of sophisticated cultures, distinguishing the transitional demarcation from nomadic wanderers through to settlers, farmers and urban bureaucracy. The possibility of surface canals around Nazca fired his imagination, and he set sail for Peru immediately.

In 1941, using aerial photography to search for canals along almost 800 kilometres (500 miles) of the south Peruvian coastline, he was shaken by what stared up from the desert below. From the air the 'canals' became pictures of giant birds, 45 metres (150 feet) across; snakes and animals, including a fox and a monkey; several whales as long as 24 metres (80 feet) from nose to tail; and strange circles and labyrinths, all seemingly carved into the surface of the desert below. The pictures until then had never been seen before. At ground level they appeared as simple ancient tracks or shallow infilled canals due to their colossal size.

Kosok considered what the baffling lines and pictures might represent; who had drawn them? How could they have been drawn? Were they simply pretty pictures or were the lines, which resembled airline runways, testament to a once-great civilisation that used aircraft to land in the region? How else could these lines and drawings have been seen? Inspecting one of the pictures at ground level, Kosok noticed that the sun set directly above one of the long vertical pathways on midwinter's day, 22 June. Was this just chance or were the lines some kind of giant astronomical theatre?

Kosok reminded himself of the real purpose of his trip to Peru. The lines would have to come second to his new discoveries of underground aqueducts in the desert which would take years to collate and catalogue.

Figure 62. The Dead-Straight Lines of Nazca

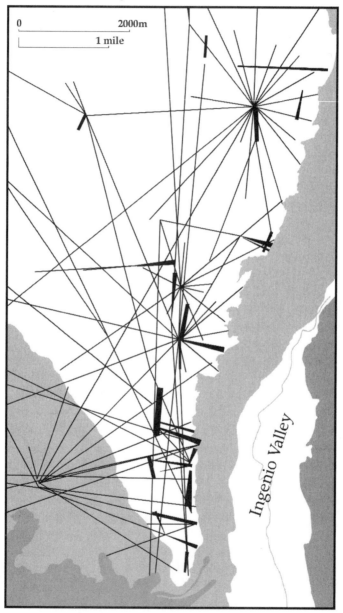

Schematic of the mysterious lines around the hills and plains of Nazca *(see figure 3 for loca-tion)*. Many researchers believe that the straight lines have an extraterrestrial purpose: runways for visiting alien spacecraft. But the creature drawings found scattered along the lines suggest an altogether more plausible explanation *(see main text)*.

Plate 17. Gateway of the Sun, Tiahuanaco, Bolivia

(a) Front (east-facing wall) of the Gateway of the Sun (in situ) that today stands in the north-west corner of the Kalasasaya. (b) West-facing wall of the gateway (rear). (c) Detail of the Viracocha iconographic bas-relief, on the centre of the front-facing lintel. (d) Line drawing of (c). (e) Iconographic bas-relief carving of Xipe Totec, Maya god of rebirth, fire and skin. (f) Line drawing of (e). (g) Xipe Totec, from the Maya Borbonic Codex 14.

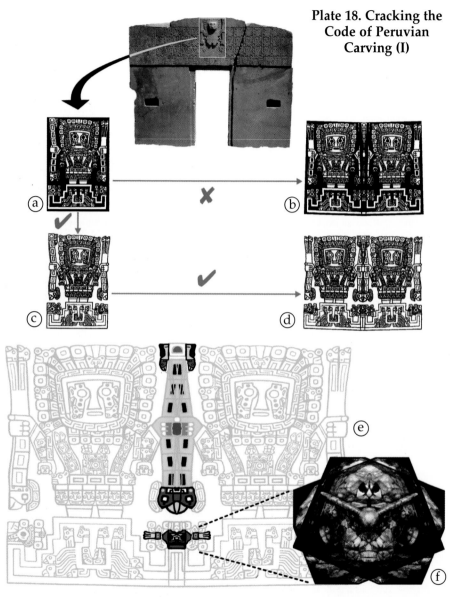

Plate 18. Cracking the Code of Peruvian Carving (I)

(a) Bas-relief Viracocha carving. This Transformer, unlike Maya Transformers, contains a built-in decoding 'inhibitor'. Attempts to decode the carving in this condition are defeated because black areas obscure the underlying line patterns, as in (b). Instructions contained in the carving *(see main text)* call for the conversion of black areas into a line drawing, as in (c). Once converted, the transparencies may be overlaid using the Maya Transformer decoding process to reveal hidden pictures. The first composite picture to appear, when the two red semicircles (located in the corners) are overlaid, is the picture of a snake with a bird's head, above a snake's head with wings (e) (a similar representation appears in a picture from the decoded Mosaic Mask of Palenque (f)). The two semicircles represent two halves of the sun. Hence, this composite picture tells us that Viracocha, the man with the beard who was known as the feathered snake, was the sun.

Plate 19. Cracking the Code of Peruvian Carving (II)
Images of the Sun-God

Representations of the sun-god from various American Indian tribes. **(a)** From the Aztec calendar **(b)**; **(c)** from Nazca textiles, Peru; **(d)** from the Mayan Lid of Palenque **(e)**; **(f)** golden sun-face from Sipan, Peru; **(g)** Viracocha carving from Tiahuanaco, Bolivia. These last two, (f) and (g), differ from the others in that the extended tongue of the sun-god is missing.

Plate 20. Cracking the Code of Peruvian Carving (III)
The Secrets of the Viracocha Statue

Statues from Tiahuanaco conceal secret instructions. The facial markings of this one from the Kalasasaya are similar to those on the Viracocha carving found on the Gateway of the Sun, suggesting that this statue is another representation of Viracocha. However, (i) we note that the hands of the Viracocha statue (a) correctly carry five fingers, unlike the Viracocha carving on the Gateway of the Sun, which has one finger missing from each hand; (ii) the Viracocha statue carries a figure of a male in his right hand and a figure of a female, upsidedown, in his left. This tells us, firstly, to make an image (male) of Viracocha (the Viracocha Transformer from the Gateway of the Sun) then make another image, this time the (opposite) mirror-image (female). Finally, we are instructed to turn the mirror-image (female) upside-down. When these instructions are followed, another secret message is revealed *(plate 21)*.

(b) and (c) show different profiles of the same statue. We note that (c1) is a different piece of stone from (c2); the statue is broken at the knees. This instructs us to break the Viracocha Transformer into two separate pieces *(figure 55)*, taking us on to a second level of the decoding process.

Plate 21. Cracking the Code of Peruvian Carving (IV)

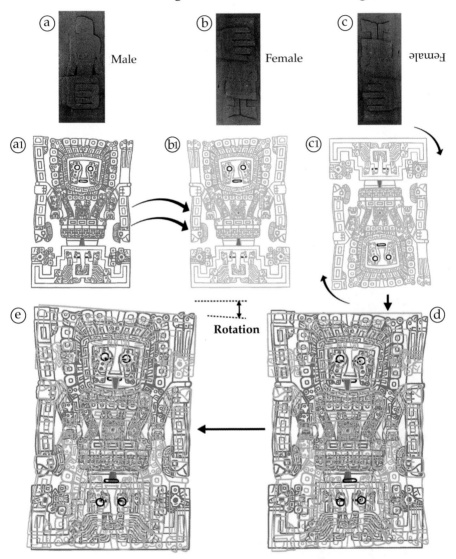

(a) Male

(b) Female

(c) Female

(a1)

(b1)

(c1)

Rotation

(e)

(d)

Following the instructions given by plate 20: **(a)** make an image of Viracocha (male), as in **(a1); (b)** make another image, the opposite of the Viracocha image (female), as in **(b1); (c)** turn the second image (female) upside-down, as in **(c1)**. Now, by using the Maya Transformer decoding process, the two images are overlaid **(d)**. The missing tongue from the Viracocha Transformer *(plate l9g)* is now restored (located). Rotating the acetates back and forth **(e)** about the epicentre (the red circle located in the centre of the composite arrangement), the tongue of Viracocha waggles from left to right. At the same time Viracocha closes each eye alternately. We again note that the Viracocha carving has one finger from each hand missing. The message here is that the observer should stand behind the doorway of the Gateway of the Sun raising one finger of each hand so that one finger frames either side of the doorway *(figure 54)*. The angle of the sun can now be measured through the doorway using parallax error derived by alternately opening and closing each eye in turn.

Plate 22. The Temple of Stone Heads

(a) Temple of Stone Heads, Tiahuanaco. (b) Statues of Viracocha (large) together with the two children of Viracocha, from the temple courtyard. (c) and (d) Detail of two of the hundreds of stone heads that protrude from the inner walls of the temple. (e) and (f) Statue of a Chaac Mool figure, from Chitzen Itza, Mexico, the head and face of which resemble those found in the temple. Chaac Mool figures were common throughout Mexico during the Maya-Toltec periods.

Plate 23. The Amazing Lid of Palenque
Story: The Reincarnations of Viracocha

Plate 30 lies beneath the scene shown on this layer. Here, in the lower foreground, Lady Death *(green)* bends down, her upstretched arms holding the head of the man with the hat, the Sipan sun-king. The Lord of Death *(pink)* stands directly behind her. The sun-king is shown with an extended tongue (representing life, or breath). The face on the tongue is that of Lady Death *(from plate 30)*. The Sipan sun-king hence brought life and brought death, just like Lord Pacal of Mexico. An odd-looking character *(yellow)*, with fang-like teeth and an extended tongue, partially covers the hat. The tongue carries the face of the Lord of Death *(from plate 30)*. 'Yellow face' hence also brings life and death. We also note that the fangs of 'yellow face' are made from sunspot loops (featured in other stories in the Amazing Lid of Palenque), suggesting that 'yellow face' is the sun. A white man *(brown)* with a beard, representing Viracocha, emerges from 'yellow face'. Plate 24 confirms the overall message, which reads: the Lord of Sipan was the sun-king who brought life and death. When he died he returned to the sun. The sun brought death through magnetic disturbance (fangs infer mastication) and, finally, he was one and the same as Viracocha of Tiahuanaco and Lord Pacal of Mexico (who also carried the man with the hat across his face).

Plate 24. The Reincarnations of Viracocha
(from archaeological evidence)

The interpretation of the decoded story featured in plate 23, the reincarnations of Viracocha, is supported by archaeological evidence. **(a)** Statue of Viracocha, the white man with the beard, from the Temple of Stone Heads, Tiahuanaco, Bolivia. **(b)** A golden long-toothed feline sun chamber, one of many found in the tomb of the Old Lord of Sipan, Peru. **(c)** The man with the hat, one of many depictions found in the tombs at Sipan. **(d)** Decoded image from the Amazing Lid of Palenque *(plate l0d)* showing the man with the hat (from across the face of Lord Pacal of Mexico). These representations tell us that Lord Pacal was one and the same as the Lord of Sipan, the Old Lord of Sipan, the sun and Viracocha.

Plate 25a. The Stones of the Incas

Close-up of an Inca building-block from Ollantaytambo, similar to ones found at Tiahuanaco, showing the difference between the 'pinkish' outer casing that carries the copper strap and the inside which is brown. It is as though the stone has been veneered, suggesting that the outer casing has at some time in the past been softened and later hardened or 'modified' in some way, permitting the introduction of the ready formed copper strap.

Plate 25b. The Amazing Lid of Palenque
Story: Cosmogonic Destruction

The story of 'Cosmogonic Destruction', one of many stories detailed on the Amazing Lid of Palenque. The two dragon heads *(green)* represent fertility. The central cross *(orange)* adorned with loops *(yellow)* and marker-pegs *(yellow and orange)* represent the four quadrants of the sun's magnetic fields covered in magnetic loops and sunspot marker-pegs. Beneath this a female reclines following the birth of two 'solar babies' *(shown upside-down with the solar symbol on their stomachs)*. Their sad mouths and downwards direction suggest they are stillborn. Tonatiuh *(brown)*, the sungod *(upside-down in between the babies)*, licks the female in an attempt to increase fertility. The story suggests that the sun's radiation failed the reproductive needs of the people. The female is shown opening her legs to the sun to improve fertility levels.

Plate 26. The Amazing Lid of Palenque
Story: The Four Previous Ages

Epoch 2 The Age of Air
This age was represented by Ehecatl, the god of wind. After this period, which lasted for around 4,000 years, the world was destroyed by high winds and hurricanes. Some men were turned into monkeys, enabling them to survive the winds by clinging to trees.

Epoch 1
The Age of Water

This age was represented by the goddess of water, Chalchiuhtlicue *(the one who wore a jade skirt)*, wife of Tlaloc. The age lasted for around 4,000 years. Destruction came in the form of torrential rains. Some men were turned into fish to avoid drowning.

Epoch 3
The Age of Fire
This age was represented by the sun-god Tonatuh. The age lasted for around 4,000 years. Destruction came from fire and earthquake.

Epoch 4 The Age of Earth
This age is represented by Tlaloc, god of rain and celestial fire. In this epoch, which lasted for around 5,000 years, everything was destroyed by a rain of fire and earth (lava). Some men were turned into birds, enabling them to survive the catastrophe.

Plate 27. The Amazing Lid of Palenque
Story: The Five Paradises

The suckling tree had its roots in Tomoanchan. Instead of fruits it had 400,000 nipples.

Cincalco
(depicted by yellow maize seeds)
This was the home of maize that lay to the west. Women who died in childbirth came here.

Tomoanchan
(our ancestral home)
Only dead babies returned here. They could feed on the milk from the nipples of the suckling tree and so gain enough strength to reincarnate.

Omeyocan
(the place of duality)
Here lived the original divine couple, Ometeoti, god and goddess of creation *(only one of the couple is shown here).*

Tonatiuhchan
(home of the sun-god)
Those who died in battle, and sacrifice, came here to this paradise, which was located in the east.

Tlalocan *(home of the rain-god)*
This paradise, which lay to the south, was the home of Tlaloc, god of rain. Here he lived with his wife, Chalchiuhtlicue, goddess of water. This was a place filled with flowers, fresh streams and bird-song. The birds sang loudly to keep Tlaloc awake so that he would not forget to send rain to make the land fertile.

Plate 28. The Amazing Lid of Palenque
Story: The Death (and Rebirth) of Lord Pacal
Scene 5

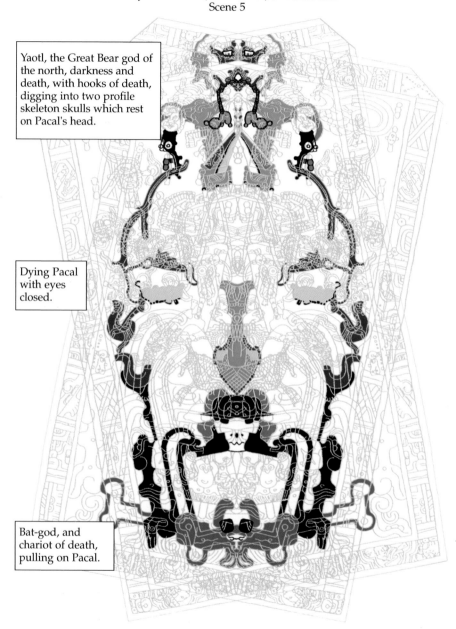

Yaotl, the Great Bear god of the north, darkness and death, with hooks of death, digging into two profile skeleton skulls which rest on Pacal's head.

Dying Pacal with eyes closed.

Bat-god, and chariot of death, pulling on Pacal.

This scene follows on from plate 9, one of a series of scenes that shows the death and rebirth of Lord Pacal. The man with the hat is now shown in skeletal form, wearing a black cloak, and in this guise represents death. He rides the bat, the god of death (*green, lower picture*), that carries Lord Pacal away to his death. Yaotl, god of the north, darkness and death, stands on Lord Pacal's head. The message reads: Lord Pacal died.

Plate 29. The Amazing Lid of Palenque
Story: The Death (and Rebirth) of Lord Pacal
Scene 6

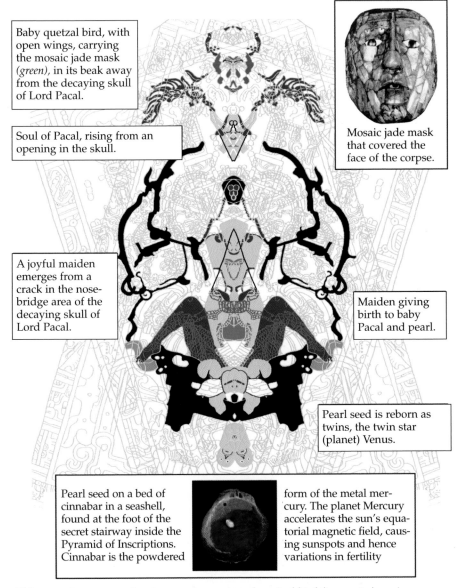

Baby quetzal bird, with open wings, carrying the mosaic jade mask *(green)*, in its beak away from the decaying skull of Lord Pacal.

Soul of Pacal, rising from an opening in the skull.

Mosaic jade mask that covered the face of the corpse.

A joyful maiden emerges from a crack in the nose-bridge area of the decaying skull of Lord Pacal.

Maiden giving birth to baby Pacal and pearl.

Pearl seed is reborn as twins, the twin star (planet) Venus.

Pearl seed on a bed of cinnabar in a seashell, found at the foot of the secret stairway inside the Pyramid of Inscriptions. Cinnabar is the powdered form of the metal mercury. The planet Mercury accelerates the sun's equatorial magnetic field, causing sunspots and hence variations in fertility

This scene is very complex; here an open-winged quetzal bird *(top, centre)* carries away the green mosaic mask, the physical identity of Lord Pacal when he was alive, in its beak. At the same time it carries away Lord Pacal's soul, in its tail-feathers. A maiden now appears across the face of Pacal with her legs wide open. A baby emerges from her womb and delivers a pearl from its mouth. The pearl becomes two 'solar babies', the twins, Venus, the morning and the evening star. This tells us that Lord Pacal was reborn as Venus, brightest of the night-time heavenly bodies.

Plate 30. The Amazing Lid of Palenque
Story: Quetzalcoatl Descends into the Underworld

On death, Lord Pacal became the twin star (planet) Venus, the brightest and purest source of light in the heavens. He was thus Quetzalcoatl, the highest of gods. Legend has it that Quetzalcoatl journeyed to the underworld to collect the bones to make mankind in the fifth age of the sun. Here we see the twins, suckled by the twin star Venus, carried into the underworld by Lord and Lady Death. Bare-breasted Lady Death kneels and steers the V-shaped bat *(green)*. The Lord of Death stands behind carrying the twins in a basket.

Plate 31. The Amazing Lid of Palenque
Story: The Twins Journey through Purgatory

Mythology tells the story of the goddess of filth. She was the house-fly that lived in the underworld. Her job was to round up sinners and bring them before the priests who would listen to their confessions. Confession purged the heart of sin, so the place of confession became known as purgatory. In time the goddess of filth became known by the more endearing name of 'goddess of hearts'. Here Quetzalcoatl (the twins), carried by the goddess of hearts, takes us on a journey through the underworld. A priest *(green, at the rear)* accompanies Quetzalcoatl.

Plate 32. The Amazing Lid of Palenque
Story: Rebirth of the Twins in the Arms of the Earth-Goddess

(a) This scene shows the twins sucking and squeezing the many nipples of the earth-goddess, Coatlicue. As the mother-goddess she suckled the new-born and brought death through earthquakes. She is usually shown *(figure 80)* as she is here, with massive clawed hands and feet with which she shook the earth and, at the same time, rocked babies in the cradle. She wore a necklace of hands, hearts and skulls, showing that she both gave life and took life away. The interpretation of this final scene, from the Amazing Lid of Palenque, therefore suggests that the twins were reincarnated on <u>earth</u> after their journey through the underworld.

(b) Instinct is fundamental knowledge which accompanies species through different incarnations on earth. Such knowledge, for example, enables the bird to build its nest without knowledge of nest construction techniques. The bird knows how to build its nest because it was a bird in its previous life (incarnation).

With regret, it was time to push the lines of Nazca to one side.

One of the translators working for Kosok, in Lima, was a middle-aged German mathematician, Maria Reiche, who in 1946, fascinated by Kosok's discoveries, hitchhiked to Nazca, taking over from where he had left off. There she embarked on a one-woman crusade, until her death in 1998, intent on solving the mystery of the lines.

The geological development of the plains around Nazca began around the end of the last ice age with the melting of glaciers in the polar regions. Heavy rains lashed the coast, washing volcanic debris, sandstone, clay and calcite down the Andes into the basin sandwiched between the Rivers Ingenio and Nazca, below. Rising sea-levels changed the route of ocean currents, bringing fog to the coast. The rains stopped and the land, due to the mini-greenhouse effect described in Chapter 1, turned to desert. Ultraviolet radiation from the sun bombarded surface rocks and pebbles in the basin, causing the upper surfaces of the stones to oxidise with a dark browny-black hue, in contrast to their shaded underside which remained primarily reddish-brown. In time, winds stripped away the lighter fine particles of surface sand leaving behind a layer of heavier stones and chippings. Whoever set down the lines, in antiquity, capitalised on the phenomenon by clawing back areas of surface stone to expose the lighter-coloured calcite beneath. The lines were simply scraped into the surface of the desert. Lack of rain, together with minimal surface activity, ensured their preservation, though many of the lighter lines have since faded due to exposure to solar radiation. One of Maria Reiche's first jobs was to rake back stones along line pathways to redefine the original designs.

Many of the locals saw Reiche as a hermit, living in a single room of a run-down hotel near the outskirts of Nazca, but her dedication eventually attracted the attention of officials at San Marco University in Lima, who agreed to fund her work with a meagre research grant. She begged and borrowed most of the surveying equipment, from the simple theodolite that measured vertical and horizontal angles to the common stepladder. She called on the air force to provide flights on board military aircraft and helicopters, photographing everything she could with her primitive box camera. Within two years, building on Kosok's earlier work, she located and cleaned pictures of a 46-metre (150-foot) long spider, and within four years a 91-metre (300-foot) wide monkey. These were followed by drawings of three killer whales, two lizards, a fox, a flower, plant-like seaweed, eighteen birds, including three frigate birds, one of which spanned 182 metres (600 feet) between wing tips, and more than a hundred spirals.

The creature designs are relatively few compared with the hundreds of lines and trapezoids running dead straight in all directions (*figure 62*), some shooting from 'star centres' that radiate for miles along the plains. Most designs are confined to a region around 19 kilometres (12 miles) north of Nazca, covering an area of around 240 square kilometres (93 square miles) in the flat-lands between the Nazca and Ingenio Valleys and further north between the Viscas and Palpa Valleys.

Despite her dedication, enthusiasm and hard work, Maria Reiche might best be remembered for bringing the lines to the attention of a wider public and for her caretaker role, preserving and protecting the lines for future generations. She came no closer than anyone else to answering the perplexing questions of why an ancient people should go to so much trouble. There was no evidence, more than chance, to suggest that any of the straight lines and trapezoids were associated with astronomical alignments, as Kosok and others had claimed.

As early as 1954 author Harold T. Wilkins, in his book *Flying Saucers*, was the first to suggest that the lines may have an extraterrestrial purpose, as 'markers' for visiting alien spacecraft. He was followed in 1960 by George Hunt Williamson, who in his book *Road in the Sky* devoted a whole chapter to the 'beacons for the gods'; in 1968 German author Erich Von Däniken, probably the best known extraterrestrial theorist, in regard to the Nazca lines, received popular acclaim with the publication of *Chariots of the Gods*, which stirred the imagination of the public during a period which, for the first time in human history, began seriously to speculate about the possibilities of manned space-flight. In 1980 Georg A. Von Breunig proposed that the lines were 'tracks for running contests', although why anyone would wish to run around a picture of a spider or a bird is not known. Another writer, Zsoltan Zelco, believes that the Nazca plain represents a map showing the Tiahuanaco empire. Dr Johan Reinhard, in *The Nazca Lines*, believes the lines portray a fertility cult that prevailed in the Andes at the time.

Archaeologists, when confronted with an object they cannot explain, generally refer to it as being of 'ceremonial significance', or as a 'religious ritual object', or some kind of bizarre 'sexual rite implement'. And so it is with the lines of Nazca. Kosok's favoured argument (notwithstanding his astronomical alignment theory) is that they represent 'badges or totems of a particular ancient community', while the shallow piles of stones so frequently found throughout the desert were 'probably altars for offerings'.

If you believe that then you'll believe anything. Put yourself in the shoes of whoever commissioned the lines in the first place (the fact that they exist seems to prove that someone at some time must have conceived the notion in the first place). First came consideration of the possibilities, and then the logistics that would demand a workforce of perhaps 500 men raking millions of tonnes of stones in the desert, 10 hours a day, 7 days a week for, say, 2 years. Where would the food come from to feed them? What about the sanitation and medical facilities? What about the surveying equipment, the stepladders, the theodolites and the rest? And anyway, when we think about it, the boots of the 500 men would trample the lines underfoot, destroying them as they moved around. More to the point: what would be the use of such a futile undertaking? Archaeologists, it seems, have never stopped to consider such questions; to them there is nothing unusual or mysterious in a people expending the gross national product of a nation in a totally useless project that takes two years to complete. After all, whoever built the pyramids felt the same way (didn't they?), and whoever cut the corners off the Amazing Lid of Palenque did so quite simply because they didn't like corners (?). In their eyes anyone who suggests anything different is simply quite mad.

Could it possibly be that whoever took the trouble to set down the lines in the desert did so for a very good reason? One we cannot understand or appreciate and therefore cannot come to terms with, the same reasons that motivated the pyramid-builders to build their pyramids and inspired the Mayas to carve their Transformers; to set down an important message for themselves to rediscover in the future?

Maria Reiche was not the first or the last to notice that each of the drawings was made by one single continuous line that circumscribed the creature (with the exception of the pictures of killer whales – where the lines ventured inside the body – and two solid infilled llamas, which will be discussed shortly). A similar technique is used in a common children's game where one of the *rules* of the game requires that the pencil should not be lifted from the drawing surface until the picture is completed in its entirety.

Taking the reasoning above a step further, this rule gives rise to an incredulity confounded by impracticality. Whoever organised the workforce of 500 men must have issued an instruction like this:

> Once the men and equipment are in place, the drawing [raking of the stones] can begin; but only within the rules . . . rakes must not leave the ground until each picture is finished.

This is like asking a sculptor to fashion stone with both hands tied behind his back. It just wouldn't make sense, and here we need to remind ourselves that the pyramids don't make sense, and neither do Maya Transformers until the decoding process is used.

There are other characteristics of the drawings which probably did not occur to Maria Reiche and the many other enquirers. The first is that there must have been a *reason* for the *rule*, for not lifting the pencil (rake) from the paper (desert) and, moreover, that this reason must have had something to do with either the *method used to construct* the lines or the *message* which was intended to be conveyed by the lines (or both). Engineers familiar with electrical circuits will immediately note a similarity here; facsimile machines use either electro-sensitive or thermal recording paper. Generally, the underside of the roll of recording paper connects to one side of an electrical circuit, whereas the signal-carrying pen makes contact with the top-side surface of the paper.

Whenever a signal appears on the pen it flows through the paper to the other side of the circuit, burning a black mark into the paper sandwiched between the two conductors. It goes without saying that if ever the pen should cease to make contact with the paper then current would be forced to stop, and the paper-marking (drawing) would also stop, irrespective of the presence of a signal on the tip of the pen. This means that the pen must be in contact with the paper at all times; it must not be lifted from the paper during the period the drawing is taking place. The *continuous-line* characteristic of the lines of Nazca tells us that whoever drew the lines understood this principle; that *a continuous current-like process was actually employed in the line-drawing process.* If we recall, it was the continuous flow of ultraviolet light (the current) from the sun on the surface of the basin that oxidised the rocks in the first place and allowed the lines to be created the way that they were. This draws our attention to understanding the nature and capabilities of solar radiation. In using the continuous-line technique, the ancients were attempting to draw our attention to the power of the sun.

Another peculiar characteristic employed in the drawing process is clear to anyone who has used a modern computer to draw an outline around an object. Here, there are several considerations. A computer mouse (a pen-like computer input and switching device) can generally be used in two ways during the generation of graphics. Firstly, the underside of the mouse may be rolled across a surface (a mouse-pad) to create a free-form (hand-drawn) line which, unless the operator is particularly skilled, will wander all over the place on the computer screen, resembling the effort of someone with a shaky hand (*figure 63, arrowed*). The second method is to 'click' the button of the mouse using the 'lassoo' tool on the computer toolbox. This, as it sounds, uses a kind of graphic needle and thread lassoo process. Every time the mouse 'clicks', the line is anchored (stitched down) at that point. The thread is then dragged (in a dead-straight line) to the next anchor point by the ball beneath the mouse and is again stitched down, instantly, by clicking the mouse a second time. In this way the outline of the drawing finishes up looking like that in figure 63: a series of dead-straight lines that vaguely follow the intended path. The next step is to click individually on each section of straight line and pull and bend the intermediary connecting line into a more representative smoother line (*figure 64* shows a smoothed-out version; compare the tail spiral area of this to that in *figure 63*). Alternatively, the computer can be told to fit the points to a curve, and the computer will average out the way-points automatically, instantly smoothing out the straight sections to the best-fit curve.

This second characteristic tells us that the dead-straight lines of Nazca could have been created *on command*, without the use of theodolites or other measuring instruments. If we recall, the mythology of the Inca (Cieza de León, *see p. 81*) spoke of the white man with a beard who turned men and women into stone *by command* (implying *instantaneously*), had the power to turn the mountains into valleys and the valleys into mountains, cause water to flow from the stone and work marvels and miracles. Moreover, close inspection of the creature drawings (*figure 64*) clearly shows the lassoo technique used in the alternative modes of both 'shaky hand' and 'click, pull and bend'. The inference here is that whoever created the lines not only created them instantly but was aware of a higher technology (computer technology) that we ourselves are only just coming to terms with.

We are now in a position to examine the drawings, and the subject matter of the drawings, with these points in mind.

Figure 63. The Secret in the Style

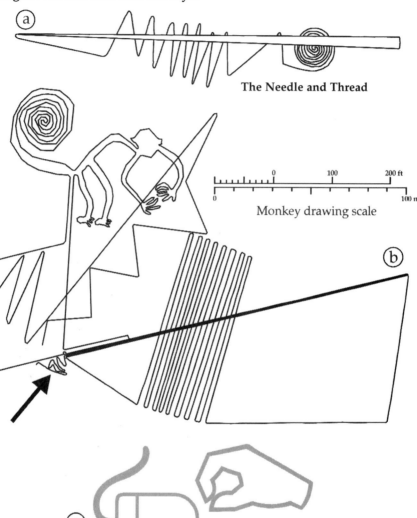

The Needle and Thread

Monkey drawing scale

(a) Desert line drawing following a needle and thread design. (b) Preliminary computer-generated drawing of figure 64. The area arrowed, on this computer-generated copy, has been drawn freehand by using the ball beneath a computer mouse device (c). The rest of drawing (b) has been generated using only straight lines by clicking the switch on top of the mouse. The straight lines, between way-points, are then bent to shape to give the final finished drawing (figure 64), an identical copy of the desert line drawing of the monkey. One of the rules of the continuous-line style of the desert drawings precludes lifting the pen from the paper. The drawings were hence generated using an uninterrupted (constant-flow) process; this tells us that solar radiation oxidised the surface pebbles, turning them blackish-brown, in contrast to the lighter-coloured subsurface pebbles of which the lines comprise.

Figure 64. The Monkey

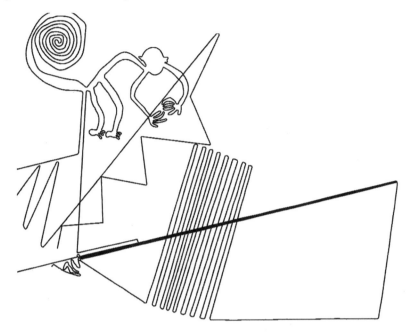

The finished version of the computer-copied monkey line drawing, smoothed to shape. The monkey has four fingers on the right hand and five on the left; one finger is missing from the hands, just like the Viracocha bas-relief carving from the Gateway of the Sun at Tiahuanaco. The monkey embraces the largest of three identical shapes (triangles). The statue of Viracocha is the largest of the three standing statues in the Temple of the Stone Heads at Tiahuanaco *(plate 22b)*. The monkey desert line drawing tells us, therefore, that the pictures were drawn by the hand of Viracocha.

The Needle and Thread *(figure 63)*

This shows a very large desert line drawing of the needle and thread design from the Nazca Valley. The main needle measures about 400 metres (1,300 feet) long. The presence of this drawing demonstrates the proposition outlined above, that the lassoo click and stitch drawing technique was used to demonstrate that the lines were created instantly and that no surveying equipment was required.

The Monkey *(figure 64)*

The monkey, for the Maya, represented 'writing' and therefore could well have had the same meaning for the Peruvians. The presence of the monkey therefore tells us that the lines and drawings in the desert are a form of writing or communication. We note that the monkey has asymmetrical hands, four fingers on the right hand and five fingers on the left. Like Viracocha from the bas-relief at Tiahuanaco, he has one finger missing, associating him with Viracocha. Next, we notice that the monkey *embraces* one large triangle from a group of three (one large and two smaller ones). This again associates the monkey with the Viracocha statue that stands alongside the two smaller statues of the 'children of Viracocha' in the Temple of Stone Heads *(plate 22b)*. The monkey's arms and hands embrace the largest of the three shapes (Viracocha), confirming the significance of the missing finger, as already pointed out. A closer look at the hands of the Viracocha statue *(plate 22b)* shows the arms and hands in an embrace, similar to those of the monkey, again supporting the interpretation that the monkey is referring to Viracocha. Note the presence of the 'shaky-hand' mouse-drawing technique employed at the end of the thick black line *(figure 63 arrowed)*, as against the precision achieved using the click and stitch lassoo method of drawing exemplified by the other lines.

The Feathered Snake

The Feathered Snake (i) *(figure 65a)*

Here the outstretched wings of a bird connect with an enormously long snake-like neck and bird's head depicting the feathered snake, Viracocha.

The Feathered Snake (ii) *(figure 65b)*

The webbed feet of a bird connect to a snake-like shape, again depicting Viracocha.

Fertility

The Spider *(figure 66c)*

Several commentators have suggested that the two parallel lines extending from the rear right leg of this spider identify it as the Ricinulei variety of the Amazon. The problem is, notwithstanding the presence of the reproductive organ, that the line drawing does not actually resemble Ricinulei, suggesting that the intended aim of the

Figure 65. The Feathered Snake Drawings of Nazca

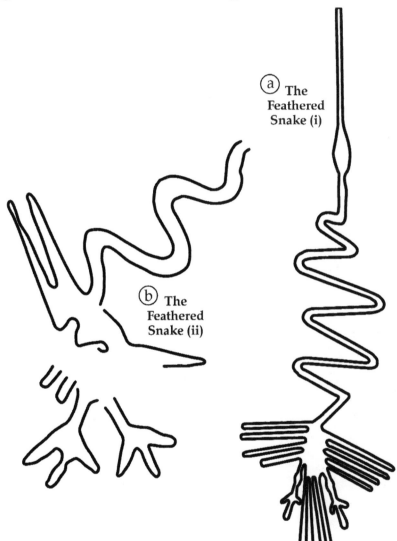

Not to scale. Orientation and position shown for illustration purposes only.

The feathered snake as depicted on two separate desert line drawings in the Nazca desert. *(a)* Bird with a snake-like neck. *(b)* Webbed feet of a bird with a snake-like neck. Parts of this drawing have been damaged (erased) over time.

Figure 66. The Fertility Drawings of Nazca (I)

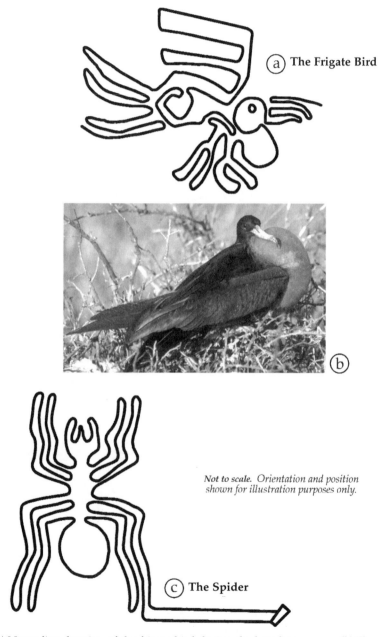

(a) The Frigate Bird

(b)

Not to scale. Orientation and position
shown for illustration purposes only.

(c) The Spider

(a) Nazca line drawing of the frigate bird during the breeding season. (b) The mating ritual of the male frigate bird showing inflation of the balloon-like sack from the throat. (c) Nazca line drawing of a spider shown with reproductive organ at the end of the right leg.

paradox is to emphasise the reproduction function, or fertility.

The spider at Nazca hence refers to fertility and might better explain the presence of the spider chambers carrying the face of the Old Lord (*figure 27*) found in his tomb at Sipan, confirming that the Old Lord was associated with fertility and hence the sun.

The Frigate Bird (*figures 66a and b*)

The male frigate bird of South America inflates a red balloon-like sac from its throat to attract the female of the species, but only during the breeding (fertility) season. The frigate bird hence symbolises fertility.

The Whales (*figures 67a, b and c*)

The three whale drawings are the exception to the continuous-line rule, discussed earlier, as though to make a point. Figure 67c shows the whale drawing comprised of one line on *both* the outside and the inside. Figure 67b shows the whale drawn from a single line on the outside; another separate single line delineates the inside, but the outside line is not connected to the inside line. Figure 67a shows a broken outside line; the inside line is continuous, but the outside line is not connected to the inside, exemplifying, on the one hand, exceptions to the continuous-line rule, while at the same time drawing our attention, importantly, to the inside of the whales. These various possibilities, all confined to one species, show that a continuous-line rule is in effect elsewhere, otherwise, probability dictates, we would expect to find a variety of broken lines among other species of drawings.

Moreover, the three whale drawings are the only drawings to feature lines *within* the outline of the creature. This unique feature draws our attention to the internal workings of the whale. Closer inspection reveals that two of the pictures (*figures 67b and 67c*) show the whales giving birth. The whales therefore epitomise birth and fertility. Most commentators agree that the physical features found in these particular drawings identify the species as killer whales. These prey on other whales, seals and seabirds, rather than just plankton favoured by the herbivore whale varieties. The sketch (*figure 87*) of a pot found in the Nazca desert features a killer whale in the vaginal area of a female. This conveys the same message as the man with the hat, featured in plate 10d, shown with the bat-god across his genital area – 'procreation brings death' (hence the significance of the type of whale – the 'killer') – and again the same as in the decoded picture of Coatlicue *(plate 32 – discussed later)* which shows the vagina of the earth-goddess covered with the skull of death. The ancients believed that physical birth in the physical world, in reality, leads to death (as against rebirth in the stars, which ensures everlasting life).

Reincarnation

The Baby Bird (figure 68a)

The Amazing Lid of Palenque *(plate 9)* shows a baby quetzal bird perched on the head of Lord Pacal. Baby birds therefore represented spiritual rebirth (rebirth in the sky). This line drawing shows a baby bird, and once again we notice that the bird has asymmetrical feet: one foot has five fingers (claws) and the other only four. The asymmetry reminds us of the Viracocha bas-relief at Tiahuanacos which had one finger missing (from each hand). The baby bird therefore represents the rebirth of Viracocha.

The Hummingbird (figures 68b and c)

The Hummingbird, *Trochilidae apodiformes*, so named after the humming sound made by its rapidly beating wings, is the smallest bird in the world with a weight of only 2.5 grammes (0.1 ounce). These characteristics permit the bird to hover and extract nectar from flowers with its long needle-like bill and tongue. It is also unique in one other way: it is the only bird in the world able to fly in a backwards and in a forwards direction, back and forth in time, and hence describes the process of reincarnation, appearance and reappearance.

The Sun

Circles (figure 69a)

Radiating concentric circles have been used by most ancient civilisations to depict the sun. The seven circles refer to the seven colours of the rainbow, red, orange, yellow, green, blue, indigo and violet, the seven levels of light.

Figure 67. The Fertility Drawings of Nazca (II)

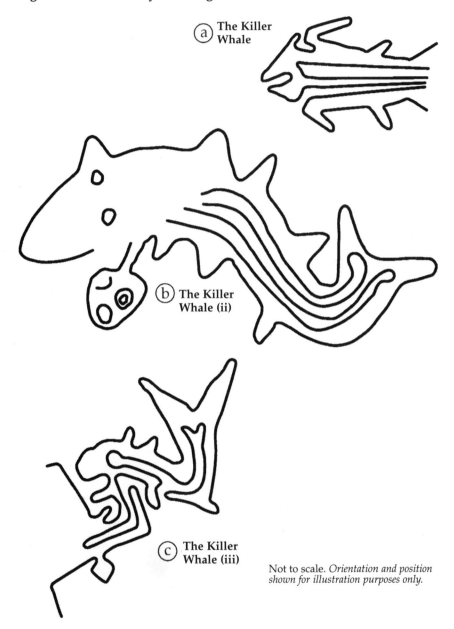

(a) The Killer Whale

(b) The Killer Whale (ii)

(c) The Killer Whale (iii)

Not to scale. *Orientation and position shown for illustration purposes only.*

(a) Nazca line drawing of a killer whale shown with intestines. (b) Line drawing of a killer whale giving birth. (c) Line drawing of a killer whale discharging intestines (afterbirth).

Figure 68. The Reincarnation Drawings of Nazca

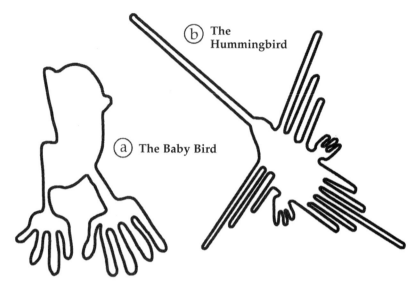

Not to scale. *Orientation and position shown for illustration purposes only.*

(a) Nazca line drawing of the baby bird with five fingers (claws) on the left foot and four fingers (claws) on the right foot. The bird has one finger missing, like the Viracocha bas-relief carving. *(b)* Line drawing of a hummingbird. *(c)* The hummingbird is the smallest bird in the world, the only one able to fly in a forwards direction and in a backwards direction (forwards and backwards over time). The hummingbird hence epitomises the notion of reincarnation: the appearance and reappearance of individuals over time.

Figure 69. The Solar Drawings of Nazca

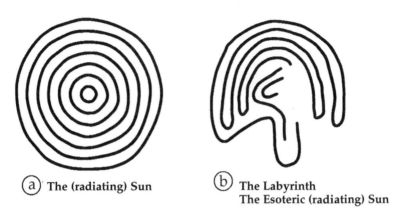

(a) The (radiating) Sun

(b) The Labyrinth
The Esoteric (radiating) Sun

Not to scale. *Orientation and position shown for illustration purposes only.*

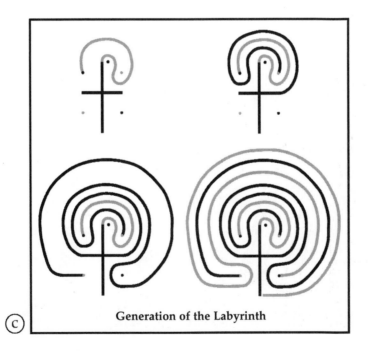

Generation of the Labyrinth

(c)

(a) The Nazca radiating sun line drawing, shown as seven concentric circles, representing the seven colours of the light spectrum. *(b)* The Nazca labyrinth line drawing; esotericists have used the labyrinth to represent the sun, light and the cross. (Parts of the drawing have been damaged over time). *(c)* The labyrinth can be constructed from a cross in four easy steps, as shown.

Figure 70. The Astronomical Drawings of Nazca (I)

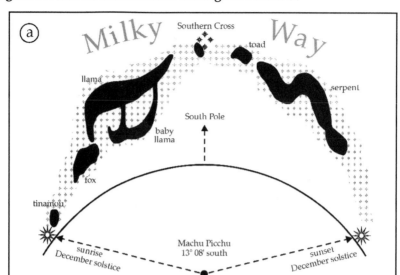

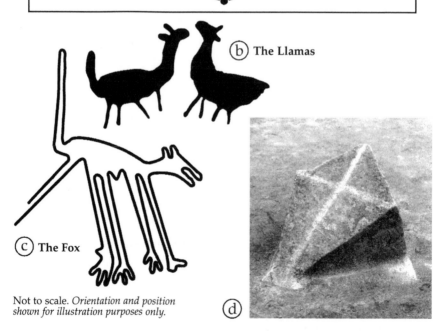

Not to scale. *Orientation and position shown for illustration purposes only.*

(a) The night sky viewed from Machu Picchu, looking south; dark patches (interstellar dust clouds) in the sky obscure the background stars of the Milky Way. Ancient star-gazers identified the patterns as creatures that crossed the heavens. (b) Nazca infilled line drawing of two llamas representing dark cloud patterns in the Milky Way. (c) Nazca line drawing of the fox, another of the dark cloud patterns featured in the Milky Way. (d) Southern Cross marker-stone carved from the bedrock outside the main temple (plate 15e) at Machu Picchu.

The Labyrinth (figure 69b)

The enigmatic labyrinth, or maze, has been patronised in rock carvings and works of art throughout history by most of the world's civilisations. A particularly beautiful labyrinth greets the visitor just inside the door on the floor of Chartres Cathedral in France. Another can be found at Tintagel Castle, in Cornwall, England, and others further afield in Knossos, Finland, North America and India have for ages perplexed the traveller. In Greek legend the maze was the home for the Minotaur, a monster, half-man, half-bull. After killing the monster, Theseus, prince of Athens, was guided out of the labyrinth by a thread given to him by the king's daughter, Ariadne.

The significance of the maze is undoubtedly mystical. Only with the greatest difficulty and determination can the enquirer journey to the centre of the maze, which is seen as the great allegory of life; the difficult search for the true self within. At the same time, those who reach the centre can never return to their previous perceptions given the revelatory profundity of the knowledge.

Geometrician and numerologist Patricia Villiers-Stuart put forward a novel way of labyrinth construction (figure 69c). The design begins with a simple cross and a single dot positioned in each of the four quadrants and one other dot positioned to the right of the top centre vertical. Figure 69c shows the step-by-step construction of a labyrinth by progressively connecting each dot in turn with each cross terminal. The maze therefore embodies, and owes its existence to, the most fundamental of spiritual tenets, the cross, featured in ancient civilisations as the sun, the source of light, the seven colours of the spectrum, the halo and those associated with light, the spiritual teachers, the Supergods.

Astronomy

There is little doubt that the early Peruvians understood the constellations of the night sky, the motion of the stars and planets and the effects of the sun on the earth. As we have seen, monuments at Tiahuanaco have been shown to have astronomically significant alignments. The Incas constructed their observatory at Machu Picchu, the Intihuana, and used a stone monolith (figure 70d) to track the motion of the Southern Cross, the group of stars in the southern hemisphere synonymous with the astronomical attributes of the Pole Star in the northern hemisphere.

Several researchers have written about the ancient Peruvian preoccupation with the heavens.

The Inca, like the ancient Egyptians and the Maya, revered the Milky Way as the celestial river that flowed through the heavens. It is therefore not surprising that the ancients, who lived in the mountains, were inspired by the heavens. On a clear night the sky is so brilliantly packed with stars it is difficult to find a dark place anywhere, with the exception of several black areas that exist within the Milky Way itself. Modern astronomers appreciate that those dark areas do in fact contain stars that are obscured from observers on earth by clouds of interstellar dust. The Incas, familiar with the dark patterns, identified them with animals in much the same way as we do the constellations of the zodiac. The dark pattern shapes of the llama, the fox, the toad, the tinamou (a kind of partridge), and the serpent all crossed the sky during the rainy season and were therefore associated with rain, new growth and fertility. Most of the dark cloud creatures fail to climb above the horizon of the night sky during the Andean summer. The largest of the black cloud shapes is that of two llamas, one said to be suckling the other.

The Two Black Llamas *(figure 70a)*

Drawings of two black llamas appear like infilled silhouettes, distinguishing them from the other drawings, which are line drawings.

The Fox *(figure 70c)*

Fray Martin de Morúa, in *Historia del origen y genealogia real de los reyes Incas del Perú*, Chapter 2, gives the following account of the deluge:

An Indian tethering his llama where there was good pasture noticed that it displayed signs of grief, refusing to eat and crying yu' yu'. The llama told him it was sad because in five days the sea would cover the whole earth, destroying everything in it. Under the guidance of the llama the Indian went to the top of the mountain called Villcacoto, taking food for five days. There he found so many animals and birds assembled that there was barely room for them all. The sea began to rise, the waters filled the valleys and covered all the hills except Villcacoto. They were so crowded that the fox's tail dipped into the water, which is the reason why the tips of the foxes' tails are black. After five days the waters abated and from this sole

Figure 71. The Astronomical Drawings of Nazca (II)

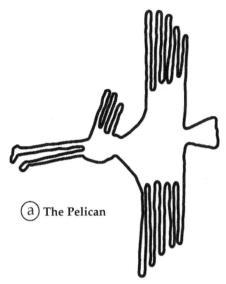

Not to scale. *Orientation and position shown for illustration purposes only.*

(*a*) Nazca line drawing of the pelican (*b*). The pelican was identified as a group of stars in the constellation of Orion, home of Osiris (the Egyptian god of resurrection).

survivor are descended all the people now in the world.

The fox was also associated with one of the dark cloud patterns in the Milky Way *(figure 70a)*.

The Pelican *(figure 71a)*

The pelican represented a group of stars in the constellation of Orion.

The Viracocha Vase of Tiahuanaco *(figure 72c)*

This earthenware vase, which orthodox archaeologists believe dates from around AD 600, was found at Tiahuanaco. Here, for the first time ever, we have hard evidence of the unexpurgated identity of Viracocha, who also appears in iconographic form in the bas-relief of Viracocha on the Gateway of the Sun. This fleshed-out depiction provides us with a much more comprehensive portrait of Viracocha than any other. Each eye is shown as the earth, divided vertically into semicircles of daylight and darkness. The sun, which shines above each of the eyes, carries the wing of a bird on one side, and a crescent shape (a snake) on the other, together showing the sun as the feathered snake.

A miniature smiling human face connects to the sunward-side of each of the eyes, showing that sunlight brings happiness. Three more smiling faces hang from a feathered snake belt around the waist. These, as we shall see, most likely refer to the five ages of creation on earth. The head of Viracocha is circumscribed by two parallel lines that carry a labyrinth-type border pattern. Snake-like rays, radiating from the border, depict the profile heads of emanations of Viracocha (separated by maize plants, symbols of fertility and rebirth); a profile of a bird's head, a smiling human face, and a jaguar profile-head, in the following order: *(clockwise)* a jaguar, a bird, a smiling human face, a bird, maize, a jaguar, a bird, maize, the tail-feathers of a bird, maize, the head of a bird, jaguar, maize, the head of a bird, a smiling human face, the head of a bird, and a jaguar; unlike the rays from the bas-relief of Viracocha *(figure 72b)* that feature only sunspot marker-pegs separated by jaguar heads.

In each hand Viracocha holds the slender body of a snake-like creature which, from all the possibilities of maize, bird, human and jaguar, features the *jaguar*; unlike the ones on the bas-relief which terminate with *birds' heads*. The number of fingers in each hand, like

Figure 72. The Squared Circles of Viracocha

(a) *(left)* **The Amazing Lid of Palenque Sub-Transformer**

(b) **Bas-relief Viracocha**

(c) **Vase Viracocha**

(a) The squared circle in the centre of this composite picture, from the Amazing Lid of Palenque, tells us that the solar magnetic reversal duration amounts to 20 (shown by the 18 full-size radiating marker-pegs plus 4 half-as-narrow-size pegs - *see also figure 74*) sunspot cycles (indicated by the 2 completed magnetic loops along the vertical centre line). The magnetic reversal duration hence amounts to 20 x 187-year periods, 3,740 years *(figure 44a)*. (b) The squared circular head of the bas-relief Viracocha is likewise fashioned along the lines of *(a)*. (c) Vase depicting Viracocha. Again, the head, with radiating ray-like creatures, is designed along the lines of the radiating sunspot marker-pegs shown in *(a)*. Similarities between these two representations of Viracocha, together with other archaeological evidence, suggest that Viracocha was one and the same as the Old Lord of Sipan, who lived in Tiahuanaco around AD 500, took the highland route north to Cuzco and then the coastal route to Sipan via Nazca, where he created the lines in the desert.

bas-relief Viracocha, is again unusual: this time the right hand has six fingers, whereas the left hand has the correct number, five, urging us once again to re-examine the number of fingers of bas-relief Viracocha.

The rectangles along the body of the snakes on the vase consistently alternate from black to white, as naturally as the night and day captured in the eyes, meaning that there is no need to make a line drawing (or a transparency) of this design; it can be seen for what it is, unlike the bas-relief Transformer which carried the instruction to turn the black areas into white.

Some of the pictures featured in the Amazing Lid of Palenque can be seen by simply colouring in (highlighting) different areas of the lid design to reveal stories supported by Maya mythological belief. Plate 26 tells one of the many accounts of how the world was created and periodically destroyed, according to a version set down in an Aztec document, the *Vatico-Latin Codex 3738*, using the gods to represent each age, or epoch, of creation, that they referred to as 'ages of the sun'. In the centre a female reclines on the back of a turtle (shown with a green head and brown front legs/flippers). Her left heel touches a cross-sectioned shell of the sea-snail, the conch, which associates her with water. She carries a lily leaf in her left hand and wears a skirt made from precious jade stones, chalchiuitl. This is the goddess of water, Chalchiuitlicue (chal-chee-whit-lick-wee), the one who wore a jade skirt. This age was said, by the *Vatico-Latin Codex 3738*, to have lasted for around 4,000 years before destruction came in the form of torrential rains that brought the deluge. Legend says that some men were turned into fish to avoid drowning. Epoch 1 was the most distant age before that of our own.

Then followed the second age (according to the *Vatico-Latin Codex*), which was ruled by the wind-god Ehecatl (air-cattle), represented by the bird at the top of the picture. This period was said to last for around 4,000 years before hurricanes and high winds brought destruction. Legend says that some men were turned into monkeys, enabling them to survive by clinging to trees.

At the bottom (upside-down), the six-toothed Tlaloc (clal-ok), god of terrestrial fire (lightning, which is synonymous with 'earth fire') and rain, then destroyed the world through a rain of lava from volcanic eruptions. That age was thought to have lasted for around 5,000 years. Some men were turned into birds to avoid the catastrophe.

Tonatiuh (ton-a-too), the sun-god (upside-down in the centre), brought destruction to the fourth age of the sun through movement, earthquakes. That age lasted for around 4,000 years.

The *present* age (as far as the Maya were concerned) is the age of the jaguar. The jaguar can be seen as a major composite picture (story) in the Lid of Palenque (not shown here) but only by using the Transformer decoding process. The composite picture story clearly shows the jaguar to be the 'fifth age of the sun'. During that age, the jaguar was thought to have devoured men, bringing destruction, but this is probably an allegory saying that the jaguar (the golden sun covered in black spots) devoured (or will in the future) the population through solar-inspired infertility and solar-inspired drought.

We know that the age of the jaguar was the current age for the Maya and that the Maya classic period, which ended at around AD 750, falls within that age. That age was therefore the most important period of concern to them and explains why they went to such great lengths to encode the picture of the jaguar into the Amazing Lid of Palenque. Encoding hence distinguishes the age of the jaguar from the other four ages that can be seen on plate 26 without recourse to the decoding process. (The Maya believed that the most important things in life cannot be seen. This is why they removed the corners from the Lid of Palenque; the decoding could not begin until the missing corners were found. The pieces that are missing are therefore the most important; hence the absence of the jaguar renders it the most important of the ages.) But the order and duration of the other four ages is uncertain.

The Aztecs (who came after the Mayas in Mexico) set down another account of mythology in their monolithic calendar stone *(plate 19b)* which was found buried beneath the streets of Mexico City. Unlike the Lid of Palenque, this features all five gods that represent the five ages. The centre of the stone is dominated by Ollin-Tonatiuh *(plate 19a)*, the sun-god who, they believed, would bring destruction through earthquake and movement. The current age for the Aztecs, at that time (during the age of the Aztecs, around AD 1325 to 1520, when their civilisation reached its zenith), was therefore the age given most prominence in the centre of the calendar stone; destruction in that age (our own age of today) would come, they believed, through solar-inspired movement: earthquakes brought by the sun-god.

The other four gods, representing the other four ages, appear in square boxes that touch the central circle of the stone: to the top right of the centre circle the head of a jaguar and (clockwise) Tlaloc (volcanic rain), then a representation of Chalchiuitlicue (flood), and at the top left Ehecatl, the bird (wind). The positions of the four boxes again gives no clue as to the sequence of ages. We note, however, that Ehecatl, the bird in the top left-hand side box, is positioned next to the jaguar in the top right-hand side box. And we know, from the Amazing Lid of Palenque, that the previous age, as far as the Aztecs were concerned, must have been that of the jaguar which preoccupied their Mayan predecessors. So although the order of the ages is uncertain, it seems that the age of Tonatiuh of the Aztecs followed the age of the jaguar of the Maya, which itself (suggests the Aztec calendar stone) had followed on from the age of Ehecatl. The sequence of the other two ages must therefore have preceded that of Ehecatl, although which came first, again, is uncertain.

Yet another Aztec account is given in an anonymous manuscript of 1558, believed to have originated either from the *Chimalpopoca Codex* or the *Cuauhtitlan Annals*, which Paso y Troncoso entitled the *Leyenda de los soles*. This says that the first sun, Nahui Ocelotl *(Jaguar)*, lasted for only 676 years. Those who lived then ate only pine nuts and were devoured by jaguars. The second sun, Nahui Ehecatl, lasted for only 364 years. Those who lived then ate only shrubs and were destroyed by high winds. The third age of the sun, Nahui Quihahuitl, lasted for only 312 years. They ate water maize, similar to wheat, and were destroyed by rain. The fourth sun, Nahui Atl, lasted for 676 years. Men were destroyed by a flood. We are now living in the fifth age, although no name for the age is given (Fernandez, Chapter 1, pp. 20–21).

Returning to the vase, we note that Viracocha as portrayed on the vase (vase Viracocha) differs from the bas-relief Viracocha in several ways.

The bas-relief Viracocha holds in each hand a snake that terminates with a bird's head, whereas those featured on the vase terminate with jaguar heads. This seems to suggest that a transition in ages of the sun took place, from the age of the bird (Ehecatl) at Tiahuanaco, to the age of the jaguar, which coincided with a time difference between the construction of the Gateway of the Sun and the manufacture of the vase. This makes sense if the Gateway of the Sun dates to around or before AD 500 and the vase to AD 600 (the classic period of the Maya which coincided with the age of the jaguar); these dates of AD 500 for the Gateway of the Sun and AD 600 for the vase are the ones favoured by archaeologists. The rays around the head of vase Viracocha, alternating as they do between bird and jaguar (separated by maize), seem to confirm the changeover in ages by showing the various alternating identity possibilities of Viracocha, from bird to jaguar, from age to age. (Synthesising the various confused mythological accounts, we hence have to assume that a transition occurred from the age of Ehecatl (the bird) to the age of the jaguar between around AD 500 and AD 600. The age of the jaguar must have been short-lived, perhaps only around 676 years (in accordance with the account given in the *Leyenda de los soles*), lasting up until the appearance of the Aztecs in around AD 1325. They then must have revered the sun-god Tonatiuh in favour of the sun-god the jaguar (that was associated with sunspots). The changeover in ages would therefore have fallen around the middle of the sunspot minimum that subsisted between AD 440 and 814 and led to the decline of the Maya civilisation by around AD 750 *(figure 45)*.

The belt around the waist of Viracocha is again consistent, but only in so far as the terminating heads on the belt are the *opposite* of those carried in the hand in both cases, vase and bas-relief. On the vase the bird-headed belt directly contradicts the jaguar heads carried in the hands; in the case of the bas-relief, the jaguar-headed belt contradicts the bird heads carried in the hands – drawing attention to, and emphasising, the contradiction between the bird and the jaguar and therefore emphasising the importance between the distinction. The contradiction, though, as we shall shortly see (below), is important in itself.

Vase Viracocha wears a tunic similar to the white one, belted at the waist, worn by the Lord of Sipan *(plate 5a)*. The labyrinth-like design again appears, this time along two sets of parallel lines that run from the belt to the shoulders.

As we noticed earlier, vase Viracocha, on the left hand, has five fingers (four fingers and a thumb), and six fingers on the right hand (five fingers and a thumb). This again identifies the main character as Viracocha, but this time the discrepancy is more revealing; not only is one of the fingers missing (with respect to the other hand), but the hands can never be correct, even if one finger were added, unlike before. (If one finger were added, to the left hand on the vase – to overcome the asymmetry – the two hands would together amount to an *incorrect* sum of twelve fingers, not ten). This incongruity therefore confirms our suspicions that the paradoxical enigma, presented by incorrect finger-counts, prevalent on both the vase and the bas-relief versions of Viracocha, is intentional and important in that both share a common feature (although, cleverly, in different ways), suggesting that vase Viracocha and bas-relief Viracocha were one and the same; the feathered snake, the jaguar and the sun (light).

We also note that the heels of vase Viracocha carry circular stud-marks, identical to markings found on the man with the hat from the tombs of Sipan *(plate 10b)* and that the Viracocha Transformer depicts one of the Nazca line drawings of a bird *(figure 61)*.

These clues suggest that Viracocha, from Tiahuanaco, must have passed through Nazca. The desert drawings tell us that he was connected with the labyrinth (the sun). He was the mind behind the lines of Nazca. He was the largest of the three triangles embraced by the monkey, and the largest of the three statues that stand in the Temple of Stone Heads at Tiahuanaco, Viracocha, the man with the beard *(plate 22b)*. The heel-studs carried by vase Viracocha associate him with the heel-studs carried by the man with the hat *(plate 10b)* which, by implication, associate vase Viracocha with the man with the hat found in the tombs of the Lords of Sipan. At least one of the Lords of Sipan must therefore have been the Viracocha of Tiahuanaco who, legend says, took the highland route north (probably via Cuzco) and then the coastal route from Nazca, where he created the lines and pictures in the desert. From there he must have journeyed to Sipan, working miracles along the way, turning the mountains into valleys and valleys into mountains before disappearing into the foam of the sea.

In creating desert drawings, visible only from the air, Viracocha ensured that understanding, or decoding, of the lines would have to wait until modern man was in a position to understand the super-science they embraced. That level would coincide with the arrival of powered aircraft flight and the (near) simultaneous arrival of the computer. Only then could we understand the method and the deep underlying message of the lines of Nazca; we have been here before and we have done it all before; reincarnation.

The Riddle of the Mixed-Up Dates

The picture of Viracocha that appears on the vase is much more comprehensive than the iconographic line drawing from the bas-relief version, suggesting that the bas-relief version was a shortened form of the vase version. (The simpler iconographic bas-relief Viracocha could be drawn from the vase, but the more comprehensive portrayal that appears on the vase could not have been compiled from the more basic bas-relief version.) This presents us with a dichotomy. The simpler bas-relief version carries a snake in each hand that terminates with a bird's head (corresponding to and representing the age of the bird, Ehecatl). The vase shows Viracocha carrying the two long snakes that terminate with jaguar heads (corresponding to and representing the later age of the jaguar). This contradicts the notion that the *earlier* basic bas-relief version must have been fashioned along the lines of the more comprehensive later vase version (conjectured above), putting the age of the jaguar *before* the age of the bird, which we know, from our analysis of the ages of the sun given by the *Vatico-Latin Codex 3738*, the Lid of Palenque, the Aztec Calendar Stone and the *Leyenda de los soles*, is unlikely. This is the contradiction that the belt heads and the snake heads warned us about earlier.

The dates, as they stand, preclude the possibility that Viracocha of Tiahaunaco was one and the same as the Lord of Sipan who was buried (if we believe the radiocarbon dating of the roof timbers from his tomb) in around AD 290. For Viracocha, from Tiahuanaco, to be one and the same as the Lord of Sipan, either the gateway was built, and the vase manufactured, around AD 250 (around the time of the supposed birth of the Lord of Sipan) or alternatively the Lord of Sipan must have lived around AD 500 to 550, but this would mean that either the radiocarbon dating of the roof timbers, from the tomb of the Lord of Sipan, is wrong or that seasoned timbers (200 years old) were used to construct the roof of his burial chamber (which is possible).

There does seem to be a real problem with the orthodox dating of the tombs of Sipan. Why have archaeologists released radiocarbon dates of the tomb timbers but not the dates of the bones of the occupants or the fabrics found in the tombs? Are they confused by the evidence and therefore erring on the side of caution?

They have asked us to believe that the tombs at Sipan date from around AD 100, for the Old Lord, and from around AD 290 for the Lord of Sipan. But this does seem odd; why would a sun-king, the *Old Lord*, wish to visit earth around AD 100 during a sunspot *maximum*, during a period *unaffected* by infertility? The Lord's appearance, placed at around AD 250, is only just appropriate, creeping in as it does at the beginning of the reversing solar minimum (*figure 41*). It seems more likely that *both* of these sun-kings would appear sometime between AD 250 and 650 (the approach to the first half of the infertility period) to warn of the

Figure 73. Revised Chronology and Identification of the Sun-Kings

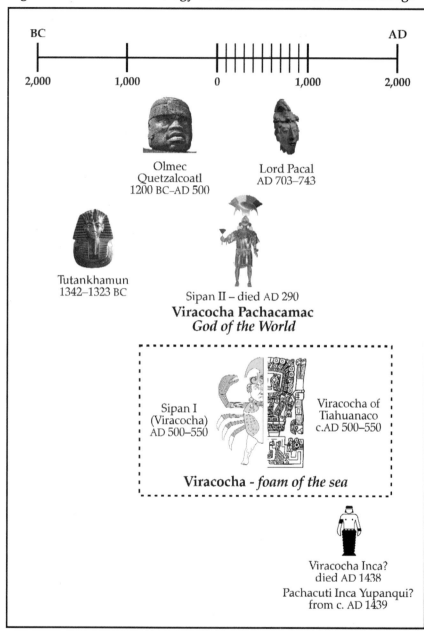

Revised chronology and identification of the sun-kings, given the new evidence of the contradiction in dates revealed by the vase Viracocha. This suggests Viracocha of Tiahuanaco was one and the same as the Old Lord of Sipan (Viracocha) who lived in around AD 500 – 550.

impending solar-inspired fertility crisis. This discrepancy would be explained if the *Old Lord* had lived and been buried at around AD 550, 450 years *after* his tomb was built. But how could this be the case? After all, his tomb was located in the lowest level of the Sipan pyramid complex, which must, surely, have been built before the top level?

The purpose of a secret timber-covered tunnel, running across the width of the Huaca Rajada, on the third level up from the bottom *(plate 1c)*, has baffled archaeologists since it was discovered during the excavation. What purpose could the passageway leading to nowhere, concealed only by a narrow layer of outer surface casing, have possibly served? And how come the bones of the Old Lord, and the fabrics in his tomb, were far better preserved than those of the Lord, above, who was supposed to have been buried 200 years later?

The fact is that a previously prepared tomb, on the lowest level, may have remained empty for 450 years before receiving the body of the '*Old Lord*' of Sipan. Access to the empty chamber could have been made later, firstly through the secret tunnel and then by a previously prepared shaft, vertically down. This would mean that Viracocha of Tiahuanaco must have been the *Old* Lord who died around AD 550 and not the *Lord* of Sipan as previously proposed. The Old Lord, personified by the crab man in his tomb, must therefore have been Viracocha, the Foam of the Sea. This would explain why the bones of the Old Lord, and fabrics from his tomb, were in a far better condition than those of the Lord of Sipan at the top. The later burial would have been made easier by wrapping the 'Old Lord' together with his treasures inside the rolls of fabrics. Then the whole bundle could have been slipped into the empty chamber; this would explain why this, the greatest of kings, was buried, so untypically, without a coffin. But why go to such lengths to confuse the dates?

By burying the Old Lord, the last of the Sipan sun-kings, on the lowest level of the pyramid (which should have contained the first of the Sipan sun-kings) the most important message brought by Viracocha was again conveyed: the first will be last and the last will be first – reincarnation.

This new interpretation of the evidence allows us to reformulate the identity and chronology of the Lords of Sipan and Viracocha *(figure 73)* to recognise explicitly that Viracocha, of Tiahuanaco, was the same physical being as the Old Lord of Sipan.

CHAPTER SIX

The Amazing Lid of Palenque Sub-Transformer

The Sun and Venus

Sceptics would no doubt argue, with some justification, that the 'assertions' put forward in the caption of figure 72a are insufficient proof that the centre squared circle delineates the duration of solar magnetic reversals. Who says, they might ask, that the head of Viracocha on the bas-relief is meant to portray the same thing as the head on the vase? Who says that either of these is connected in any way with the squared circle composite in the Amazing Lid of Palenque? Who says that the 20 marker-pegs refer to the 20 sunspot cycles that make up one computer-calculated magnetic reversal? What proof exists to support such assertions?

The proof to each of these rests in the Lid of Palenque itself, where each discovery leads on to another. Familiarity with Maya Transformers allowed the breaking of the code of the bas-relief Transformer which showed characteristics not previously considered or encountered. For example, the statue of Viracocha from the Kalasasaya (*plate 20*) informed us that the bas-relief Viracocha Transformer could be 'broken' at the knees. Figure 55 then showed that the lower section of that Transformer may then be rearranged as a Transformer in its own right, a 'Sub-Transformer'. This feedback allows a re-evaluation of the squared circle composite (*figure 72*). Close examination of this (*figure 74*) shows that the semicircular magnetic half-loops, either side of the vertical centre line, become complete loops only when the acetates are sliced and rotated by 1.36°. If we recall, the heart shape of the man with the hat featured in figure 25 was completed only when the acetates were juxtaposed by *14.4°*, and the composite featured Lord Pacal with *144*,000 written on his forehead. The *1.36°* rotation of the squared circle composite hence refers to the *1,366,040* days of the solar magnetic reversal. The 20 marker-pegs therefore rightly describe the 20 sunspot-cycle periods that make up the 1,366,040-day solar magnetic reversal period. The peg-carrying squared circle must therefore represent the sun, which means that the head of bas-relief Viracocha also represents the sun, as does the head of vase Viracocha. But this is only the first of many such proofs contained in the Amazing Lid of Palenque which all confirm that the peg-carrying squared circle refers to the sun.

The astute reader will have noticed that figure 75 also shows (in grey) two horizontal magnetic half-loops along the horizontal centre line inside the squared circle. These loops could only ever be completed by overlaying another squared circle composite on top of itself. In other words, the squared circle composite must be a Transformer in its own right, just like the lower section of the bas-relief Viracocha Transformer. The two pieces that make up this new Sub-Transformer contain the proofs referred to above.

Figure 76 shows the border codes (not yet discussed) along one side of the Amazing Lid of Palenque. A border-code pattern in the region of one of the missing corners resembles semicircular magnetic loops. At the other end another pattern resembles 'spotty-sun' markers. The acetates are now arranged so as to complete the magnetic loops. In this position the spotty-sun marker becomes a twin-star marker, representing Venus. Shading in the patterns along the length of the edge reveals composite border-code pictures of four small faces: at the top a bird's head and beneath this a human face wearing a blindfold, a tiger face and a dog face wearing a blindfold. These pictures are not persuasive in themselves but this need not concern us unduly; we know they represent only the index, a list of contents, of composite pictures which may be found inside the Amazing Lid of Palenque.

Figure 74. Decoding the Squared Circle

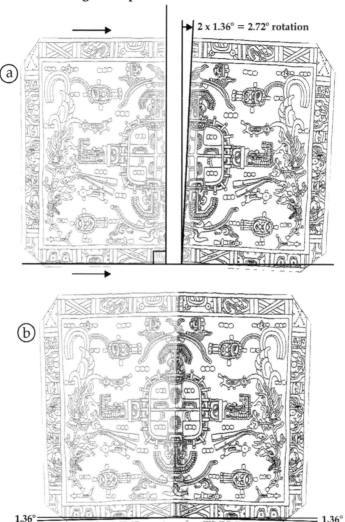

Proof that both the Amazing Lid of Palenque, the Viracocha bas-relief and the vase of Tiahuanaco all portray the sunspot cycle. (Proof I): the squared circle composite (*figure 72a*) is produced by slicing the lid design through the central cross portion of the picture (*a*). The half-loop marks on two complementary acetates may now be buttressed together to provide the final composite arrangement (*b*), as long as each acetate is rotated by 1.36°, as shown. In figure 25 (which shows Lord Pacal with **144**,000 on his forehead), the acetates required **14.4**° rotation; here, in the same way, the **1.36**° rotation refers to the **1,36**6,040-day solar magnetic reversal period. The half-loop marks hence refer to solar magnetic activity, and the 20 marker-pegs (which can be seen only when the half-loop marks are brought together to become complete loops (cycles)) refer to the 20 magnetic cycles of one solar magnetic reversal period (*figure 75*).

Figure 75. The Squared Circle and the Sunspot Cycle

(Proof II): the Amazing Lid of Palenque squared circle composite *(above)* contains 20 marker-pegs (18 full-size marker-pegs plus 4 half-size narrow marker-pegs, either side of the centre line). Figures 79a, b and c also show that the marker-pegs <u>are</u> intended to represent sunspot cycle periods of 68,302 days duration. 20 x 68,302-day periods amount to 1,366,040 days, the duration of one solar magnetic reversal period. Hence the 20 marker-pegs featured here refer to 20 sunspot cycles.

Figure 76. The Amazing Lid of Palenque
Decoding Patterns in the Border

Bird's head

Magnetic half-loop symbols

Composite magnetic loop symbols

Human face with butterflies covering lips wearing a blindfold made from skin

Tiger face

Spotty-sun symbol

Twin star symbol, Venus

Dog face wearing a blindfold carrying bones between teeth

End section of the Amazing Lid of Palenque *(left)*. The shaded composite border-code pattern *(far right)* shows a bird's head, a human face wearing a blindfold (butterflies cover the lips), a tiger face and a dog wearing a blindfold carrying bones between its teeth. These four characters symbolise four gods of the Maya *(see main text)*. This border-code instruction reads: *find these four characters in the main section of the lid and the story of the sun and Venus will be revealed.*

Figure 77. The Amazing Lid of Palenque
Story: Xolotol, the god of Fire and the Sacrificed Victim

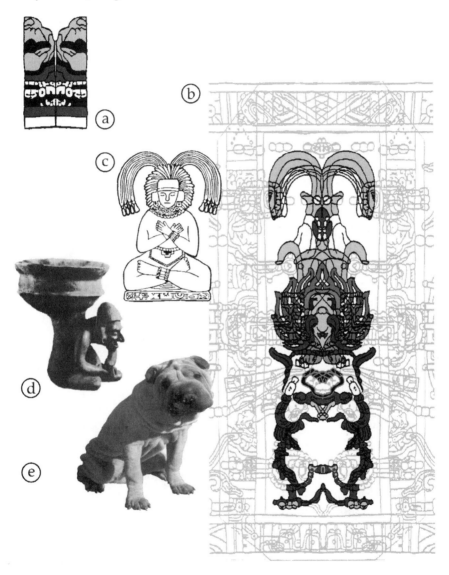

(a) Border-code indicator for the composite picture (b) showing (*from bottom to top*) a dog (*similar to e*), representing Xolotol ('the blind dog', Venus in the evening) and Xiuhtechutli, the god of fire (d), carrying a sacrificed victim in the brazier on his back. The blind dog, Xolotol, carries bones between its teeth. Xiuhtechutli stands above him, the pads of its feet covering the eyes of Xolotol below (making him blind). The sacrificed victim offers his heart in between his raised praying hands as his spirit, fountainlike, leaves his body like the meditating priest (c).

The Bird Face

Mythology tells of a green heron named Quilatzli (pronounced kill-atz-lee). She was a sorceress who was able to transform herself into different living things. Hence she had many names: 'woman serpent', 'woman eagle' and 'woman warrior' among many others. She was said to have accompanied the Mexicas (early Aztecs) as they migrated to the Valley of Mexico. Legend has it that she was perched on a cactus disguised as an eagle when two warriors, intent on killing her, approached. In a ploy to escape she turned herself into a likeness of their sister. On seeing this they decided not to kill her. Knowledge of this well-known story helps find the composite picture of Quilatzli perched on a cactus featured in the inner part of the Amazing Lid of Palenque. The story is shown in two separate scenes (not illustrated here) that show Quilatzli, as a little girl (their sister), emerging from the chest of an eagle. The bird face in the border code hence points to the presence of the encoded story in the inner lid. What has this got to do with the sun or Venus? Not a lot. But turning this composite arrangement upside-down (rotating both acetates together by 180°), another composite picture appears which features a dog. The scene of Quilatzli, in the inner lid, thus helps locate the more difficult-to-recognise scene containing the dog.

The Dog Face

When Quilatzli *(scene 1)* is turned upside-down and the composite picture shaded in, three pictures appear *(figure 77)*. A dog with bones in its mouth sits facing the observer at the bottom of the arrangement. Its eyes are covered by the soft feet-pads of Xiuhtechutli *(shown in figure 77d)*, the Maya god of fire who was a similar emanation to Xipe Totec mentioned earlier. He carried a brazier on his back within which sacrificed victims were cremated. His feet therefore obscure the sight of the dog below, making the dog blind. This is why the corresponding border code *(figure 76)* shows the face of a dog wearing a blindfold. Mexican mythology tells of the story of Xolotol (shol-o-tol), the dog who cried so much that his eyes fell out of their sockets. Because he was blind he could find his way in the dark and was thus chosen to assist Quetzalcoatl steal bones from the underworld to create mankind in this the fifth age of the sun. This is why the dog in this composite, and the corresponding border-code dog-face, are both shown carrying bones between their teeth.

Xolotol, as the faithful servant of his master Quetzalcoatl, followed his master wherever he went. Xolotol hence journeyed to Venus to become one of the twin stars, Venus in the evening (darkness).

Legend also has it that the underworld consisted of nine levels through which the soul of the deceased had to travel on death. The first level consisted of a swift-flowing river. The only way for the soul to cross the river would be to hold on to a dog that could see through the darkness and paddle across the river into the next level of the underworld, which explains why dogs were buried along with their owners in South and Central America. The border codes in the composite *(figure 77b)*, beneath the feet of the dog, feature a solar symbol with a single star in between these two, two more stars (the twin star Venus) side by side (this is not clear in black and white but persuasive in colour).

Xiuhtechutli, consumed in flames in this composite, wears a helmet to protect him from the fire in the brazier on his back that cremates the sacrificed victim. The dying victim can be seen above the flames, hands clasped together in prayer with the spirit, his departing soul, radiating from his head. This scene therefore introduces us to Xolotol the dog, Venus in the evening (the evening star), as well as Xiuhtechutli, the god of fire and sacrifice.

Now we slide the acetates along to a new position. This composite picture is more complex.

The God of Ice

Tlahuizcalpantechuhtli (pronounced clar-wheat-cal-pan-tee-coot-lee) was the god of ice who was blinded by a dart that came from the sun. He was therefore, like Xolotol, chosen as a helper of Quetzalcoatl in the underworld. Tlahuizcalpantechuhtli also journeyed to Venus with Quetzalcoatl and became known as the other star of Venus, the morning star, because as the god of ice he was associated with the morning frost in the mountains and ice crystals, or daggers. His nickname was 'twisted knife'. The knives associated him with human sacrifice. He is usually depicted wearing a blindfold made from human skin, and a hood made from feathers that carried two shields. The composite *(figure 78)* shows the large face of the god of ice wearing a blindfold and a

Figure 78. The Amazing Lid of Palenque
Story: The God of Ice

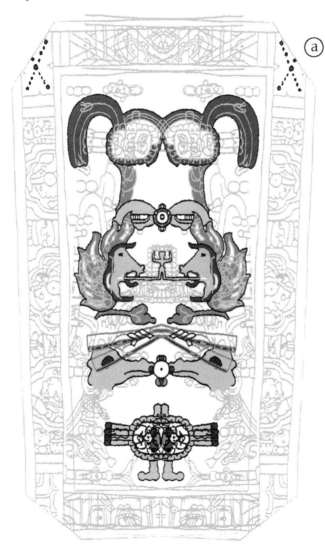

Composite
border-code
picture showing
a human face,
with butterflies
covering the lips,
wearing a
blindfold made
from skin

(a) Composite scene showing the face of the god of ice, Tlahuizcalpantechuhtli, Venus in the morning. He was injured by a dart from the sun and so, like Xolotol, was blind. Here we see him wearing a blindfold made from human skin, which explains the meaning of the border-code picture (b). He was the god of ice, whose nickname was 'twisted knife' after the ice daggers, or frost crystals, that he brought every morning. Here he wears two sets of twisted knives, like a bow tie. His jowls are formed by the complementary heads of two butterflies that grip a sacrificial victim between their teeth. Two hummingbirds, beneath the 'bow tie', sip nectar from a flower. Beneath the flower the skin of a flayed victim stands prostrate.

conical hat embossed with two shields. His jowls are made up from what looks, at first glance, like the complementary profile heads of two horses facing each other. The 'horses' seem to be gripping a human figure in a cage, between their teeth. The figure and cage form the nose and mouth of the god of ice. The figure in the cage assumes the stance of the man with the hat from Sipan. Beneath this, two sets of 'twisted knives', like tails of a bow tie, confirm the identity of the character.

Those familiar with Mexican mythology will have heard the story of the two butterfly gods.

Iztpapalotltotec (its-papa-lot-al-totec), lord obsidian butterfly, and his wife Iztpapalotlcihuatl (its-papa-lot-al-kee-wattle), lady obsidian butterfly, were two gods (stars) that shone in the sky. One day they visited earth to pick wild flowers when they carelessly snapped the branch of a tree which gushed forth blood. The two gods became synonymous with: butterflies, because the accident happened when they were picking flowers; sacrifice, because the tree shed blood; and with obsidian (sharp volcanic rock), which the other gods hailed down on them as a punishment for their wrongdoing. The pair were banished from the sky, which suffered the loss of two stars. They were hence associated as a duo of two stars, rather than two individual stars, and hence became associated with the twin star Venus. They were also associated with a 'twisted knife' because their wings were thought to have been made from sharp obsidian knives. As butterflies they were associated with sipping the nectar from flowers, like hummingbirds. Hummingbirds represented purification, through sacrifice and, as we have already seen with the lines of Nazca, reincarnation. This story sheds light on the identification of the 'horses', mentioned above, which can now be seen as the detailed heads of two butterflies that grip a sacrificial victim between their teeth. Their lips form the mouth of the god of ice. The raised arms of the victim held between their teeth must therefore depict sacrifice, as must the raised arms of the man with the hat from Sipan. What we learn from this is that the small man with the hat, with raised arms, found in the tombs at Sipan, signifies that the Lords of Sipan, the sun-kings, died through sacrifice.

Beneath the two twisted knives (the 'bow tie'), the profile heads of two hummingbirds sip the nectar of purification from a flower. Beneath the flower the skin of a flayed victim stands prostrate, with arms outstretched and internal organs exposed.

The butterflies also carry a hooked 'messenger's staff' (stick), indicating that the sacrificed victim would carry a message to Venus, who in turn would take it to the sun. Such a gift of amelioration would be graciously accepted by Tonatiuh, who would, in return, ensure that a climate of wellbeing prevailed.

All these pictures explain that the god of ice was Venus in the morning and that purification comes through sacrifice and reincarnation. Now we can understand why the human face in the border code wears a blindfold made of human skin and carries butterflies over the lips.

The Tiger Face

The tiger face, featured in the border code, refers to the story of the tiger in Mexican mythology. The god Yaotl was the great bear that lived in the northern sky. Deprived of light, it was difficult to make out his features; he was hence associated with darkness and deceit, and so became known by the nickname 'two faces'. Legend has it that Quetzalcoatl, the good god of the west, fought with Yaotl, who fell from the sky into the dark ocean. All that could be seen were his eyes, shining in the darkness, like two stars. So on the one hand he was known as the tiger (cat's eyes) and on the other the great bear (stars from the Great Bear constellation in the sky).

The presence of the tiger among the border codes of the Lid of Palenque is revealing in its novelty; it is the only character to appear in the border code which does not, *and yet does*, appear as a story in the main Lid of Palenque – the tiger appears in his *other guise*, his *other face*, that of the Great Bear, which stands on the head of Lord Pacal *(plate 28)*. This clever nuance suggests that the Lid of Palenque was meant to be decoded only by someone who understood the subtleties of Mexican mythology.

The Sun, Venus and the 20 Marker-Pegs

The Lid of Palenque Sub-Transformer features the final scene in this series that confirms that the squared circle does indeed represent the sunspot cycle.

At the top of the Sub-Transformer *(figure 79a)* the face of the dog can be seen with bones in its mouth. Its eyes are filled with tears. This

Figure 79. Viracocha and the Sunspot Cycle

The Amazing Lid of Palenque
Story: the Sun and Venus

Xolotol the Dog, Venus in the Evening.

The God of Ice, Venus in the Morning.

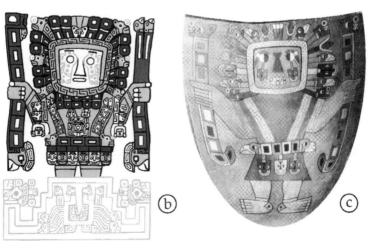

(Proof III): the Amazing Lid of Palenque *(a)*, the Viracocha bas-relief *(b)* shaded, and the vase of Tiahuanaco *(c)* all portray the sunspot cycle. *(See main text for commentary.)*

must be Xolotol, who cried so much that his eyes fell from their sockets. Two miniature faces (twins), one on either side of the bones, identify the dog as one of the twins, Venus in the evening.

At the bottom of the Sub-Transformer a head with daggers on the cheeks suggests that this is the head of the god of ice, Venus in the morning. Two miniature faces (twins), one on either side of each ear, confirm the identity as one of the twins.

The squared circle is now positioned between Xolotol at the top and the god of ice at the bottom, *between* the evening star and the morning star. The squared circle must therefore represent the sun, just as the sun appears, at different times, *between* the morning and evening stars (*figures 31b and c*).

Further examination of the squared circle and radiating marker-pegs confirms the association with Viracocha: the squared circle shows the upward-looking face of Viracocha and the outstretched arms of Viracocha holding long-bodied birds in each hand, exactly like bas-relief Viracocha.

All this confirms that whoever designed the Lid of Palenque designed the bas-relief Viracocha and the vase Viracocha and that the squared circle with radiating marker-pegs, featured in each of the representations of Viracocha, indeed represents the sun.

And what about the other contents of the newly discovered Lid of Palenque Sub-Transformer?

That's another story.

CHAPTER SEVEN

Reincarnation

The Secret of Purification

In a recent BBC radio interview the presenter asked the Dalai Lama, the Tibetan Buddhist leader, two questions, both of which he declined to answer: where would the Dalai Lama go when his body died? And why did the Dalai Lama and other religious orders believe that physical sex was sinful, unless it was undertaken for the specific purpose of having children? The reason for evading the first question is straightforward: in keeping with Buddhist philosophy, only the purified who are free from desire make it to heaven. This means that those who *want* to go to heaven are by definition excluded from entry. The Dalai Lama could not therefore say that he *wanted* to go to heaven, safe in the knowledge that he would, in conformance with the Buddhist Parable of the Hen, which, for those unfamiliar with *The Supergods*, is reproduced below:

> Just as when a hen has eight, ten or twelve eggs, and the hen has properly brooded over them, properly sat upon them, properly sat herself around them, however much such a wish may arise in her heart as this, 'Oh would that my little chickens should break open the egg-shell with the points of their claws, or their beaks, and come forth into the light of safety.' Yet all the while those little chickens are sure to break the egg-shell with their beaks, and to come forth into the light of safety. Just even so, a Brother thus endowed with fifteen fold determination is sure to come forth into

the light, sure to reach to the higher wisdom, sure to attain to the supreme security. The lesson is that the result is quite certain, however much doubt the hen or the believer may have about it (Oldenburg, Vol. x, verse xi).

The answer to the second question is much more involved and, in the case of readers unfamiliar with *The Supergods* and *The Tutankhamun Prophecies*, cannot be understood without an introduction explaining how the purification process works.

I explained, in *The Tutankhamun Prophecies*, how New Zealand researcher Bruce Cathie, dissatisfied with the inadequacy of Albert Einstein's figure of 300,000,000 metres per second for the speed of light, had recalculated the value taking into account recently discovered gravitational anomalies. His figure, calculated in angular degrees (in recognition of light travelling over the surface of the globular earth rather than in metres per second along a straight line), amounted to 144,000 minutes of arc per second. As we know, this number, revered by the Supergods, represents the chosen few who will enter the Kingdom of Heaven.

Bruce Cathie's discovery allows a new interpretation of the true meaning of the Supergod teachings: those who radiate light (144,000) from their foreheads, represent the chosen few who will enter the Kingdom of Heaven.

This is not new. Throughout history the nimbus, or halo, has identified the pure of spirit. Indian and Tibetan teachings maintain that the true mystic radiates light from the head. This is enabled through the sustained practice of intellectual meditation, which allows the endocrine centres within the body, the chakra centres, to reach equilibrium.

Each chakra (Sanskrit for 'wheel') is likened to a flower with a specific number of petals corresponding to a particular vibration *(figure 88b)*; the base chakra is centred on the adrenal gland located at the base of the spine. This controls the sympathetic (stimulating) nervous system and is represented as a flower with 4 petals; the sacral chakra corresponds to the ovaries (testes in the male) that release fertility hormones – 6 petals; the solar plexus chakra is the pancreas, which produces insulin and digestive juices – 10 petals; the heart chakra corresponds to the thymus located in the chest. This produces lymphatic tissue – 12 petals; the throat chakra refers to the thyroid (and parathyroid) glands in the lower throat region that produce iodine and regulate the metabolism of calcium and phosphorus – 16 petals; the brow chakra, centred in the light-sensitive pineal gland, produces the timing hormone melatonin which regulates biorhythms and sexual activity – 96 petals; and the crown chakra, located deep within the pituitary (and hypothalamus) regions of the brain, control the entire endocrine system – 1,000 petals. When the chakra centres are balanced, the wheels are said to spin at their designed vibration. Energy then surges from the base chakra, up the spine, activating the pituitary, which radiates light *(figure 88c)*. Esotericist Alice Bailey (1880–1949) has pointed out (*A Treatise on White Magic*) that the number of petals, of the lower 6 chakra centres, adds up to 144. When these lower 6 centres resonate, they act on the crown chakra (1,000 petals), producing, as a product, a vibrational resonance of 144,000, which corresponds to the vibrational resonance of light, a halo.

Most of us know when the chakras engage and operate; feelings of *desire* stimulate the solar plexus (pancreas), producing a 'butterfly' sensation in the stomach; *grief* wrenches the heart chakra (the thymus), producing heartache; *trepidation* causes the throat chakra (the thyroid) to tingle and the mouth to dry; *fear* rattles the door of the base chakra (the adrenal gland), sending a surge of adrenalin around the body for it to fight or run. Is it any surprise, given the cacophony of physical stimuli that bombard the senses, that the chakras seldom harmonise? But how many, or few, have known the peace that flows, say the mystics, when a thin stream of light-like honey trickles through the brain, from the pituitary to the hypothalamus? How many have sensed the golden wave that overpowers the body, drenching the senses, before radiating, in a heavy silent pulse, through space?

Body and Soul

There are two distinct schools of thought in regard to the true nature of man. The first suggests that the *self* is simply the physical body. This type of person perceives the physical world as *reality* and the self as a mere biological organism, like a bird or a fish or a cow, that lives and dies. Within this scheme of things every day is spent in the pursuit of pleasure. The senses and emotions simply provide a feedback mechanism intended to maximise the objective. The fallback position of those who subscribe to this view is to live painlessly for as long as possible. This type of person believes that death is the end of the self and that on death the self ceases to exist.

The second type believes that there must be *more* to the self than the body. After all, if a man were to lose his arm he would still be himself but his arm would not. If he lost his other arm and both legs he would still be himself, but his dislocated limbs would not. If he had a heart-transplant, a liver-transplant and a lung-transplant, he would still be himself, but those organs would not. If he stored his memory on to a computer disc (technology permitting), he could have a brain-transplant and then retrieve (download) his memory into the new brain and he would, presumably, still be himself, but his old brain would not. All of which goes to show that he cannot be the same thing as his body, which means, therefore, that 'he' must be something else. This man subscribes to the notion of the *soul*, believing his true *self* to be the soul, some kind of *energy*, inside his body. The body is seen as the home of the temporal *personality* whereas the soul is seen as the home of the all-pervading *individuality*, which continues to exist after the death of the physical body; it therefore must have existed before birth, which gives rise to the notion of reincarnation, the transmigration of the soul from one body to the next during different physical lifetimes on earth.

Memory, or the lack of it, has forever dogged the reincarnation debate. We have no memory of any previous physical life; therefore, the argument goes, there was no previous physical life. But we have no memory of existence in the womb, or of the first few years of life. Does this mean we did not exist at those times? There are other days in our adult lives which we cannot remember at all, not in any way: does that mean we did not exist on those days? The Egyptians warned us about this by carefully preserving the internal organs of the dead – the liver, lungs, stomach and intestines – inside canopic jars following the process of mummification. As we have already noted, there was no need to keep the most precious organs, the brain and the heart; they knew that if they were to reincarnate they would receive a new heart (with new emotions) and a new brain (with a clean memory).

But this raises another question: if we have all lived many times before, why are we not, as individuals, more aware, further developed, more advanced than we are? Why has mankind not progressed in any way (apart from technologically – and whether that is progress is debatable) since history began? The fact is that man suffers from the same old vices – anger, avarice, envy, gluttony, lust, pride and slothfulness – as he always did. If you were to tread on the toe of a passer-by today, he would react just as angrily as would a Roman centurion, a medieval carpenter, or a Babylonian boatman. If your wife was more beautiful than theirs, they would, in all likelihood, envy your good fortune. If they or their offspring succeeded in some particular endeavour, they would no doubt imagine that they deserved some of the credit, that they, in some way, should be proud of what has been achieved. But the ancients tell us that this is the way of folly. This is the way of the physical body. Our senses – sight, sound, touch, taste, and smell – make sure that we, today, receive all the same messages as we have done throughout history. After all, if you couldn't *see* your friend's wife, you could hardly be envious.

So our senses betray us, and yet we value them. Where, indeed, would we be without them; without anger, avarice, envy, gluttony, lust, pride and sloth? Not here in the physical world, that's for sure.

As noted earlier, when studying the Viracocha vase of Tiahuanaco, the decoded Amazing Lid of Palenque reveals more about this life, and the afterlife, than any other archaeological artefact yet discovered (and decoded). It teaches that the most important things in life cannot be seen; the decoding of the lid could not begin until the missing corners were found and the lid 'repaired'. The pieces that do not exist are much more important than the large piece that does. The important things in life are beyond our senses and can be reached only after a long search and a great deal of thought (*The Popol Vuh*, the long-lost sacred book of the Mayas, if we recall, was hidden from the searcher and the thinker).

The Archaeological Evidence

Plate 25b highlights areas of the Amazing Lid of Palenque that together tell the story of 'Cosmogonic Destruction', how the world was destroyed through solar-inspired catastrophe. The central cross of the picture represents the cross-sectional schematic of the sun's magnetic structure (*figure A1, iii*) covered in sunspot loops. The yellow and red marker-pegs represent longer-term magnetic activity on the sun. The central cross is flanked by dragon heads. Dragons appear all over the world in various myths. There does not appear to be a consensus of what the creatures, with their forked tongue and feathered tail, glaring eyes, flared nostrils, scorching breath, sharp teeth, eagle talons and scaled snake-like body are meant to represent. The word 'dragon' derives from an ancient Greek word meaning 'to see', suggesting that the glaring eyes can 'see beyond the obvious'. In the Old Testament of the Bible the dragon is mentioned in the same breath as the owl, another creature that, known for its wisdom, can 'see beyond the obvious'. Many cultures associate the dragon, despite its formidable appearance, with good luck and prosperity, particularly in the Far East.

In around 350 BC the early Chinese astronomers KanTe, Shih Shen and Wu Hsien compiled the first great astronomical almanacs, which contained the first accounts of sunspots. In China the dragon is believed to have the head of a stag, the claws of an eagle and the body of a snake, a *feathered snake*, which is part stag. (This remarkable coincidence will be covered in greater detail in my next book.) For now we accept that, for the Maya, the feathered snake, as Quetzalcoatl, represents wisdom and that the stag, Camaxtle, represents rebirth and fertility. The presence of the dragon's heads, on either side of the central cross *(plate 25)* of the sun (which we know control's human fertility on earth), can thus reasonably be identified and associated with fertility and rebirth.

Beneath the cross *(plate 25b)*, a female, reclining with her legs open, is licked by the sun-god Tonatiuh (turn the picture upside-down to see the sun-god with his tongue extended). The sun-god is framed on either side by a 'solar' baby that carries the sun on its stomach and a sad 'magnetic loop' for a mouth. The sad-looking babies point south towards the underworld. The overall story reads: *Radiation from the sun failed the reproductive needs of the female(s). The female opened her legs to receive more radiation from the sun. Despite this the babies died.*

Plate 27 tells the story of the Five Paradises, the various destinations for the dead. The central cross here depicts a tree, rooted in the lower part of the picture. The cross is adorned with nipples and therefore depicts the suckling tree; instead of fruits it was said to have 400,000 nipples.

A female reclines in the centre of the picture. She represents one half of the original divine couple known as Ometeotl (o-mee-tee-owe-tal), the equivalent of Adam and Eve in the West. The other half (Adam) is missing and can be seen only when the transparency decoding process is used. Ometeotl lived in the paradise known as Omeyocan (o-mee-owe-can).

A few maize seeds can be seen just behind the left heel of the reclining figure. Maize represented the paradise known as Cincalco (sin-cal-coe); women who died in childbirth came here.

Tlaloc lived in his own paradise, Tlalocan, which lay to the south. He was the consort of Chalchiuitlicue, the goddess of water. This place was home to flowers and birds, which would sing loudly to keep Tlaloc awake, ensuring he sent rains to make the ground fertile.

Babies that died at childbirth went to the paradise of Tomoanchan (tom-owe-one-chan), our ancestral home. There grew the roots of the suckling tree that they would suckle to gain enough strength to reincarnate.

There was only one other paradise, as far as the Maya were concerned, and that was the one known as Tonatiuhchan, home of the sun-god Tonatiuh. This was the destination for those who died in battle and sacrifice.

Plate 28 shows the next scene that follows on from plate 9 (the death and rebirth of Lord Pacal) and of course can be seen only once the transparency decoding process is used. This scene is quite complex; the face of Lord Pacal now appears with his eyes closed expelling his final breath. The Great Bear, Yaotl, god of the north (one of the four corners of the sky), death and darkness, stands on Pacal's head, with the symbol of the four corners (shown as red, black, yellow and blue) hanging from his neck. In each hand he carries, in profile, the head of a skeleton with an extended tongue. Pacal's mouth is covered by a skeleton (black) which, as the god of death, wears a cloak and a hat. (This scene, incidentally, was decoded the first time around, before any knowledge emerged of the treasures of Sipan, or the man with the hat from Sipan.) The god of death (the skull with the hat) is carried away by the bat-god (of death) with outstretched bony wings at the bottom of the picture (green). The meaning of the message contained in plate 28 therefore reads *death carried Lord Pacal away.*

Plate 29 shows the next scene from the same series. Lord Pacal has now degenerated into a simple skull (outlined in black). At the top of the picture a baby quetzal bird with outstretched wings carries a mosaic mask in his beak away from the face of Pacal and in so doing removes the heavy burden of physical life (his physical identity; personality) from the dead man's face. The tail-feathers of the quetzal bird come together to form the soul of Lord Pacal as it departs through an opening in the top of the skull. At the same time a young maiden emerges from Pacal's skull, opens her legs and gives birth to a baby with wings, which crawls towards the viewer. A pearl emerges from

Figure 80. Coatlicue, the Earth-Goddess

Coatlicue, the earth-goddess, wearing a skirt of snakes and a necklace of hands and hearts and a skull.

the mouth of the baby to become two solar babies (pink in the lower picture) that carry the joint solar symbol on their stomachs. The joint solar symbol resembles an eight-pointed star. The maiden who has given birth smiles joyfully and points, using two converging lines (one from each hand), to a point on her forehead, the pineal gland.

If we recall, the message of plate 9, given in Chapter 1, read: *Lord Pacal died and was reborn as Quetzalcoatl.* The message of this scene reads: *When Lord Pacal died, his soul was carried away by the quetzal bird.* And moreover: *He was reborn as the twin star Venus, the brightest and purest source of light in the heavens.* And finally: *Rebirth is a function of the pineal gland.*

Quetzalcoatl, as the morning star and the evening star, as we have seen, was associated with Tlahhuizcalpantechuhtli, the god of ice, Venus in the morning and the evening star Xolotol. He accompanied Quetzalcoatl when he journeyed into the underworld to collect the bones to make mankind in the fifth and final age of the sun. Plate 30 shows the twins (Quetzalcoatl) carried in a basket held by the Lord of Death (who wears the sign of the bat, the god of death, across his mouth). Bare-breasted Lady Death (who wears the mark of the bat across her chest) kneels in front, steering the V-shaped bat-god home into the darkness of the underworld. The twins suckle the twin stars Venus, confirming their identity.

Mayan mythology tells the story of the goddess of hearts *(plate 31)*; she was originally the goddess of filth that lived in the underworld where she would round up sinners and carry them to the priests, before whom they would confess their sins. Confession purged the heart of guilt and so the place became known as purgatory. The goddess of filth became known by the more endearing term of 'goddess of hearts' (because she helped purge the hearts of sinners). This scene tells us that in the afterlife sinners must journey through purgatory before they can spiritually progress.

Figure 80 shows a stone statue of the earth-goddess Coatlicue. Her face is made from the profile heads of two serpents, representing birth and rebirth. She wears a skirt of snakes, representing fertility. Around her neck hangs a necklace of hands and hearts, showing that as the mother of life she gave life. But she also shook the earth with her heavy clawed feet, causing earthquakes and death, so she was also identified with death. The shaking of the earth associated her with the rocking of babies in the cradle. Plate 32 shows the twins (Quetzalcoatl) suckling, and squeezing with each hand, the many nipples of Coatlicue. She wears the necklace of hands and hearts and a skull which covers the genital area, indicating that procreation brings death. This story tells us that the twins, Quetzalcoatl, came back to earth (reincarnated) in the arms of the earth-goddess.

These pictures, just a few of the many composite pictures hidden in the Amazing Lid of Palenque, tell the story of the afterlife; of the various destinations of the dead; of rebirth in the stars for the pure of heart and reincarnation on earth for the rest. And they tell us that Lord Pacal was both cleverer and wiser than we are today, that he was the white man with a beard, the feathered snake who, when he died, went to the stars.

The Legend of the Feathered Snake and the White Man with a Beard

The ancient Chinese were the first to notice that sunspots appeared and disappeared at regular intervals, approximately every eleven and a half years. The cause of the cycle of magnetic activity is today put down to the differential rotation of the sun's magnetic fields *(figure A3)*. The eleven-and-a-half-year cycle is carried on top of a longer magnetic cycle of 187 years, which is associated with the tilted, warped equatorial region of the sun *(figure A4)*. Interplay between the two cycles causes magnetic reversals to occur on the sun every 3,740 years (1,366,040 days), which, as we know, was very close to the number worshipped by the Maya (who used complete revolutions of the planet Venus to measure the cycle; 2,340 revolutions of Venus = 1,366,560 days). Magnetically inspired solar radiation thus regulates the production of fertility hormones in females and hence human fertility on earth.

The Maya, like the Egyptians and the Peruvians, worshipped the sun as the god of fertility; they called it the 'feathered snake'. In *The Tutankhamun Prophecies* I explained the derivation of the name; when the eleven-and-a-half-year sunspot cycle is superimposed on the 187-year solar cycle the combined shape takes the form of a 'feathered snake' *(see figures A4–A7)*. This is why the Egyptians worshipped the symbol of the sun's disc, with wings and serpents *(figure A8)* and why Tutankhamun, the son of God (light), carried the vulture and the snake (feathers and snake) on his forehead *(figure A9)*. We also note that the beard of Tutankhamun carries the pattern of a snake skin along its length and the tail-feathers of a bird at the end.

The statue of Viracocha from the Temple of Stone Heads *(plate 24a and detail 24d)* shows Viracocha as the white man with a beard, and we now know that the Viracocha Transformer shows Viracocha as the feathered snake *(figure 81)*. One of the scenes from the decoded Mosaic Mask of Palenque *(see The Tutankhamun Prophecies, plate 7)* shows Lord Pacal as a man with wings. Another *(figure 82 and plate 18f, herein)* shows a clear picture of the head of a snake resting on feathers. The snake also carries wings on its forehead. The message here reads: *Lord Pacal was the feathered snake (light)*. Figures 58b and 59b confirm that he was also the white man with a beard.

Treasures from the tombs at Sipan inform us that the Old Lord of Sipan was also the feathered snake *(figure 83)*.

The Amazing Lid of Palenque *(plate 23)* tells us that Viracocha was a reincarnation of one of the Lords of Sipan (associated with the man with the hat) and that Lord Pacal and the Lords of Sipan all came from the sun (represented by the gilded feline sun chambers *(plate 24b)* from the tomb of the Old Lord of Sipan.

The riddle of the mixed-up dates tells us that the Old Lord of Sipan was the same physical man as Viracocha of Tiahuanaco.

Other decoded stories from the Amazing Lid of Palenque *(plates 29 and 30)* say that on death Lord Pacal became the twin star Venus, the brightest of the night-time heavenly bodies. The raised-arm stance of crab man Viracocha *(figure 29)*, from the tomb of the Old Lord of Sipan, associates the Old Lord with Lord Pacal (the raised-arm stance of the man with the hat corresponds to the raised-arm stance of the small man with the hat that covers the mouth of Lord Pacal in plate 9), and hence the rebirth of the Old Lord as Venus.

As mentioned in Chapter 1, treasures from the tomb of Tutankhamun associate him with Osiris, who lived in Orion. Figure 84 shows Tutankhamun with his Ka (his soul), or twin, embracing Osiris, god of

Figure 81. The Feathered Snake of Tiahuanaco

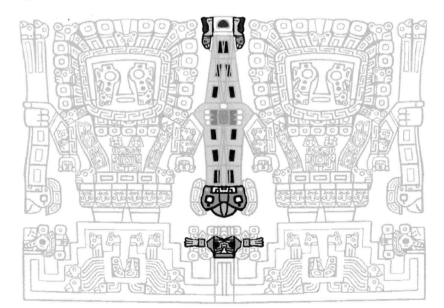

The Viracocha Transformer from the Gateway of the Sun, Tiahuanaco, showing Viracocha as the feathered snake.

Figure 82. The Feathered Snake of Mexico

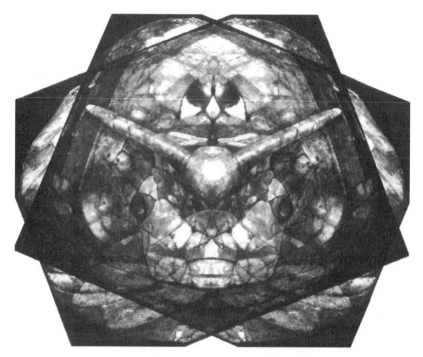

Lord Pacal as the feathered snake, from the decoded Mosaic Mask of Palenque.

Figure 83. The Feathered Snake of Peru

The Old Lord of Sipan, as the feathered snake, featured on the golden spider chambers from his tomb at Sipan.

resurrection and everlasting life. This says that on death Tutankhamun became twins and joined Osiris in the heavens, as the twin star Venus. The statues of Viracocha and the children of Viracocha (in the Temple of Stone Heads at Tiahuanaco, *plate 22b*) are laid out in the same way as the stars in Orion's belt *(figure 85)*, which hence associates Viracocha with the stars. The statues of Viracocha in the Temple of Stone Heads at Tiahuanaco hence tell us that when Viracocha died he, too, was reborn as a star, like Tutankhamun, as two children, the twins, Venus in the heavens.

Do we need any more evidence? The legends of the feathered snakes (sun-kings of Mexico) of Egypt and Peru are clear; from time to time a being in possession of higher knowledge visits earth to teach mankind the higher orders of science and spirituality. He has walked among the ancients many times. They call him Viracocha, the feathered snake, the white man with a beard. Whenever and wherever he appeared his presence was marked by sun-worship, a fertility cult, an awareness of spiritual purpose and destiny, and by an explosion in scientific accomplishment, epitomised by stonework and archaeological treasures, that remains beyond the understanding of modern man. We have been told that these feathered snakes were all one and the same man, who has reincarnated on earth many times, each time bringing the same knowledge and each time leaving the same knowledge behind.

Mechanisms of Reincarnation – the Archaeological Evidence

The Mosaic Mask of Palenque *(figure 58b)* shows an Olmec head looking down on a fruit bat. The bat carries the face of the bearded white man on its forehead, similar to that of the jade figurine of the bearded white man found in Lord Pacal's tomb *(figure 59b)*. The mask covering the face of Lord Pacal was also jade, suggesting that Lord Pacal was the white man with a beard.

Lord Pacal also appears in the Amazing Lid of Palenque *(figure 57)*. That scene shows Lord Pacal watching over his own birth, that of the feathered snake. In the same picture is an Olmec head (that carries a conch shell on his head, identifying him as Quetzalcoatl, the white man with a beard). But clearly the Olmec head was a black man without a beard. How are we meant to interpret the message here? The Olmec head *(figure 57)* is featured with a bat covering his mouth, indicating that the Olmec head is dead. The Olmec head must therefore have come first, before Lord Pacal. Which means that the black man

Figure 84. Tutankhamun's Journey to the Stars

Tutankhamun *(right)* meeting his escort Nut, goddess of the night sky and the stars. Tut-ankhamun, after death *(centre)*, and his Ka (soul/twin) meeting Osiris, god of resurrection.

Figure 85. Viracocha's Journey to the Stars

Orion's Belt

Statues of Viracocha and the children of Viracocha at the Temple of the Stone Heads, Tiahuanaco, laid out to reflect the stars in Orion's belt.

(Quetzalcoatl) must have preceded the white man (Quetzalcoatl) with a beard. This means, if both were Quetzalcoatl, that the black man without the beard reincarnated as the white man with the beard.

This interpretation is confirmed by information from the tomb of Tutankhamun. The sealed-up doorway to his burial chamber was 'guarded' by two black ebony figures of Tutankhamun *(one of which is shown in figure 86a)* that clearly portray the boy-king as a black man, suggesting that the next time Tutankhamun walked on the earth he would do so as a black man without a beard. Two other clues suggest that this may indeed be a rational appraisal of the evidence; a footstool found in the tomb shows a procession of 9 men that alternate from white man to black man *(figure 86c)*. The footstool belongs with the ecclesiastical cross-legged throne *(figure 86b)* also found in the tomb. The cross-legged feature allows the stool to be used and then folded away in a closet, then used again, and again folded away in the closet, emulating the birth–rebirth characteristics of reincarnation. The back of the throne carries two different names of Tutankhamun, suggesting that the characters on the footstool shared the same name. Together, these clues suggest that Tutankhamun reincarnated from black man to white man during alternate incarnations.

The Bible also comments that: 'many that are first will be last and the last shall be first' (Matthew xix, 30). This implies that the principles of reincarnation incorporate an inversion mechanism: black people reincarnate as white people and white people reincarnate as black people. Taking this one step further, it becomes clear that such a notion accommodates the principle of karma (the universal law of action and reaction); for if fat people reincarnate as thin people, thin people as fat people, men as women, women as men, and so on, then all of our sins and prejudices in one life will be re-presented to ourselves in the next.

The Scientific Argument

The scientific argument for reincarnation was set down in *The Tutankhamun Prophecies* (an abridged explanation is provided for new readers in Appendix 4 herein). The scientific argument is much more straightforward than orthodox scientists and atheists might wish to consider; the archaeological evidence left to us by the Supergods (who were far more intelligent than ourselves) suggests three worlds exist *(figure A10)* that accommodate the physical and spiritual states

Figure 86. Reincarnations of the White Man with a Beard

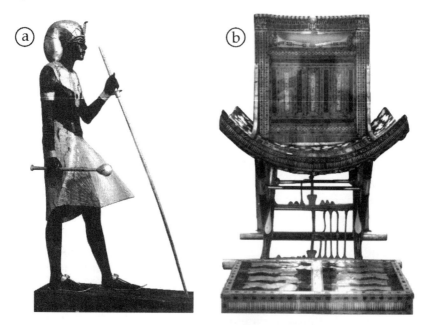

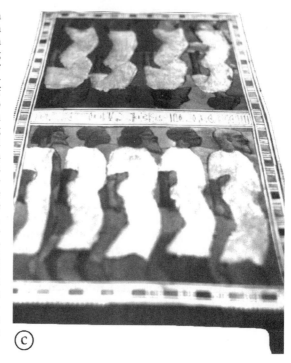

(a) Gilded ebony statue from the tomb of Tutankhamun showing him as a black man without a beard. (b) Folding ecclesiastical throne together with the footstool that carried two different names of Tutankhamun. (c) Close-up of the footstool showing a procession of alternating bearded white men and Olmec-style Nubian (north African) heads. The pattern around the edge of the footstool resembles that of the Amazing Lid of Palenque (without the border codes). The folding chair symbolises the principle of reincarnation (it can be folded away and reused [reborn] many times). The procession informs us that the white man with the beard reincarnated as a black man, who in turn reincarnated as a white man with a beard.

of being. These are the God World, where resides the creator of the universe; the Physical World, which includes the stars, planets, trees, birds and all living and non-living tangibles; and the Soul World, the place where impure spirits subsist in between existence in either the Physical World or the God World.

Before we can progress towards a true understanding of the meaning of life and our own place in the universe we must first consider the religious argument for reincarnation, previously set down in *The Supergods*; this recognised that all the world's religions agree on certain propositions: in the beginning God the creator existed; God the creator was *light* (electromagnetic energy); God was *good* and God was *love*. Christianity adds that *God made man in his own image.*

We can now examine the religious argument. If God is good and God is love, then the only thing better than God must be more God. God's objective must therefore be growth, more God *(figure A11)*. But God made himself in man's image, and we know that man cannot grow unless he sacrifices a part of his physical being, a sperm containing chromosomes, to produce more offspring. In the same way, a woman cannot grow unless she sacrifices an ovum containing chromosomes. This must mean that God cannot grow unless he likewise sacrifices a part of himself, throws a part of himself away, as it were. So in the beginning God, electromagnetic energy, must have detached a part of himself *(figure A12)*, a portion of electromagnetic energy (light). That energy (E) was then converted into mass (m), the physical universe. Physicist Albert Einstein tells us that energy cannot be destroyed, only converted from one state to another; energy may be converted to mass (physical things), at least in a mathematical sense, and mass may be converted to energy.

The energy contained in a particular mass is proportional to the atomic weight of the mass (the sum of the constituent parts of the atom) and to the speed of light squared ($E=mc^2$). When a heavy (radioactive) element is smashed to pieces, the energy released is proportional to both its atomic weight and the speed of light (300,000,000 metres per second). The result is a very large bang; a nuclear explosion. We must assume that some kind of *inverse* bang took place when God converted himself into the physical universe and that this event is what orthodox scientists nowadays refer to as 'the big bang' from which our universe was created.

In the beginning, in the spiritual world, there was no such thing as time. The only thing that existed was light. Nothing ever happened. Nothing happened before anything else and nothing happened after anything else, which means that time did not exist. Time began with the creation of the physical universe. Things began to happen after the big-bang. Things then happened before other things had happened, and things happened after other things had happened. Time embraced evolution, and mankind biologically advanced. In time, man became more complex and intellectually advanced. The brain developed operating voltages, the opposite charge to that which created them; when +E (positive E) moves across the equation it must convert to -m (minus m), a simple rule of algebra which explains why biological man has a propensity to be attracted back to God.

These voltages then began to attract further packets of energy, soul energy, from the creator energy. This marks the evolutionary moment at which mankind acquired a soul and became a complete being.

The physical world differs from the spiritual world, just as the physical world differs from the intellectual world; if I have a £1 coin in the physical world and you have a £1 coin in the physical world and we exchange them then we still each have only £1. However, if I have one idea and you, too, have one idea and we exchange them, we both finish up with two ideas, at no cost. Taking this one step further, in accordance with the scriptures, it seems that (at least in the spiritual world) if I love you my soul voltage increases, grows, at no cost, whereas if I hate you my soul voltage depletes. If my soul voltage has grown, it is attracted with greater force back to the creator energy (God) on physical death of the body. Conversely, if my voltage has fallen during its lifetime it instead returns to earth, next time as a lower being, attracted to a lower voltage body, for another try at purification. In this way God grows, the universe grows and those who have not loved their neighbour suffer again during another incarnation on earth.

The Sacred Secret of the Sun-Kings

Bruce Cathie's speed of light (144,000 minutes of arc per second) means that light travels around the *physical earth* (a circle) 6.66 times every second. In the Book of Revelation in the Bible, the number 666 represents the opposite of God, the devil. Cathie's discovery, therefore, suggests that the number 666 in Revelation may in fact refer to the earth, meaning that the physical earth is the devil.

The fact that everything in the physical universe is of the opposite polarity charge to that of the creator energy (heaven) also means that everything in the physical universe must likewise be hell, including physical biological bodies. God, the creative energy, is electromagnetically attached to each and every one of the biological bodies. When we look at life in this way, everything begins to make sense. For every happiness there is unhappiness, for every gain there is loss, for every life there is death, and for every day there is night. Esoteric societies, and the Church, know this already. They know that this place is hell. They, like you, know the sacred secret of the sun-kings. On the one hand they wish to escape from this endless hell, and yet they know that they cannot escape unless they love God and their neighbour. And therein lies the difficulty: love for God implies love for God's objective, which is growth. God made sex pleasurable to ensure a steady supply of babies that would attract more and more souls from the God World *(figure A12)*, thus enabling perpetual God growth for eternity. Looked at in this way, mankind is a conduit that facilitates the objective of divine reconciliation, enabling God to grow. This is why the Church opposes birth control and abortion. The objective of individuals in the Church and those in the esoteric societies is therefore to allow God to grow and yet at the same time escape from hell. This is the reason for the secrecy; by keeping this knowledge secret, and loving God and their neighbour, the esoteric orders can purify their own soul and escape, leaving others behind to have more babies, most of which will repeatedly reincarnate on earth. Physical birth amounts to eternal imprisonment on earth. This is why prisoners appear with erect penises on the walls at Huaca Cao Viejo and why prisoners appear in the tomb seals of Tutankhamun, bound by ropes that terminate with the divine lotus. Life on earth amounts to divine imprisonment.

The mechanism of karma (the universal law of cause and effect, action and reaction) provides the final link in the chain of understanding; bad (lower-voltage) souls reincarnate into lower-voltage bodies and suffer during the next incarnation on earth. Suffering in the next life increases the soul voltage during that lifetime, leading to reincarnation again, next time in a higher-voltage body. In this way each earth-life alternates between more suffering or less suffering. This is why the ancients left the message of *inverse transmigration*; black reincarnates as white, white as black, men as women, women as men, healthy as sick, sick as healthy and so on. In time each soul

Figure 87. The Killer Whale of Nazca

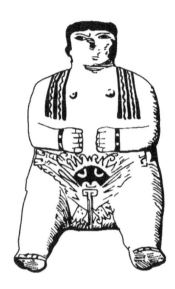

Pottery effigy from Nazca showing a female with the killer whale symbol covering her vagina, conveying the message 'procreation brings death' in the physical world.

experiences every condition until purification is attained. This was the 'sacred secret' put forward in *The Tutankhamun Prophecies*.

But the bound prisoners of Huaca Cao Viejo, parading with their erections, a killer whale symbol featured on the vagina of a Nazca ceramic *(figure 87)* and the presence of the bat-god covering the genitals of the man with the hat on the decoded face of Lord Pacal suggest an additional, hitherto unknown, step in this process: the man with the hat tells us that purification comes only to those who do not procreate. The prisoners of Huaca Cao Viejo tell us that those who have erections are forever imprisoned, and the Nazca pottery, together with the bat-god, tells us that those who give birth bring only death. We need to ask why this should be the case and what physical mechanism might be employed to ensure the propagation of such a scheme.

The Ultimate Secret of the Universe

An examination of the chakra centres *(figure 88)* shows that purification of the spirit is possible only when the physical, emotional and intellectual bodies achieve coordinated equilibrium. This can happen only when the physical, emotional and intellectual bodies are at perfect peace with the universe, God and our neighbour. When we love our neighbour more than ourselves, energy, known as sushumna to the mystics, ascends the spine and light radiates from the head, and we become one of the 144,000. It seems that any unbalance between the three bodies results in disequilibrium.

For males, physical sperm-production places great demands on the physical being. Sperm is rich in protein and essential minerals. Ejaculation of sperm results in reverse energy flows down through the body (*figure 89a*), and sushumna flows in the wrong direction. At the same time the great loss of protein means that the body must now produce more, drawing on all its energy reserves and leaving less energy for sushumna production. Ejaculation of sperm hence precludes coordinated equilibrium and purification of the spirit. This is why monks, clergy and those belonging to the higher esoteric orders take vows of celibacy, why masturbation is frowned on by the Church and why some religions have adopted circumcision as an impediment to male masturbation.

As far as women are concerned, motherhood, in conjuction with the endocrine system, brings with it a maternal bonding with the offspring greater than with any other. The mother loves her own child more than herself. In effect (*figure 89b*) the chakra centres direct energy towards the offspring, preventing the rise of sushumna and the radiation of light in the mother.

The Dalai Lama's Dilemma

Now we understand the reason why the Dalai Lama refused to answer the second question. He dare not reveal the secret of the sun-kings. If people became aware of the reality of existence, of the true purpose of their presence on earth, they might stop producing babies, and God would stop growing. At the same time (*figure 89*) those who produce babies are excluded for consideration in the purification process and hence are excluded from entry into heaven.

Herein lies the dilemma of the Dalai Lama, and the great paradox of existence: those who produce babies create the conditions for expansion of heaven and yet, at the same time, those who produce the babies exclude themselves from entry into heaven.

How could the Dalai Lama explain in a radio interview what we have learned from the ancients? He could not. So he held the line, the traditional view, saying that sex was allowed only for the production of children.

Figure 88. Chakras: the Nine Gateways to Heaven

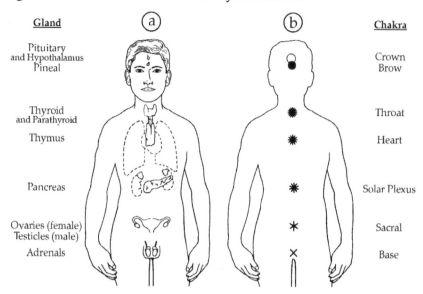

(a) Chief glands of the endocrine system; (b) chakra (energy) centres; (c) positive (ida), negative (pingala) and light (sushumna) energy flow patterns around Chakra centres when the physical, emotional and intellectual bodies achieve coordinated equilibrium; (d) the caduceus representing the cancellation of positive and negative energies, which gives rise to the generation of light, the feathered snake.

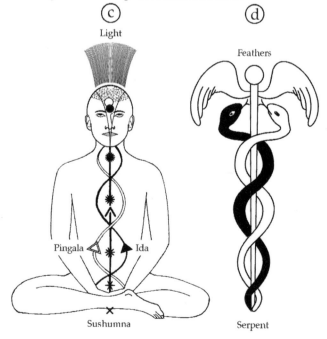

Figure 89. Closing the Gateways to Heaven

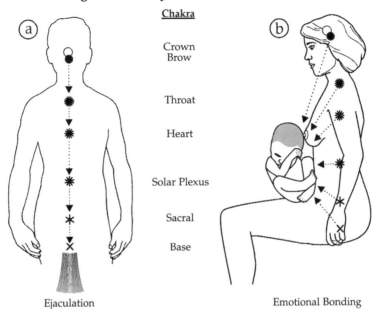

Chakra

Crown
Brow

Throat

Heart

Solar Plexus

Sacral

Base

Ejaculation   Emotional Bonding

In the male, ejaculation directs energy away from the chakra centres, precluding co-ordinated equilibrium of energy flows through the body and hence the generation of light. In the female, emotional bonding with the infant directs energies away from chakra centres in the same way.

And this is not the only reason for secrecy. In both *The Supergods* and *The Tutankhamun Prophecies* I introduced the reader to the Taoist view on the need for secrecy:

> On hearing of the Way, the best of men will earnestly explore its length. The mediocre person learns of it, takes it up and sets it down. But vulgar people, when they hear the news, will laugh out loud. And if they did not laugh, it would not be the way.

And the Christian view:

> Give not that which is holy unto the dogs, neither cast ye your pearls before swine, lest they trample them under foot and turn again and rend you (Matthew ix, 6).

Disclosure invites ridicule. This is not paranoia. The mob rules today just as it did during those heady days in Jerusalem when chants of 'Barabas, Barabas' filled the air, denying Jesus the justice he deserved. Those subscribing to the ethos of 'love thy neighbour' have, throughout history, been persecuted and crucified for their convictions.

In England, in January 1999, the manager of the England football team dared to reveal his views on reincarnation to a journalist from *The Times*. The manager had let slip his personal beliefs on reincarnation, saying, in a radio interview, that 'disabled people are suffering for their sins from a previous life'. He omitted to mention that he, you, me and everybody else were also here suffering for the sins of a previous life.

The Times, that great British literary institution, ignoring the many charitable events the manager had organised for the disabled during his career, decided publicly to take the manager to task over his comments which, the newspaper insisted, had no place in modern society. There would be no penalty shoot-out between the editor and the footballer to decide the issue, no. Instead, the editor of *The Times* would take on the footballer in a war of words; which is rather like the heavyweight boxing champion of the world taking on an eight-year-old boy except that, amid cries of 'thuggery', the contest would never be allowed to take place.

The mob had a field day. 'Resign', cried the sports minister; 'if he said those words he should go', said the Prime Minister; 'a load of mumbo jumbo', scorned the press; it was just a load of *rubbish*, they all agreed.

It seemed that the press, and the mob they incited, wished, in some way, to discriminate between the disabled and the rest of the population, to exclude them from the model of reincarnation, although why they wished to do this is not yet clear.

The sports minister, who proclaimed it was just 'medieval madness', denounced reincarnation on the television news, in hourly bulletins, 'because it has no place in modern society', as if universal laws, which embrace electricity, magnetism, gravity and reincarnation, somehow diminish with the passage of time; but if that were true then we would, surely, all float free of the planet.

If these people could explain how to build pyramids as the Egyptians did, or how to encode a carving as the Mayas did, or how to melt stone as the Peruvians did, then I would be the first to congratulate them. If they could explain why we are born, why we die or why this has to be, then I would admire them. If they loved each other or had ever helped the disabled, as had the manager they so readily crucified, then I would revere them; instead they simply shout 'Barabas', unaware that the physical world exists to teach us about the spiritual world.

The Transmigration of Souls

Two-thirds of the world's population believe in reincarnation, although not all in the same way. Some believe that low-voltage (impure) souls return to earth into low-voltage (sick) *human* bodies and that transmigration across species is not possible. This, if it were true, would explain instinct; a bird, for example, would know how to build a nest because it must have been a bird in its previous life *(plate 32b)*. Others believe that low-voltage souls can return to earth as lower life forms, from animals to insects, presumably to a level of intellectual awareness that permits variation in voltage commensurate with *intent*. This view would accommodate the notion of 'soul shatter', which would explain why shoals of fish all swim and turn in unison, why insects like midges fly in 'bundles' or 'spherical balls', and why birds flock together; soul shatter, as the name implies, might result from soul breakdown, analogous in the physical world to a 'nervous breakdown', or a car windscreen shattering into many fragments. The once-unified soul of, say, five volts shatters into many parts, perhaps a thousand pieces, each of which carries a charge of only five-thousandths of a volt. These mini-souls are attracted to individual five thousandths of a volt mini-cells that reincarnate as lesser creatures, like fish or insects or birds. But those mini-souls would be all part of the same single soul, which means that the whole bundle would during that incarnation *move together*. In time the mini-souls would recombine, as each mini-soul again increases in voltage following suffering and purification on earth.

The truth, in regard to the possibilities of reincarnation, no doubt lies somewhere between these two views, or embraces both.

The message is simple for those who do not wish to come back and live again on earth: listen to the secrets of the ancients. You were once one of them. You will again be one of them. Listen to your *self* and save yourself the suffering.

Nature, the Great Redeemer

'Can I,' the anxious parent asks, 'get to heaven this time around or will the gates be firmly closed when this life ends?' In a purely pragmatic sense, it seems unlikely that those who procreate face automatic exclusion from entry into heaven. If that were the case then, mindful of the Theory of Divine Reconciliation, God would not grow by very much very quickly. But then again, because time does not exist in the spiritual world, time cannot, of itself, be of the essence in regard to God-growth. The answers we seek, therefore, in this regard will not be found in this line of reasoning.

Mystics say that the first 20 years of life are for learning, the second 20 years for procreation and the final 20 years for spiritual redemption.

The Tutankhamun Prophecies (Appendix 1, xiv) explains how the magnetic interaction between the sun and the earth shifts by around 30 degrees each year, resulting in a 12-year magnetic cycle between the two. That cycle affects the pineal gland and the biorhythmic performance of the body causing menstruation to commence in females at around 12 years after conception, around the age of 11 years 3 months on average. The cycle is naturally modified by environmental factors that affect the biorhythmic harmony of the body. After 4 of these cycles, following conception, 47 years 3 months on average, the body and the sun conspire to ensure decreasing levels of female fertility hormones; the ageing pineal gland produces less melatonin, the pituitary less of the follicle-stimulating and luteinising hormones and the ovaries less oestrogen and progesterone. The perfectly natural menopause is not just nature's way of ensuring that the youngest and fittest of females carry the healthiest of offspring; it is nature's way of closing the gates on sexuality and opening the gates of enlightenment and spiritual awareness, although many fail to follow the plot or see perfection at play. Male testosterone declines at the same time, concentrating the mind on the more important issues of soul purification.

It would seem, then, that even those who procreate *can* be admitted to heaven, although 20 years or so of distraction, rearing offspring, naturally leaves 20 years' less time available for the pursuit of spiritual purification. Time *is* of the essence in the physical world.

Mystics also acknowledge that we live in a perfect world where nothing is left to chance. But if God created a perfect world, you may ask, how do we account for natural disasters, and accidents, which take such great loss of life?

God indeed created a perfect physical universe; the sun radiates light and energy that fuels the solar system. The gravitational force of the sun captures and interns the planets.

Over billions of years the once-molten surface of our own planet has cooled sufficiently to support life on its hard outer crust that flexes with the gravitational pull of the sun and the planets. Crustal sections, the great continental plates, drift around the surface, colliding, causing earthquakes that dislodge surface structures.

As the earth turns on its axis it divides night from day, accommodating the rest and regeneration of all living things.

The axial tilt of the earth, together with its orbital movement around the sun, brings the seasons and with them cycles of growth. As it spins, it generates circulating winds and ocean currents that together, with energy from the sun, regulate evaporation, precipitation and glaciation. These geophysical phenomena may not always suit human life, but by accommodating catastrophe cycles that bring periodic destruction and death they do suit the divine objective of perpetual God-growth. If the continental plates did not move gradually and repeatedly, the planet would have been torn apart by torsional stresses caused by the sun and other planets and, in the same way, if the winds did not blow, or the rains fall, then life on earth would cease and all 5.5 billion occupants would perish.

What would you prefer, if you were the great creator? The loss of 5.5 billion people and with it an end to a perfect world and unlimited God-growth or the sacrifice of 50,000 people, through *natural* disasters, every year? If you truly understood the perfection that confronts you, that the soul is imperishable, indestructible, immortal and everlasting, then you would understand that the 50,000 souls will either be reborn on earth or elevated to heaven to live with the creator; you would also be relieved of your intellectual and emotional anxieties.

Perhaps an awareness of reincarnation is not so bad after all; would men pointlessly kill men knowing that killing *releases* the victim from hell, assuring rebirth on earth or escape to heaven? And if killing is not the final solution for man's inhumanity to man, where could enmity seek refuge?

Would the rich be unkind to the poor, men to women, women to men, black to white or white to black if they truly understood that, next time, their roles would be reversed, the first becoming the last and the last becoming the first?

And yet, still, the many laugh, seeking light amid the darkness, unaware that light comes from light. Now you know why *if they didn't laugh, it would not be the way.*

APPENDIX 1

How the Sun Determines Personality

In 1957 James Van Allen, an engineer working at NASA, discovered radiation belts encircling the earth *(figure A1, iv)*. Further studies showed that the belts captured space-borne charged particles that would otherwise cause damage to life on our planet.

In 1962 *Mariner II* spacecraft relayed data to earth showing that the sun gave off considerable amounts of charged particles, collectively described as the 'solar wind' *(figure A1, i)*.

In 1969 Jeff Mayo, a British astrologer working with Professor Hans Eysenck at the London Institute of Psychiatry, compiled a psychological profile from respondents to a questionnaire that supported personality assertions of sun-sign astrology *(figure A1, v)*.

In 1979 a British physicist, Professor Iain Nicolson, discovered that the earth's magnetic field varied whenever the Van Allen belts were bombarded by solar particles. New words and expressions soon evolved to describe these discoveries; scientists began talking about how 'solar wind' particles collide with the 'magnetosphere', the magnetic bubble that surrounds the earth, how it compresses the magnetosphere on the sunward side (the bow shock) and elongates the magnetic field lines on the leeward side, how they entered the Van Allen belts and spiralled from North Pole to South Pole every second and how the earth's 'geomagnetic field', the magnetic field at ground level, varied in sympathy with the Van Allen belt particle bombardment.

Figure A1, i shows a cross-sectional view of the sun's idealised

Figure A1. How the Sun Determines Personality

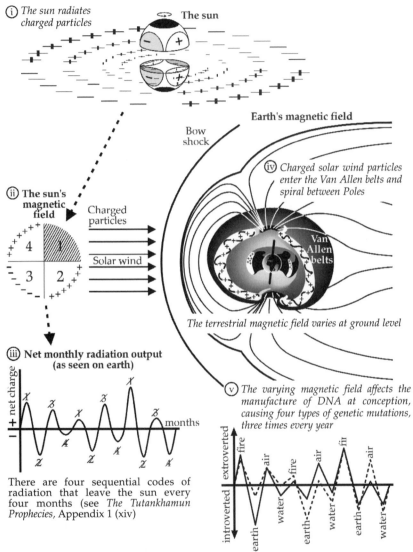

(i) The sun radiates charged particles

The sun

Earth's magnetic field

Bow shock

(iv) Charged solar wind particles enter the Van Allen belts and spiral between Poles

Van Allen belts

(ii) The sun's magnetic field

Charged particles

Solar wind

The terrestrial magnetic field varies at ground level

(iii) Net monthly radiation output (as seen on earth)

months

(v) The varying magnetic field affects the manufacture of DNA at conception, causing four types of genetic mutations, three times every year

There are four sequential codes of radiation that leave the sun every four months (see *The Tutankhamun Prophecies*, Appendix 1 (xiv)

(vi) The 12 genetic mutations every year correlate with the 12 signs of the zodiac (above graphs from two studies by Jeff Mayo and Professor Hans Eysenck, London Institute of Psychiatry). The positive 'signs' are extroverted, the negative 'signs' are introverted. This suggests that the sun is responsible for the determination of personality (sun-sign astrology) through genetic mutations beginning at the moment of conception

191

magnetic fields; the black areas illustrate the magnetic field that exists between the Poles (the vertical polar field). Four more 'bubbles' of magnetism exist around the equator (the equatorial field).

The sun spins on its axis, causing the equator to revolve once every 26 days (28 days when observed from the moving earth), while the more slowly moving polar regions take 37 days to complete one revolution (40.5 days when observed from the moving earth). The resulting turbulence showers the distant earth with charged particles. (The shaded area of the sun's magnetic field indicates a non-charged field sector which slides, anticlockwise, through field sectors 1, 2, 3 and 4, causing the net radiation to polarise monthly from positive to negative, as shown in figure A1, iii.)

The polarity of solar particles (i) can be seen to coincide with the rotating equatorial magnetic field sectors of the sun. This girdle (figure A1, ii) hence shows *the sectored structure of the solar wind.*

In 1984 a team of geneticists at the Naval Medical Research Institute at Bethesda, Maryland, USA, led by Dr A. R. Lieboff, discovered that changing magnetic fields cause genetic mutations in test-tube babies at the time of conception. The strength of the field needed to cause such changes was calculated to be less than that caused by solar-wind-inspired magnetic activity in the Van Allen belts.

In 1986 I discovered that the sun releases a sequence of 12 types of radiation each year; a different sequence every month. Putting the pieces of the puzzle together, it became clear that these 12 types of radiation bombard the Van Allen belts, causing 12 types of magnetic modulation of the earth's magnetic field. These magnetic changes cause genetic mutations in the developing chromosomes of early-impregnated ova at the time of conception.

It was known since the 1920s that personality was genetically determined. The solar-inspired magnetic modulations hence result in a dispersion of 12 types of personality among the new-born each year. Here was the scientific basis for astrology *(figure A1, v)* as determined empirically by astrologer Jeff Mayo and Professor Hans Eysenck.

It was not a popular notion, not what astrologers wanted to hear. After all, they believed that the moment of birth, not conception, was the crucial moment in astrological understanding, so they ignored it, as did the biologists, the physicists, the astronomers and the psychologists.

In 1987 Dr Ross Aidey, White House chief medical officer for the

Reagan administration, discovered that production of the biological timing hormone melatonin was greatly affected by magnetic fields. The biorhythm cycle had already been determined by others as lasting 28 days, which corresponded exactly with the sun's period of rotation (as seen from earth). It was a simple step to make the connection between the 28-day biorhythm period and the rotational periodicity of the sun.

The investigation had raised the question of whether solar-inspired magnetic variations could affect the production of a hormone (melatonin), but measuring the effect solar-inspired magnetic variations might have on the manufacture of the hormone melatonin, and hence biorhythms, is more difficult because behaviour is difficult to quantify.

There is another way to assess the impact of solar-inspired magnetic modulations on the endocrine system, and that is by examining the effect magnetic modulations have on the female menstrual cycle, which is also hormone-driven and better understood. In 1989, comparing the 28-day production cycle of the female follicle-stimulating hormone and the luteinising hormone, it became clear that these were driven by the 28-day magnetic cycle of the sun (*figure 32*). The investigation confirmed that solar-inspired magnetic modulations were converted within the brain into chemicals – hormones.

This means that hormone levels are dependent on the combined influence of both the earth's magnetic field and that of the sun; whenever an organism is removed from the magnetic field that prevails at the time of conception, magnetically induced hormone levels change, causing variations in the timing hormone melatonin. This explains why geographical movement of the human body across the earth's magnetic field gives rise to behavioural inertia, the reluctance of the body to adopt modified magnetically induced biological rhythms, resulting in symptoms ranging from jet-lag to homesickness. This is how the pigeon finds its way home; it simply circles, to ascertain the most favourable direction of magnetic field. The direction that causes the least anxiety is that direction which corresponds to where it was conceived. It simply flies in the direction of home.

What it doesn't explain is why all females menstruate at different times during the 28-day cycle (*see Appendix 2*).

APPENDIX 2

The Reason for Asynchronous Menstruation

Dr Ross Aidey's scientific paper 'Cell Membranes, Electromagnetic Fields and Intercellular Communication', published in 1987, announced that:

> ... about 20 per cent of pineal glands in pigeons, guinea-pigs and rats respond to changes in both direction and intensity of the earth's magnetic field ... [Semm, P., 1983] ... causing variation in the peptide hormone melatonin, which powerfully influences circadian rhythms ... (Welker, H. A., *et al.*, 1983).

This explained why the biological rhythm cycle corresponded exactly with the sun's 28-day rotation. It becomes clear that an individual's biological clock is locked on to the sun's 28-day radiation pattern from the moment of conception, meaning that each individual's clock is synchronised to the solar cycle at a different moment in time. Only those conceived at identical moments would share biological clock synchronisation and hence biorhythms.

Menstruation is affected by each individual's biological clock, which begins at the moment of conception (just like astrological personality determination covered earlier). It is for this reason that females will *not* all menstruate at the same time, because each individual's clock began at a different moment in time. This can be illustrated using the 'carousel' analogy *(figure A2)*.

Imagine that for every revolution of the carousel the horses and riders rise to the top of their respective pole and then descend to the floor once. Each passenger queues to alight the carousel at point 'A'. One passenger mounts the first horse, and the carousel moves forwards slightly. The first passenger rises from the floor of the carousel as the horse rises. The carousel now stops, allowing the second passenger to mount the second horse, which has descended to the floor. Once the second passenger has mounted, the carousel moves forwards again. The first two riders rise higher up their respective poles. The third horse descends to the floor, allowing the third rider to mount the third horse, and so on until all the horses are occupied with riders. Then the ride begins.

All the riders rise and fall once with each revolution of the carousel (in the case of the analogy with the sun, every 28 days). Each is synchronised to the sun's 28-day radiation. But each rises and falls at a different moment in time. This is because they each took their respective seats at different moments in time. The rise and fall of each rider relative to the next is therefore 'asynchronous'. Women do not all menstruate at the same time because each was conceived (alighted the earth) at a different moment in time. Hence biorhythms (and endocrine activity) commence at a different time for each female. But each endocrine system is locked into the 28-day biorhythmic solar clock.

There are exceptions to this general 28-day rule:

(i) The duration of the cycle will vary when the polar magnetic field of the sun interferes with the equatorial magnetic field of the sun. This means that the cycle will vary (quite naturally) from between 24 to 32 days (28 days +/- 4 days, with the average duration amounting to 28 days).

(ii) Anything that affects the biorhythm or metabolic rate will cause variation in the duration of the cycle. These agents could be stimulants like coffee or tobacco, or artificial hormones, or anything that interferes with the biorhythmic signal from the sun, such as overhead power cables or electromagnetic interference.

(iii) Females radiate hormones as a natural bodily emission. These radiating hormonal emissions, if stronger than those induced by the sun's electromagnetic emissions, will cause females in close proximity to synchronise menstruation for as long as the interference continues.

(iv) Scientific evidence shows that females placed under ground, shielded from the sun's radiation, will stop menstruating and their biological clocks will malfunction (see *New Scientist*, June 1989;

NASA's experiment using Stefania Follini, under ground, in the caves of New Mexico).

Figure A2. A Carousel Analogy of Menstruation

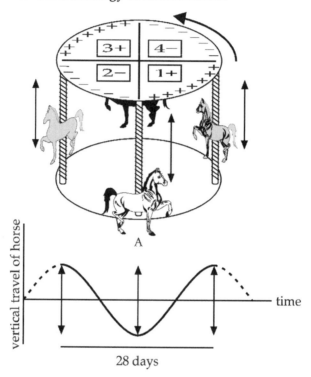

Here a carousel analogy explains why women menstruate every 28 days on average and yet do not menstruate simultaneously; the four quadrants of the sun's magnetic field *(figure A1, ii)* are shown as the roof of the carousel (the shaded sector has been omitted to simplify the illustration). Imagine that the carousel revolves once every 28 days, corresponding to the revolutionary period of the solar equatorial field. Before the carousel ride begins, the passengers mount the horses at point 'A', at different moments in time, as each horse reaches the lower extremity of vertical travel. The ride begins once all the passengers have taken their seats. Each horse moves up and down every 28 days, as indicated by the sinusoidal wave beneath the carousel, but each horse moves up and down at different times. The horses are all synchronised to the 28-day period. Females all menstruate at different times because they alighted the earth at different times and their biorhythms, like the mounting of the horses, commenced at different moments in time.

The Sun

Figure A3. Solar Radiation and Sunspot Activity

The sun's polar magnetic field, shown as + and - on the diagrams below, revolves once around the sun's axis every 37 days (every 40.5 days when measured from earth). The equatorial region, which has its own magnetic field, revolves faster; every 26 days when measured on the sun's sur-face, 28 days when viewed from earth. The different rotational speeds of thse two magnetic fields are known by scientists as 'the differential rotation of the sun's magnetic fields'. It is this magnetic interaction which causes charged particles to leave the sun's surface and bombard the earth.

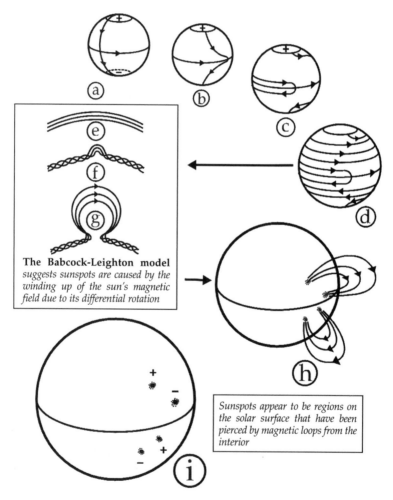

The Babcock-Leighton model
suggests sunspots are caused by the winding up of the sun's magnetic field due to its differential rotation

Sunspots appear to be regions on the solar surface that have been pierced by magnetic loops from the interior

Radiation from the sun is known to vary with changes in sunspot activity. In 1961 engineers Babcock and Leighton proposed that sunspots were caused by the winding up of the sun's two separate magnetic fields. Hence, radiation from the sun and fertility on earth can be expected to correlate with sunspot activity.

Figures A4–A8. Solving the Mystery of the Feathered Snake

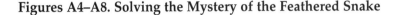
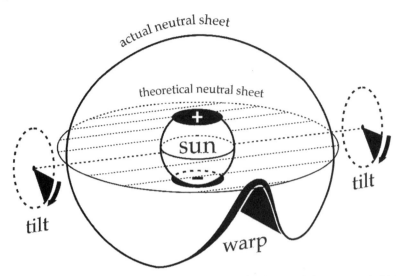

Figure A4. This diagram shows the sun's magnetic field around the equator (which is neither north or south polarity) to be distorted. This area of null magnetic activity is also tilted and hence is known more commonly to scientists as the warped, tilted neutral sheet of the sun.

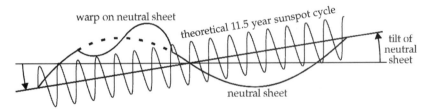

Figure A5. The smaller cycles represent a theoretical 11.5-year sunspot cycle. It is this that distorts the neutral sheet into its observed warped shape.

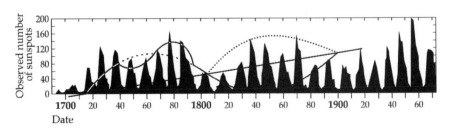

Figure A6. The distorted neutral sheet amplifies and suppresses sunspot activity, leading to variations in the number of observed sunspots over time. The variations in numbers follows the shape of the neutral sheet.

199

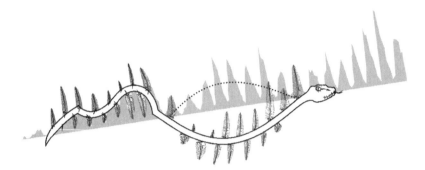

Figure A7. The sunspot cycle as the feathered snake.

Figure A8. The sun, as the feathered snake, was worshipped and depicted in carvings and paintings throughout the whole of Egypt.

Figure A9. The Feathered Snake of Egypt

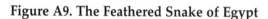

Tutankhamun carried feathers and a snake on his forehead. His beard was the body of a snake which ended with the tail-feathers of a bird. Like Lord Pacal, he was the perfect combination of spirit and flesh.

Reincarnation

The Lid of Palenque *(plate 27)* explains that the souls of those who die at childbirth, in battle and in sacrifice migrate to the paradises, various destinations of the dead, to enjoy heavenly bliss, presumably before proceeding to the God World. Plates 28 and 29 explain how the soul leaves the body for either rebirth in the stars (the heavens and the God World) or *(plate 32a)* rebirth on earth (reincarnation). Plate 30 describes the journey of the soul into the underworld and Plate 31 the journey of the soul through purgatory. The Mayas also believed that there were nine levels to the underworld through which the departed soul had to travel prior to moving on, either to the God World or to reincarnation on earth. (It seems that perfectly purified souls fast-track through the Soul World to the God World and that impure souls suffer in the underworld (purgatory) for their earthly sins before acquiring the energy to reincarnate on earth for another chance of soul purification.)

Figure A10. The Three Worlds

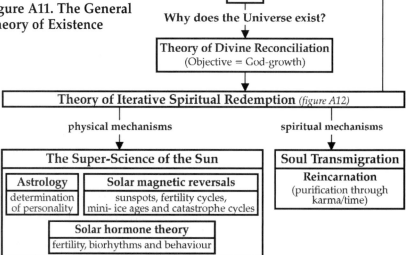

Figure A11. The General Theory of Existence

Treasures from the tombs of the sun-kings suggest that the purpose of the universe is to accommodate God-growth (in accordance with the Theory of Divine Reconciliation, as detailed in the main text). Figure A12 resolves the Theory of Divine Reconciliation and The Three Worlds hypothesis into a working model.

Figure A12. The Theory of Iterative Spiritual Redemption

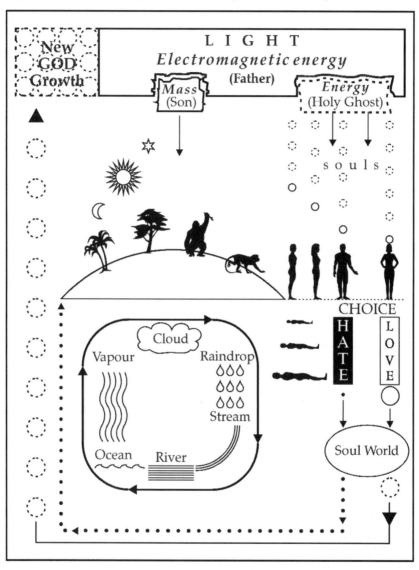

The scriptures tell us that God is light. Light is electromagnetic energy. Einstein tells us that $E = mC^2$, which means that energy (E) can be converted into physical mass (m) and mass can be converted into energy. The equation tells us that the release of energy, when mass is converted, is proportional to the speed of light squared (C^2). This suggests that in the beginning God sacrificed a part of himself, creating the physical universe (the Son). Physical bodies then evolved to attract discrete packets of electromagnetic energy (souls) away from the source of energy (God). The journey of the soul is analogous to that of a raindrop, which is reborn many times. Purification comes from love and sacrifice. Purified souls return to the creator. As a result, the creator grows. Bad souls return to earth, attempting purification once again.

Bibliography

Acosta, Father José de, *Historia natural y moral de las Incas*, Seville, 1590, translated by Grimston, E., 1604

Aidey, Dr W. Ross, 'Cell Membranes, Electromagnetic Fields and Intercellular Communication', Basar, E. (ed.), from a paper presented at the International Conference on Dynamics of Sensory and Cognitive Processing in the Brain, Berlin, August 1987

Allen, J. M., *Atlantis, The Andes Solution*, The Windrush Press, 1998

Alva, Walter, *Sipan*, Backus y Johnston, Peru, 1994

Arellano, Alexander, *All Cuzco Peru*, Universidad de San Martín de Porres, 1998

Bailey, Alice, *A Treatise on White Magic*, Lucis Publishing, New York, 1892

Bawden, G., *The Moche*, Blackwell, 1996

Burger, Richard L., *Chavín and the Origins of Andean Civilization*, Thames and Hudson, 1995

Burland, C. A., *Peoples of the Sun*, Weidenfeld & Nicolson, 1976

Cáceres Macedo, Justo, *The Ancient Moche Society of Peru*, Nueva Arqueológia-APA, Asociasión Peruana de Arqueología, 1996

Cáceres Macedo, Justo, *The Prehispanic Cultures of Peru*, Nueva Arqueológia-APA, Asociasión Peruana de Arqueología, 1996

Cathie, Bruce L., *The Harmonic Conquest of Space*, Nexus, 1995

Cavendish, R., *An Illustrated Guide to Mythology*, W. H. Smith, 1984

Cobo, Father Barnabé, *Historia del Nuevo Mundo*, Cuzco, 1653

Collier, John, *Indians of the Americas*, Mentor, New York, 1947

Cotterell, M. M., *Astrogenetics*, Brooks Hill Robinson & Co., 1988

Cotterell, M. M., *The Amazing Lid of Palenque*, Vol. 1, Brooks Hill Perry & Co., 1994

Cotterell, M. M., *The Amazing Lid of Palenque*, Vol. 2, BHP & Co., 1994

Cotterell, M. M., *The Mayan Prophecies*, Element, 1995 (co-authored)

Cotterell, M .M., *The Mosaic Mask of Palenque*, BHP & Co., 1995

Cotterell, M. M., *The Mural of Bonampak*, BHP & Co., 1995

Cotterell, M. M., *The Supergods*, Thorsons, 1997

Cotterell, M. M., *The Tutankhamun Prophecies*, Headline, 1999

Dixon-Kennedy, Mike, *Native American Myth & Legend*, Blandford, 1996

Egerton Sykes, *Dictionary of Non-Classical Mythology*, J. M. Dent and Sons, 1952

Elorrieta Salazar, Fernando E., and Eliorreta Salazar, Edgar, *The Sacred Valley of the Incas*, Sociedad Paraitanpu Hatha, 1996

Eysenck, H. J., and Nias, D. K. B., *Astrology: Science or Superstition?*, Maurice Temple Smith, 1982

Fernandez, Adela, *Pre-Hispanic Gods of Mexico*, Panorama, 1987

Flemming, John, *The Conquest of the Incas*, Macmillan, 1970

Frost, Peter, *Exploring Cusco*, Nuevas Imagens, 1989

Garcilaso de la Vega (El Inca): *Primera parte dos los comentarios reales de los Incas*, Lisbon, 1609; *Segunda parte de los comentarios reales de los Incas: Historia General del Perú*, Cordoba, 1617. Parts I and 2 translated by Livermore, Harold V., London and Austin, 1966

Goetz, D., and Morley, S. G. (after Recinos), *Popol Vuh*, University of Oklahoma Press, 1947

Hadingham, E., *Early Man and the Cosmos*, Wm. Heinemann, 1983

Hadingham, E., *Lines to the Mountain Gods*, Wm. Heinemann, 1987

Haining, P., *Ancient Mysteries*, Sidgwick & Jackson, 1977

Hapgood, C., *Earth's Shifting Crust*, Chilton (Philadelphia), 1958

Hemming, John, *The Conquest of the Incas*, Macmillan, 1970

His Majesty's Special Command (translation), *Holy Bible*, Eyre & Spottiswoode, 1899

Hitching, F., *The World Atlas of Mysteries*, Wm. Collins & Son, 1978

Hoogendoorn, Ambanta de, and Hoogendoorn, Willem, *Chavín de Huantar*, E. Oswaldo Pucar Cabrera, Lima, 1995

Jordan, M., *Encyclopaedia of Gods*, Kyle Cathie, 1992

Kolata, Alan L., *The Tiwanaku*, Blackwell, 1993

Lafferty, P., and Rowe, Julian (eds), *The Hutchinson Dictionary of Science*, Helicon, 1996

León, Cieza de, *Crónica del Perú*, Seville, 1553

Leonard, Jonathan Norton, *Ancient America*, Time-Life, 1967

le Plongeon, Augustus, *Sacred Mysteries among the Mayas and the Quiches 11,500 Years Ago*, Macoy, 1909

Mackenzie, Donald A., *Myths of Pre-Columbian America*, Gresham, 1921

Molina (of Cuzco), Cristóbal de, *The Fables and Rites of the Yncas*, translated and edited by Markham, C. R., in *Rites and Laws of the Yncas*, Hakluyt Society, London, 1873

Moore, Hunt, Nicolson and Cattermole, *The Atlas of the Solar System*, Mitchell Beazley, 1995

Morúa, Fray Martín de, *Historia del origen y geneologia real de los reyes Incas del Perú (1590–1611)*, ed. Ballesteros-Gaibrois, Manuel, 2 vols, Madrid, 1962, 1964

Morúa, Fray Martín de, *Historia general de Perú, Origen y descendencia de los Incas (1590–1611)* , Madrid, 1962

Oldenburg, Prof., *Sacred Books of the East*, Vol. x, Oxford, translated by Müller, Max, Clarendon Press, 1881

Osborne, Harold, *South American Mythology*, Chancellor Press, 1997

Oswaldo, E., *Chavín de Huantar*, Paucar Cabrera, Lima, 1995

Pearson, R., *Climate and Evolution*, Academic Press, 1978

Pierpaoli, Walter, and Regelson, William, with Colman, Carol, *The Melatonin Miracle*, Simon & Schuster, 1995

Pinnillo, R., *Chán-Chán*, Oro Chimu Collection, Peru, 1989

Posnansky, Arthur, *Tihuanacu, the cradle of American man*, J. J. Augustin, New York, 1945

Prescott, William H., *History of the Conquest of Peru*, G. Routledge and Sons, 1893

Price, Glickstein, Horton and Bailey, *Principles of Psychology*, Holt Rinehart and Winston, 1982

Reader's Digest, *The World's Last Mysteries*, 1977

Reiche, Maria, *Nazca, Peru, Mystery of the Desert*, Hans Shultz-Severin, 1968

Reinhard, Johan, *The Nazca Lines: A New Perspective on their Origin and Meaning*, Editorial Los Pinos, 1985

Santa Cruz Pachacuti-Yamqui Salcamayhua, Juan de: *Relación de antigüedades deste reyno del Pirú*, c. 1615; ed. Jiménez de la Espada, M., in *Tres relaciones de antigüedadas peruanas*, Madrid, 1879, translated by Markham, C. R., Hakluyt Society, 1873

Shaw, I., and Nicholson, P., *British Museum Dictionary of Ancient Egypt*, British Museum Press, 1995

Shri Purohit Swami, *The Geeta*, Faber & Faber, 1935

Thomson, W. A. R., *Black's Medical Dictionary*, A. & C. Black, 1984

Velikovsky, I., *Earth in Upheaval*, Doubleday & Co., 1995

Velikovsky, I., *Ages in Chaos*, Sidgwick & Jackson, 1953

Velikovsky, I., *Worlds in Collision*, Book Club Associates, 1973

Von Däniken, Erich, *Chariots of the Gods*, Corgi, 1969

Von Hagen, W., *The Ancient Sun Kingdoms of the Americas,* Thames and Hudson, 1962

Warner, R. (ed.), *Encyclopaedia of World Mythology*, BPC, 1970

Welker, H. A., Semm, P., Willig, R. P., Wiltschko, W., Vollrath, L., 'Effects of an artificial magnetic field on serotonin-N-acetyltransferase activity and melatonin content of the rat pineal gland', *Exptl. Brain Res.* 50:426–531, 1983

White, J., *Pole Shift*, ARE Press (USA), 1993

Willis, Roy (consultant), *Dictionary of World Myth*, Duncan Baird, 1995

Index

BOOKS OF RELATED INTEREST

THE TUTANKHAMUN PROPHECIES
The Sacred Secret of the Maya, Egyptians, and Freemasons
by Maurice Cotterell

RETURN OF THE CHILDREN OF LIGHT
Incan and Mayan Prophecies for a New World
by Judith Bluestone Polich

THE MAYAN FACTOR
Path Beyond Technology
by José Argüelles

SECRETS OF MAYAN SCIENCE/RELIGION
by Hunbatz Men

THE GIZA POWER PLANT
Technologies of Ancient Egypt
by Christopher Dunn

THE MYSTERY OF THE CRYSTAL SKULLS
Unlocking the Secrets of the Past, Present, and Future
by Chris Morton and Ceri Louise Thomas

DANCE OF THE FOUR WINDS
Secrets of the Inca Medicine Wheel
by Alberto Villoldo and Erik Jendresen

ISLAND OF THE SUN
Mastering the Inca Medicine Wheel
by Alberto Villoldo and Erik Jendresen

Inner Traditions • Bear & Company
P.O. Box 388
Rochester, VT 05767
1-800-246-8648
www.InnerTraditions.com

Or contact your local bookseller